India and the Changing World Order

India and the Changing World Order

Emerging Paradigm Shift in the Global, Political and Economic Order

S. Gurumurthy

ink | OCCAM | Vivekananda International Foundation

Title: India and the Changing World Order: Emerging Paradigm Shift in the Global, Political and Economic Order
Author: S. Gurumurthy

ISBN: 978-93-92209-48-2

First published in India 2023
This edition published 2023

Published by:
BluOne Ink LLP
A-76, 2nd Floor, Sector 136, Noida
Uttar Pradesh 201305

Website: www.bluone.ink
Email: publisher@bluone.ink

Printed and bound in India by Thomson Press India Ltd.

ink | OCCAM | Vivekananda International Foundation

Contents

Preface

When the virus outbreak at Wuhan turned into a global pandemic in 2019, many great minds said it would lead to such unprecedented, far reaching and undiagnosable changes as would change the world order forever. Against this background, there has been a dramatic change for the worse since then in the relations between Western powers and China, which points to a risky future ahead for the present global order and its institutional framework. The pent-up effect of the irrational appeasement of China by the West, kept well suppressed and deferred by suave and persuasive geopolitical diplomacy for too long, despite China being increasingly aggressive outside and regressive within, has also added to the pace, breadth, and complexity of the changes.

Yet, no one was, and even now is, sure about what that 'change forever' would mean and be. No one is clear about its depth, reach and consequences to the world and to individual nations. There is more muted and less open discussion and debate on multi-dimensional issues such as, with the rise of China, whether there would be a change in the world order and if so, what would be that change; what would be the shape of the future world order; whether today's liberal democracies would continue to lead the world order as they have been doing since the Cold War ended; whether there would be a new Cold War; whether liberal democracies which have declared China systemic adversary, would take it on; whether liberal democracies which are under attack from the left and right, would continue to be liberal at all; with the world so divided, whether there will be disorder; whether the West would seek a broader coalition of democracies to sustain the global order—and the like. All such and more issues are on the table for discussion. In the immediate context, a year-and-a-half after its outbreak, Covid-19, which has devastated the world in a manner unknown since World War II, is relentlessly savaging families, communities, business, trade, economies and most importantly, the very way of life of the people, with no end to the misery in sight. The only positive news is that a massive vaccination campaign is on which has definitely brought down the mortality, if not the infection rate. The post Covid-19 outbreak world, which is not past Covid as yet, continues to undergo monumental changes not seen since the melting of the Cold War.

Given the abnormal conditions clouding the world and India, this book is a random survey of where the world, nations, and India stand, and what is the likely future course. The momentous changes taking place are so fundamental and far reaching that the entire post-World War II and post-Cold War foundations of the world seem to need re-examination. *India and the Changing World Order* is a humble attempt to provoke a debate on larger issues, including civilisational, cultural and social diversity issues that have missed their place in the debates leading to the formation of the post-World War II and post-Cold War global order which stands challenged today.

***

India and the Changing World Order touches upon an unusual range of subjects, ranging from emerging civilisational, religious and historical issues, to the out-of-the-box suggestions for astronomy-based education for conflict avoidance, to how liberal democracies are short-termist as compared to long-termist autocratic China, to how the liberal and civilisational democracies like India are different, to how Indian democracy is under threat both from autocratic China and the liberal West, to how market economics is distinct from market societies, to contemporary geopolitical, geo-economics, geo-strategic issues with a particular reference to India and India's strategic relations with select countries and the emerging strategic relations between India and the USA, just to mention a few.

The chapterisation of *India and the Changing World Order* and introductory paragraph headings for each subject discussed is an attempt to make it as less random as possible.

India and the Changing World Order is a consensual position of Team VIF on diverse issues that confront India and the world. It is inevitably long, considering the extraordinary and multiple issues and challenges confronting the world today, which calls for a response from the Indian perspective. The expectation is that experts, scholars, fellows and associates of the VIF should study, debate and offer their views on this book so that it becomes the base from which the VIF will initiate dialogue within the strategic community in India and outside.

Introduction

The text *India and the Changing World Order: Emerging Paradigm Shift in the Global, Political and Economic Order*—originally titled as *Random Thoughts 2021*—is an endeavour to capture the state of the world before and after the Covid pandemic, the monumental geopolitical shifts forced by the Covid pandemic, and the possible changes in the global order perceived particularly by West thinkers after Covid had disturbed global relations and supply chains structured by the West. The changes which once seemed impossible before Covid and which became probable and possible with the advent of Covid, seem to have become inevitable because of the tsunami in geopolitics caused by the Ukraine War.

What is witnessed since the Ukraine war seem no more like the likely changes talked about before the war. What is happening, assumptions and 2022, is difficult to fathom—acrobatic backslidings forcing uncontrolled tectonic changes that are clearly disturbing all and established relations, obliterating all assumptions, and destabilising all global institutions that had formed the bedrock of geopolitics and geo-economics for decades as the settled and durable ways of the world without alternative forever. While the immediate consequence of the chaotic situation that is confronting the world order, led by the US and West, is the emergence of multipolar power centres all around the world setting off diffusion of global power from hegemonic powers. The long-term consequences of the changes, whose flow still continues to unfold, cannot be fathomed or foreseen. The world, particularly the West which authored and persuasively, and coercively at times, mentored the Rest into, and led, the post-World War and post-Cold War order, would never have bargained for what it is witnessing now even in its wildest dreams. This introduction which is a partial attempt to update *India and the Changing*

World Order from where it had ended to connect it to where the world in our view stands now, is in substance, an epilogue.

I. The "World Order" question

India and the Changing World Order has drawn attention to how the best minds in the world have begun talking about the world order changing forever under the impact of the Covid-19 pandemic. Now the outbreak and the endlessly prolonging war in Ukraine have almost fatally knocked down the post-World War II and post-cold-war world order. It has already forced some mighty minds of the world to ask whether the world order would get permanently restructured and wonder whether Western civilisation would collapse. What is the nexus between the world order and Western civilisation that if the former gets restructured, the latter might collapse? The answer to that question also answers why the contemporary world order seems to be failing the stress tests that it had started facing in recent times, with the Ukraine war as the latest and possibly the final and fatal stress.

A close look at the founding premises of the contemporary world order would bring out the fact that in substance and form, it was never an inclusive all-world order, but an order founded on the ideological evolution of the West and prescribed for the Rest when the West emerged strong and victorious and the Rest emerged from Western colonial exploitation and domination for centuries. The ideological premises of the post-World War II and the post-Cold War world order constitute the Judeo-Christian civilisational evolution from its dark past, the Dark Ages to the Age of Enlightenment regarded as modernity in the West and accepted by the Rest also then. But with the rise of Asia in recent times, the very assumption that modernity originated in the West and spread around the world has begun changing with the emerging alternative view that the West is not a single source of modernity but there are multiple modernities with each civilisation having its own evolution to modernity.

The Western view of the Dark Ages is not accepted by other civilisations which dispute that they had any Dark Age like the West. The theory of Oriental Despotism was seen by Western scholars as Asia's—and therefore India's—dark ages and by Karl Marx as the foundation of the Asiatic Mode of Production which he believed was a mix of political despotism and economic stagnation. In the Age of Enlightenment, this theory was sourced from Europe's empirical understanding of the Islamic world and was extended by scholars via the Mughal rule to India. The theory was found to be wrong by Oriental scholars of the West as early as in the 18th century itself as it had presumed on wrong empirical evidence that a despotic ruler controlled all rights and power and therefore there were no individual property rights in Asia, and therefore, in India. ***Orientalist Abraham-Hyacinthe Anquetil-Duperron (1731–1805) thought it was even necessary to oppose the notion of Oriental despotism because of Europe's growing economic and political interest in Asia, particularly in India, whose complex and ancient civilization would have been wronged by the use of this concept.*** As far as three centuries back, the West was warned that Indian civilisation could be wronged by the Western notions of Oriental Despotism. Yet the concocted concept was relentlessly promoted in the colonial period as it suited the colonialists to run down India to make the colonised subjects feel inferior to the colonial masters. The totally wrong assumptions underlying Oriental Despotism had become a settled part of the assessment of India by the West and that falsely aided the self-image of the West that it was the source of modernity for all of Asia, and Africa and therefore the whole world. This theoretical formulation aided by colonial power was the foundation of the Post World War II World Order which rested on the view that the West was modern, and the Rest was despotic—meaning semi-barbaric in Greek—and has to follow the West and become modern. The 'modern' West which had emerged victorious in World War II and in the Cold War later, could easily propose its ideological beliefs as universal values for all, and the West-colonised Rest, which had no matching power to resist or counter influence, had no alternative but to accept it.

But the ecosystem in which the rules of the world order were framed by the West in the post-World War and post-Cold War times has changed with the rise of Asia as the 21st century opened, and with the great financial crisis of 2008 first, the pandemic next, and the Ukraine war at last raising questions over the universality of the foundations of the present world order. The World Order conceptualised by the West has been clearly failing in the stress tests since the turn of the 21st century and now almost fatally with the eruption of the Ukraine war. One need not have to search for the reasons for it as the West had perceived, and it has been increasingly perceiving, the world through its prism of modernity and its later forms of evolution, namely liberal society, liberal democracy, market and economics as universal values for all—as a one-size-fits-all (OSFA) model for the whole world.

The first limb of contemporary Western universalism, the liberal society, is founded on the Western notion of universal human rights. This was the outcome of the euphoria of the West which had emerged victorious in World War II. The other two limbs, liberal democracy and free market, were the outcome of what was touted as the final victory of the West over the Rest in the Cold War. The rise of China—a Frankenstein Monster with total disregard for human rights raised by the sustained efforts of the US and West itself—has clearly undermined the other two limbs of Western universalism—liberal democracy and market economics also. The Western perspective of human rights has always been the cause of the friction between the West and the rest of the world. It is necessary to trace how human rights became so central to the West-led post World War II order from the late 1940s and how, additionally, liberal democracy and free market became central to the West-led post-Cold War order from the early 1990s. At both those points in history—the 1940s and 1990s—the euphoria of the victory had blinded the West into believing that it could fit the Rest into its own model.

Post-World War Order and Post-Cold War Order—The Outcome of Euphoria

The first casualty of euphoria is balance of mind, which is a basic requirement for conceptualising any durable future plan. Future plans cannot and should not be devised in an extreme state of mind resulting from either gloom or euphoria. Both the post World War order and post-Cold War order were born in euphoria. The post World War order was framed in the euphoria generated by the victory of the free world over Fascism and Nazism. The post-Cold War order was conceptualised by those who euphorically claimed the final victory of the Western liberal democracy and free market over the communist state and economy. In substance, the post-World War and post-Cold War orders were the outcomes of the euphoria of victorious forces which authored the world order. As the world, which sees the end of the present world order, stands at crossroads as to what the path ahead is, it is incumbent on it to draw appropriate lessons from its past errors of the victorious forces framing global rules based on their own perspectives and world view.

Originated in Extreme Reaction to Fascism, Nazism

The foundations of the world view of the West, born out of its own experiences during World War II of fighting Fascism and Nazism—which grew in its own backyard—had dominated the structuring of world order post-War and more emphatically after the end of the Cold War. The ideological construct of World War II was both intra-Western and reactive to Fascism and Nazism. Therein lay the structural defect in its construct. The background to the emergent post-World War II order was beautifully captured by HG Wells in his book, *Rights of Man or What are we fighting for?* The heavy hangover of the most destructive war against organised, extremist State Fascism and Nazism, both Western in origin and construct, had tormented and driven the Western thinkers who shaped the post-World War II global order to another extreme—unbridled individual rights that soon began to tower over nation-states, civilisations, cultures and even traditional family. Thus, in framing the post World War II world order, the intra-Western hangover and the guilt of its own Fascist and Nazi past—like the guilt of the Dark Ages led it to reject religion for reason—heavily influenced and explicitly manifested in its instant reaction to undermine, if not reject, any kind of collective normative restraints on the individual, including the traditional cultural and family values. This reactionary and extremist ideological drive of the West-led world order manifested in the conceptualisation of human rights sans even basic normative human duties in the Universal Declaration of Human Rights [UDHR].

Mahatma Gandhi vs H.G. Wells and Aldous Huxley

While the Western thinkers were only reactive in their response, a great Indian thinker, Mahatma Gandhi, was totally opposed to their reactive response. He wrote to H.G. Wells first and later to Aldous Huxley—both had sought Mahatma Gandhi's endorsement of UDHR—refusing to oblige them and explicitly telling them that the UDHR be exclusively duty-centric, saying that human rights are internalised in human duties and not the other way round. The Mahatma Gandhi–H.G. Wells/Aldous Huxley debate had brought out the civilisational divide between the politically powerful West, which had a decisive influence in the discourse at the United Nations, and the numerically large Asia which had little influence. With the colonised and defeated Asia and Africa looking to the victorious West for support and development, there was no possibility of any non-Western civilisational input into shaping the UDHR. The Gandhian view was Asian and civilisational and was an alternative approach to Western anthropology of modernity which shaped the post-World War II Western world view. The Gandhian civilisational approach was largely the view of Asia which, though it had its nominal presence, had little voice in shaping the world order.

Delegitimises Traditional Social Capital

The family, community, and society—the cultural and civilisational foundations of Asian and Indian way of life—constitute the intermediary institutions connecting the individual with the remote state, and socialise and integrate them into the non-formal moral order. In recent times, coinciding with the dawn of the post-Cold War world order, these intermediary institutions are regarded as social capital. The essence of social capital is that it is based on familiarity and trust. Social capital differs from financial and intellectual capital which belongs to individual owners. Social capital belongs to the normative society and not to any individual(s). Social capital is an evolution—and in most non-Western world, it is a cultural and civilisational evolution. But the Western thinkers of the 19th century regarded the culturally and civilisationally evolved societies as static or mechanical societies and those which are newly formed as industrial or organic societies. The former were regarded as traditional societies which function on the basis of relations, and the latter, which rest on contractual relations, as modern. The Western scholars, stunned by the tectonic shifts of industrialisation and urbanization, saw delegitimization and destruction of all relations and the birth of urban, contractual and modern society. While this may be true and appropriate for the West, as far as the non-Western world is concerned, this is completely wrong and as wrong as the West's own view that its Age of Enlightenment is the single source of the modern world. The contemporary Western view is that each civilisation has its own way of modernising and that there are multiple modernities. The ideology of UDHR is founded on the contractual modern societies that tend to reject all other ways and forms of social organisations as mechanical. In the process, civilisationally and culturally-shaped organic families' communities in the non-Western civilisations began to be seen as mechanical or static and delegitimised. But applying the basic rationale of social capital, the traditional family and community which rests on mutual trust constitute social capital.

A whole body of literature has come out on how development of economy, trade, business and finance in most non-Western world—even in parts of the West—centres around and is driven by traditional families and communities which constitute social capital in the non-Western world. But UDHR conceptually sees all culturally and civilisationally evolved organic societies as mechanical societies and actively promotes atomisation of the societies, and even families, into mere contractually bound and atomised individuals. The very ideology of UDHR delegitimises traditional families and communities which constitute the social capital in most non-Western world.

Impotent against Autocracies, Undermines Democracies

The declared intent of the West in institutionalising human rights through the UDHR is to democratise the world but its hidden intent is to promote the Cold War agenda of communist autocracies. But UDHR was impotent against autocracies which were impenetrable. In contrast, constitutional democracies like India, whose constitutions guaranteed fundamental rights to the citizen enforceable against the state by independent judiciary, were repeatedly undermined by the West by invoking UDHR in issues and matters which were largely internal to their democratic evolution.

Increasingly Becomes a Political Project

The exclusive rights centric UDHR aimed at creating a global society, which was diversified by nature, homogenised on individualism and atomising Western values. Later, the notion of atomising Human Rights which was used by the West selectively to suit its geo-political purposes turned UDHR into a Cold War and post-Cold War political project of the West against the sovereignty of most non-Western nations. As a consequence, the UDHR, instead of being the basis of harmonious world order, tended to become the basis of a discordant if not disorderly world because of the political use of the UDHR concept by the West, which tended to atomise the traditional societies and families generally in the non-Western world, particularly in Asia. After the West launched its globalisation project in the 1990s, the West-centric ideological drive became deeper and broader, with the reactions against it faster and even broader. After all, it was the human rights issue which broke up the quarter century of intense engagement between the US and China and which also torpedoed the Comprehensive Agreement on Investment between the EU and China in early 2021.

UDHR Transmutes into UN's One-Size-Fits-All Model

In the post-World War order, as the immediate sequence and as parallel to the UDHR, the UN decreed a development model which was merely an extension of the UDHR. The United Nations Measures for the Development of Underdeveloped Nations 1951 declared: ***There is a sense in which rapid economic progress is impossible without painful adjustments. Ancient philosophies have to be scrapped; old social institutions have to disintegrate; bonds of caste, creed and race have to burst and large numbers of persons who cannot keep up with progress have to have their expectations of a comfortable life frustrated. Very few communities are willing to pay the full price of economic progress.*** This ideological declaration acquired complete legitimacy and greater acceptance in the 1990s with the collapse of the socialist structures and with the emergence of liberal democracy and free market as the pillars of the future perfect world order in the Hegelian sense.

Rise of Asia and OSFA Model

But very soon with the rise of Asia, particularly China, the West had to soft-pedal the OSFA model after the US War on Terror commenced and the G-20 was formed. In the G20 meeting in 2005, the West compromised on the OSFA idea by declaring that there is no one-size-fits-all development model and development has to be nation-specific, signalling a qualitative dilution of the West-led global order in the development domain. In 2008, the World Bank also gave up its long-held faith in the OSFA model and finally in 2010, the United Nations which first institutionalised the idea of OSFA rooted in the Western notion of development, also withdrew from it and expressed its disapproval of it. While on the economic model the West gave up the OSFA approach, on the social side it began to deepen its human rights, liberal democracy and liberal society. Yet, undeniably, the world order of Western construction had begun to dilute after the War on Terror began and the rise of Asia, and particularly after the financial meltdown hit the US and the West more than Asia, it began to shake.

2008 Melt-down Questions the Post-World War Order

The 2008 US financial crisis, which had raised serious questions over the Western financial model, to date remains unaddressed and unresolved by the US and West within their own economies and in the global institutions like the IMF, the World Bank and the WTO created by them. The West, particularly the US, could not even address the basic cause of over-leverage in its financial system which had led to the US meltdown and hit the world and is even today an operational part of its monetary system. Not just the loose monetary policy, even the question of interest rates which had touched zero wasn't addressed till the highest inflation in four decades hit the US. Till then it was like this: When Walter Bagehot spoke of John Bull being able to stand many things, but not 2 per cent interest rates, he meant that that was too low a rate, a floor; but that 2 per cent seems to have become a kind of ceiling, above which Joe Sixpack begins to feel unwell. This is rank bad economics but worse still, the US economy has got so habituated to it, that it cannot come out of it easily and has also acclimatised the global financial order. But inflation topping 9 per cent is compelling the US to hike the interest rates and cut back the liquidity it has pumped into the US and global finance.

The US Fed had in March last, decided to cut back the liquidity by $47 billion each in April and May, and by $95 billion a month from June. Had it done as it had said it would, it would have by now sucked $236 billion away from the market. But so far it has cut back only a third of it, $75 billion. This shows not just unwillingness, but possibly, that it is not possible. While the Fed implemented its call on interest rates, it has been benign on the liquidity cut back. This year will tell whether the US Federal Reserve will have the courage to continue to normalise monetary policy, or whether like in 2017 it will become nervous and force rates down to near-zero again.

Undoubtedly the post-2008-crisis has weakened and debilitated the West-led model, particularly with the rise of an autocratic and non-transparent China, which was generously engaged first and was allowed into the transparent West-led rule-based world trade and finance, by the US believing in the euphoria of the success of its own liberal democracy and free market as the final victors. But China, more loyal to Marx than the Market, decided to hide and bide its time, took full advantage of the opening provided by the US and promoted its economics at the cost of the free market itself. The West had finally moved in 2016 to get the WTO to declare China as not a market economy at all! Even as China claimed that the very admission into WTO meant that it was a market economy! This showed how unstrategic has been the US, which many believe to be the most strategic power. After the 2008 financial meltdown and the rise of autocratic China leveraging the geopolitical position offered to it on a platter by the US and distorting the market-run world trade—the so called Washington Consensus—the West-led post-World War and post-Cold War order seemed less and less viable. Thereafter it appeared more and more like a pretence of an order than reality. To sum up, the continuing post-2008 crisis, which questioned the world order based on the balance of power cleverly crafted by Henry Kissinger in the post-Cold War period, became weak after the 2008 crisis, and the post-Cold War world order, led by the US as the sole superpower, began eroding after Covid-19 strike. The post-Covid pandemic developments were seen by Henry Kissinger as a sudden and fast-forwarded change forever in the world order, although even Kissinger would not say change from what into what.

Range of Change—'Permanent Restructure' to 'Survival of Western Civilisation'

But, the Ukraine-Russia War, however, has changed the entire scenario, causing not just a tectonic shift in the partial remains of the world order, but forcing the West to see the change as that which threatens the survival of the Western civilisation itself. Henry Kissinger, who in 2020 had warned of a change in the world order after the advent of Covid-19, went one step ahead during the World Economic Forum meeting at Davos in May 2022 and said that the Ukraine War 'could permanently restructure the world order' and desired that the war must be stopped soon, in a couple of months. But the controversial billionaire George Soros, with a net worth of $8.5 billion according to Bloomberg, who spends a large part of his wealth promoting pro-liberal agitations across the world, was more explicit in his Davos speech. He did not utter a word about the Covid challenge, climate change, or inequality, which used to be his favourite subjects, but exclusively focussed on the authoritarianism of Xi Jinping and a war-mongering Vladimir Putin, warning that 'our civilisation may not survive'. While it is not clear what he meant by 'our civilisation', given his left and liberal tendencies, it is clear that he meant that the West-led liberal world order is at risk. Soros added that Western aid to Ukraine and the latter's resistance to Russia were the only silver linings. He said the war has shaken Europe to its core and even when the fighting stops, as it must, the situation will never revert to what it was before. The media keeps reporting that Soros spends huge sums of money through his Open Society Foundation to influence geopolitics to promote liberal world order. Even though both influential men spoke using different terminologies, what they meant was that the liberal world order, which Soros equated to modern [Western] civilisation, was in danger, ranging from 'restructure' to 'risk of survival'.

Against the historic and contemporary background, it is necessary to re-examine the founding thoughts and institutions of the world order, the risk to which both Kissinger and Soros are highly concerned. It calls for a recall of ideologies and ideas that formed the basic structures of the post-World War II West-led world order, which it had thought had become unchallengeable with the emergence of globalisation founded on the victory of the Western liberal democratic social order and free market economic order—the so-called Washington Consensus—over the Rest. It is also necessary to examine how so soon and suddenly these great and momentous events seem to have become distant memories now.

The impact and effect of the tectonic changes taking place after the onset of the Ukraine war, at the speed of light as it were, are difficult to comprehend at present. The sequence and consequence of the shift will become manifest only when the full effect of the unprecedented war plays out in the future. Yet, it will be Team VIF's endeavour to throw light on the impact and effect of the war on the world and on different nations in the upcoming Random Thoughts 2022. We will delve into and dissect the ideologies that drove the ambitious Western world order project and its historical background. We see the debate initiated by influential minds like Henry Kissinger and George Soros on the emerging change in the West-led world order as a fascinating geopolitical and geo-economic development in post-World War II history.

II. Impact of the Ukraine War

The next edition of the Random Thoughts will discuss how the world is being turned upside down by the Ukraine war and try to trace how a hidden Cold War has transformed into an open Ukraine-Russia war, how the US underestimated and created Putin, and how deep had been the Russian planning for the war. We will also track the relative effects of Russian strategy and the Western counter strategy, how successful Russia's oil for rouble strategy is, and how Russia must have planned to use the very platform of globalisation—which had made nations interdependent believing that the world has entered an era permanent peace and harmony—to make entire Europe dependent on it for energy. We will also endeavour to assess what a continuing war means to Russia, Western nations and others, and its impact on European nations, their economy, and the Trans-Atlantic Alliance, and on US-Middle East relations. We will also try to capture how the war is turning traditional alliances into current problems and also contemplate on whether the outcome will be a restructured order or more disorder. We will also discuss the impact of the Ukraine conflict on the global institutions—the UN, the WTO, the UN Commission on Human Rights and other similar multilateral bodies; the impact of the Ukraine conflict on globalisation, global trade and regional trade pacts, and also how the war is creating and deepening non-Western political, economic and financial blocks. We will also try to assess the outcome and impact of the war on the different world nations, groups and alliances, on the global monetary order, trade and finance, and India's current response to it and what, in our opinion, its future responses could be. We will also discuss China-related issues, India's neighbourhood issues and finally, diverse scenarios of the emerging world order from the current threat of disorder and India's role in influencing it as we see it.

Global Monetary Order, Trade and Finance

The coming edition will endeavour to comprehend the possible shift in global trade from financial power to commodity power, the resultant possibility of a shift from the post-Cold War emphasis on the financial economy, back to the real economy, and the possible, and perhaps, inevitable changes in the global monetary and financial order and its effects, and the travel back from globalism and multilateralism to civilisational and other groups pacts to bilateralism and the increasing role of national currencies in bilateral trade.

Ukraine War, and the US and Europe

It also will try to measure the impact of the Ukraine War and its result on the global climate issue, particularly in the context of the energy crisis in Europe forcing Germany and other countries to go back to coal-based energy, which will turn the climate deal on its head. We will also discuss how the messages and outcome of the Ukraine conflict point to the emergence of an increasingly polarised world, full of distrust, where global, commercial, and financial commons are used as weapons of war, robbing the world of residual morals in global affairs and where there are no neutral geographies or actors left.

It will also discuss how the war has dented American influence and leadership, resulting in a defensive West in a world of offence. We will also discuss whether Ukraine is a trailer for Taiwan or a warning against it. We will examine the impact of US/West sanctions on Russia, the West and the Rest, and whether these sanctions are a success or failure by tracing their background. We will also try and comprehend the international strife, leadership deficiencies in the US, Russia, China and Europe, split polity in Europe and the US, and the rise of nationalism in the West—France, Ireland, and other nations—and the explosive and deepening Liberals vs Conservatives conflict.

Ukraine War and Emergence of New Global Players

It will also examine how international developments are likely to open up considerable opportunities for middle-level power players like Iran, Saudi Arabia, Turkey, Israel, and the UAE, to leverage the evolving situation to their advantage. India, which has risen from being a middle player into a higher orbit in the last few years, has a great advantage over most middle powers as its comprehensive power is far superior to theirs and its continental economy opens up unprecedented opportunities for it at a time when China has emerged as a big challenge to the West, even as global supply chains have been greatly disrupted. We will discuss how this new phenomenon also points to the emergence of a multipolar world, where hard power, which India has been quietly building, and its natural soft power, both matter. With multiple players emerging and geopolitics being used as a global policing force, what is likely to emerge is a multipolar world, where persuasion rather than pressure will be key to global relationship management.

III. Ukraine War and India's Response

India's response to the Ukraine War and how India's Ukraine Policy is the most exemplary and courageous diplomatic and strategic exercise that has protected the Indian national interest and at the same time secured and even moved India into a central place in global affairs. With the Western world harassed by the pandemic, disturbed supply chains, lack of common approach between the two sides of the Atlantic over the China question, throwing the world in throes of a recession, India had to take a position that was not only appropriate for itself, but also positioned India in the Russia vs US and West conflict as not approving or condemning either, and more importantly also not to allow Russia to fall completely into the lap of China resulting in Russia-China iron-clad ties which will neither be in India's interest, nor the World's, or the West in the interest of the world and the West itself. This second and phenomenal outcome of a brilliant diplomatic exercise by India has been that India began buying, and continues to buy, more and more Russian oil at less and less prices and for payment in Rupees rather than in Dollars. This has added a huge economic value to India. On the political side, the Indian Prime Minister balanced what the West saw as Indian tilt towards Russia, by telling Vladimir Putin to his face that 'today's era is not the era of war', which the West perceived and claimed as India's criticism of the Ukraine War. But India has consistently refused to be a part of the UN Security Council attempt to condemn Russia as the aggressor or invader, and yet it had voted against Russian resolution for a secret ballot to condemn its annexation of four regions of Ukraine.

India strategically moved with warring nations, even getting them to suspend the war, to bring back all Indians safely from Ukraine—a great and physically demanding diplomatic feat by any standards.

We will also try to comprehend the Ukraine War's impact on India's relations with different nations—the US, Russia, Germany, France, England, Japan, Israel, and the Arab world—UAE, Saudi Arabia—and China. We will try to measure India's rising stature as demonstrated by physical Indian visits and virtual meetings of heads of state, finance, trade and foreign ministers of Japan, Australia, Nepal, UK, Oman, Israel, China, even as the war rose in crescendo. Finally, we discuss the QUAD and India and India's dilemma in the QUAD.

We will try to bring out India's economic challenges, opportunities and risks in the present context and in the future, India's internal issues and challenges, India's Chinese challenge, and India's neighbourhood risks and obligations. We will also discuss how in the medium and long run, Indian democracy will stand at the Centre, mediating between the liberal and the illiberal world, and how liberal democracies, whose influence is perceived to be weakening, will have to work with India to sustain a democracy-inspired world order in a world geographically and numerically dominated by autocracies.

IV. Can China do a Ukraine on Taiwan?

We will also endeavour to figure out and explain China's economic challenges, particularly those arising from Western model real estate-driven growth, and the external and internal issues in China, including those between Xi and his adversaries, Xi and the PLA, the Xi regime and Ukraine Policy. We will also try to understand the stand-off between China and Taiwan because of the visit of Nancy Pelosi, Speaker of the US House of Representatives, to Taiwan, and whether the war hysteria China has created over the visit would turn into a war or peter out into long Cold War, tearing apart the deep engagement that has twined the two powers, the US and China, and the consequences of either to the world and also to India. How the separation of the two Siamese twins is going to take place will be a historic development to watch.

While how the Taiwan stand-off will play out is unclear, there are some clues as to how different things are between the Ukraine war and the Taiwan war, if it takes place. One would normally tend to think that the Ukraine war would be a trailer for China's Taiwan action. But the new kind of sanctions that the West levied on Russia would make the Chinese think twice before taking any unilateral, aggressive action. The Western response to Russia with sanctions involved the ban on the use of global commons like SWIFT to use multinational corporations to freeze dollar assets and so on. Russia could ward off the impact of the sanctions by leveraging its strength as the major gas and oil supplier to the European nations and on their weakness as energy-dependent on Russia. The sanctions, which the US had prematurely claimed reduced the 'rouble to rubble' have not been highly successful against Russia, whose use of energy as a weapon against the European nations has seen the rouble rise to a three-year high. While the West has shown, by its sanctions, that Russia's own assets cease to be its assets and can even become its liabilities, Russia has shown by its rouble for gas and oil that the economic and trade interdependence of the world, which the West forced on the Rest through the West-centric globalisation, can be the greatest danger to the West. Now apply the war rules of Ukraine to Taiwan.

If China moves unilaterally on Taiwan and the West responds in the same way as it did against Russia, what are the possible consequences to China? The Chinese have kept invested close to a trillion US dollars in US treasury securities. That apart, American Enterprise Institute Global China Investment Tracker says, that between 2005 and 2022, the Chinese have invested $2.25 trillion world over—of which over $850 billion is in North America, especially the USA, Europe and Australia—all falling within the areas of US influence and can be subject to sanctions in case of a Chinese invasion of Taiwan. It means that some $1.80 trillion of Chinese cash can be frozen by the West.

The US and Europe are certainly China dependent on some critical areas of the supply chain and cheaper consumer goods. But that dependence is unlike the energy dependence of Europe on Russia. Countermeasures of China to the kind of sanctions the US and West have levied on Russia, if levied on China, cannot have the kind of impact which Russia's energy weapon could produce on Europe. Any Russian kind of sanctions on China could be a lighted map to a train of gunpowder on China—the consequences could be immeasurably harmful to China. Let us examine.

The most critical issue in China's economy now is the real estate bubble. Housing accounts for 30 per cent of China's GDP. Since 2005, China has focussed on housing and related sectors, steel and cement, for its high growth, much of it financed by debt. China accounts for 57 per cent of the world's steel production. Policies like presale mortgages, which China had adopted to promote housing, resembled the subprime lending of the US to promote home values. The home values, which rose by three times between 2011 and 2020, powered China's data of GDP rise. The home values constitute 70 per cent of the personal wealth of the Chinese. But the pandemic and global slowdown, besides the aging society, appeared to have reversed the fortunes of China's housing economy. The residential property sales have crashed by 72 per cent since last year and the slide has been continuous month after month for 11 months and appears irreversible. Home buyers are refusing to pay the mortgage dues for the houses which are not completed and are agitating on the streets. On top of that, the unsold property inventories reached a 5-year high. Large firms are defaulting on debt. Experts say that 30 per cent of steel producers dependent on the housing economy are staring at bankruptcy. Even though 90 per cent of the property developers are locally funded and only 4 per cent have taken loans from abroad, the housing crisis will cause a massive impact on the Chinese regular banks, shadow banks, and the economy. The Chinese economic growth which was 8.1 per cent in 2021 is likely to be 5 per cent in 2022. The OECD EcoScope estimates that a 2 per cent fall in the Chinese economy, coupled with housing stress and higher finance in China, will cause a 2 per cent reduction in global GDP and also cause a collateral impact on prices in the world—which will also have a spin-off effect back on China's economy itself.

There are two more causes of concern to China. One, China's total Debt to GDP has risen from 146 per cent in 2006 to 258 per cent which is presently more than that of the debt-prone US. The dollar denominated debt of China is $3 trillion. China is regarded by many as a candidate for a debt crisis. With a huge dollar component in its debts, a Chinese debt crisis can, by contagion effect, get exported outside. The other issue is China's overseas lending. National Bureau of Economic Research [NBER] US estimates that Chinese overseas lending which was $500 billion in 2000 topped $5 trillion by 2018—equal to 6 per cent of the world's GDP. NBER also says that if the Chinese investment in foreign equity and Direct investment [that is the AIE figure of $2.30 trillion] is added, the total investment would equal 8 per cent of global GDP. These figures are outdated—four years old. A non-transparent China does not allow easy detection of its assets and liabilities. Yet, these are assets valuable in peacetimes. If the US-China stand-off leads to a global economic mess and it triggers a global economic crisis, as it is bound to, it will not only rebound on China, but it can also turn the global loans of China into non-performing loans.

It is true that China has dominance in rare earth supply—in 2019, its dominance was as high as 80 per cent of global supply—so critical for technology manufacturing and renewable energy products essential for green energy. In 2010, China had almost a total monopoly with India as a marginal supplier. But things are changing. With the US planning to rival China by including, in its $2 trillion infra mission, on-shoring of rare earth production for its semiconductor industry and for remaking its transport sector, the Chinese dominance cannot last too long. Rare earth may soon become not so rare. In case of a war against Taiwan, Chinese rare earth dominance cannot produce for China the effect that Russian gas produced for Russia in the war against Ukraine. Apart from rare earth, China can also hold back green energy equipment. With the green agenda being undermined by the Ukraine war, the issue will cease to be a pressing issue.

To conclude, with the change of the rules of war the West has demonstrated against Russia in the Ukraine war, it will be difficult, if not impossible, for China to respond to the West as Russia did. That is, it cannot easily do a Ukraine on Taiwan like Russia.

But the strategic difference between the Russia vs Ukraine situation and China vs Taiwan situation should not induce one to think that China would not take aggressive action. Xi Jinping's third term of five years is due for confirmation in October next, which may compel him into kinetic mode as, having unwisely hyped Nancy Pelosi visit into an issue against One China Policy that China had extracted from the US, he cannot be seen to be accepting her visit without responding—even though the international community will find it difficult to accept that Pelosi visit as a sufficient cause for China to act militarily against Taiwan. Yet, members of the international community, especially among the Quad members and ASEAN countries, should advisedly not remain complacent. While the financial and trade deterrents to military action by the People's Republic of China are obvious, there are ominous signs of heightened preparations for war on the Chinese side, apart from the pronounced aggressiveness of the military exercises it is conducting around Taiwan. Chinese are decoupling their economy by gradually pulling companies out of listings in New York; they have stockpiled semiconductors needed for their industry, especially after the difficulties faced in this regard by Huawei and ZTE; and they have launched a movement to cleanse the public space of 'sissy boys' and the 'lie flat' movement. All of this would be consistent with their medium-term strategy to sanction-proof themselves for a possible show-down. Above all, in the background of the demonstrated lack of appetite for the US and West for military involvement outside, given the US retraction from the Middle East and Afghanistan, it would be unwise to underestimate the PLA's inclination and determination to settle the matter by force, as also to underestimate the power of the PLA in decision-making on matters of national security. Prudence dictates the need to prepare in advance for any untoward development—the war in Ukraine has lessons for the West as well as for the PRC.

Another intriguing aspect is the dichotomy between its aggressive war drills against Taiwan and the latest—and bad—news about its economy. Over and above the burgeoning woes of its housing economy—the mainstay of China's GDP—China's industrial production as well as retail sales for July 2022 have slowed. The relentless fall in home sales continuing for the 11th successive month in July has ripped through the industrial sector with Chinese steel production touching the lowest since 2018. Data shows that 19.9 per cent of all youth in the age group of 16–24 are jobless—a record high, and shocking. It shows a larger malaise in the economy. This is of huge concern to the CPC as the Chinese Congress is expected to meet in mid-October to re-elect XI Jinping. The real GDP growth has also slowed below estimates indicating that the growth target of 5.5 per cent for 2022 may be unachievable and the actual could well end up at sub 4 per cent. China experts in world finance regard the sudden bad news as alarming. This has forced the People's Bank of China to cut its rate by 10 basis points—the reverse of US Fed action to hike the rates—and also inject $60 billion in lending markets. The surprise rate cut, though not significant, is seen by some economists as indicating that the entire economy is in trouble. Because of the bad economic data from China, global oil prices have dropped by 5 per cent, which is good news, though small, for the US which has been toiling to bring down the oil prices with the twin aim of controlling domestic inflation and harming Russia, a principal beneficiary of high oil prices. Whether the bad news on the economic front would dissuade China from a war on Taiwan is also a million-dollar question. What happens on the economic front before the Chinese Congress meets might also influence Xi's decision.

V. India's Neighbourhood

We will also discuss the developments in India's neighbourhood, particularly in Pakistan, Afghanistan, Bangladesh, Nepal and Sri Lanka, and the way forward. Afghanistan, in particular, looms large: the dismal performance during the withdrawal by the US and allied forces has probably played a part in emboldening America's adversaries. It will reflect on the ability of the Western consensus to sustain its values if there is any weakness shown towards the Taliban, under whatever pretext its crypto supporters will drum up. The Taliban have openly flouted the assurances they gave at the time of the Doha Agreement, particularly in terms of women's rights, minorities' treatment, and terrorism. This cannot be a cost-free approach for them.

The significance of the economic and consequent social troubles in the South Asian neighbourhood deserves special attention. At heart, this reflects predatory loan practices, without due consideration of the ability of the recipient country to absorb and repay the capital. Much of the spending done by the People's Republic of China is of this kind, done in disregard for the creditworthiness or repayment capacity of the countries. But, as we have seen in the case of Sri Lanka, it is India that has to finally work to stabilise the situation. Why all China's Belt and Road Initiative participants including Pakistan are in serious trouble, needs a probe. In this endeavour, cooperation from the Quad partners would be invaluable for the four to work together in an important new vector.

Finally

We will compare the global developments in the background of what we have seen and prognosticated in the previous edition.

In the end, we will try to build diverse scenarios about the likely future of the world and the role of India in it as we see it.

A historic, fascinating, high-risk and uncontrollable transformation of the world is taking place in front of us, which has shattered all post-Cold War positive predictions of a conflict-free world assured of peace, prosperity and harmony, through globalisation and West-led solutions to global problems. Interesting yet dangerous times are ahead for all nations in the short and the long run.

1

From the Age of Enlightenment to the Age of China Challenge: Abstract Ideas Emerging Concrete

The admission of the Western Bloc in June this year, that China is a challenge to the West, is a significant development after the Cold War in geopolitics. The question that should particularly torment Western minds is what the challenge of an autocratic China means to the liberal West and the rest of the world.

This raises more basic questions like how did this happen; why and where the West, which was almost deciding who should rise and who should not in the order led by them, erred in its judgement about China and chose to engage with it and help it to rise? Why did it promote a China that was deep under the system of a Communist ideological autocracy considered dangerous by the West? Did the West overestimate the superiority of its own system and so on.

The search for an answer to these questions must haunt Western thinkers. But the rise of China equals the rise of its aggressiveness both outside and inside, unbalances the world order and upsets its current assumptions and foundations. It is also of equal concern to the rest of the world, particularly countries like India, Taiwan and Japan, with whom China shares unfriendly to adversarial relations. The rise of an aggressive China aspiring to be a dominant global power that sees India as its regional impediment impacts on the latter as a nation and people, since both share a 4000-km-long border with each other.

In the context of the post-Covid-19 world order, which some of the best minds say will change forever, with China challenging the West, that the West itself has acknowledged, there are bound to be tectonic shifts in the global system and order. These shifts are bound to be unpredictable and will touch a wide range of issues—abstract and unsettled issues of the past, and present issues, like how world history and the history of different civilisations that had been cast in Western perspectives in the past, will be reviewed and recast in their own perspectives, to whether there is a one West-centric modernity as the West has been saying, or multiple modernities as the rest of the world has been saying; to how the West-led socio-economic theories that ruled the world may get altered, to how the multilateral world turns into a multi-polar world, to how the single global supply chain may become diverse and so on. In this process, some of the hitherto seemingly abstract issues of the past may become concrete issues in the future.

Seemingly Abstract, but Actually Concrete Issues

We see China's challenge as a context for revisiting, rethinking and reassessing the way the West-centric world order has moved post-World War II, and more particularly, post-Cold War. This is bound to raise some fundamental questions which may seem abstract if looked at from the current and short-term perspectives that the world has got used to in the last few decades.

But a deeper and closer look shows that these questions would raise long-term and future issues, in the background of accumulated and hidden deficiencies in the discourse of the past, and, therefore, not abstract. There is near total consensus that, post the Covid-19 pandemic, the world order will change forever, with no one being able to say what that change forever will be and mean. Obviously, such changes, some of which are forced by accumulated but suppressed causes, will not produce only short-term effects. The perceived changes won't be just changes with continuity from the past, or just improvements over the current status quo, but ones with long-term consequences, in which the past and its accumulated and unsettled balances among nations will play a constitutive role.

This will need a 360 degree look into the past, present, and future.

When the world order changes forever, the unsettled balance of issues of the past, be it civilisational, cultural, political or economic, will all open up in geopolitics. Here is an illustrative attempt, not an exhaustive account, of such issues, some of which may seem abstract, but may emerge as concrete ones. One such is the likely emergence of a civilisational paradigm.

Civilisational Paradigm Emerging?

That China, which had been for 70 years under the Communist paradigm of rejecting the past and even went through a Cultural Revolution to obliterate it, has shockingly begun recalling and asserting its ancient civilisation more than its Communist ideology. This is an important U-turn in global history.

China, which hated its past and disconnected from it, and the West, that dismissed its past as the Dark Ages and disconnected from it, were similarly positioned till the other day. No nation or civilisation other than China and the West, has ever declared its past as Dark as did the West, and as worthy of destruction as did China. China did not just engage in an intellectual battle with its past but used its Cultural Revolution to launch a bloody civil war against it. In Communist ideology, history only moves forward, never looks back. Communism generally shares an adversarial relation with the past, wanting it discredited and obliterated. That is why it is shocking to see China racing at hectic pace to reconnect with its 5000-year-old civilisational past with both pride and enthusiasm. In contrast, the West continues to regard its own past as the Dark Ages and views the contemporary period as a new beginning since the Days of Enlightenment. As opposed to China, its civilisational disconnect continues. But Communist China has overcome its hate for the past and views it with pride. This is likely to cause a significant shift in the global discourse on the civilisational paradigm.

Not stopping at characterising its own past as dark, less than a matter of pride and even barbaric, the West has moved ahead and tarred everyone's past and every civilisation with the same brush, making them feel that their past was unworthy of recall. Rejecting the past came to be regarded as the first index of modernity.

This universalisation of the Western anthropology of modernity has destroyed the self-pride of many nations and almost all colonised nations. This trend has been changing slowly in recent times, with a gradual rise in the civilisational consciousness of different peoples and nations.

Most nations have always been internally proud of their ancient past and unlike the West, none have regarded their past as dark. But they could never openly speak about it in the West-centric anti-civilisational liberal world order, lest they be misunderstood as anti-modern at the minimum and xenophobic at the maximum. But of late, even nations which had reservations about their past, have begun recalling it with pride. China is a late and new entrant to a class of nations that openly celebrates its ancient past. China getting onto the civilisational paradigm has significant potential for the emergence of a global civilisational paradigm.

It is surprising that this potential has not been fully noticed in global discourse or diplomacy. This shift, when it becomes more explicit, will have far-reaching consequences for the West and the rest, as the former has continuing reservations about the very word civilisation.

Its stunning attempt at intellectual, academic and geopolitical abuse and rejection of Samuel Huntington's thesis of civilisational clashes without even a modicum of dignified debate, underscores its apprehension that civilisational consciousness is not only backward, but antithetic to the idea of a liberal world and global harmony.

To make matters worse, Huntington centralised his thesis on 'clash' of civilisations, which is common in Western, particularly Abrahamic religious history, ancient and modern.

The shift towards the civilisational paradigm will also redefine the idea of democracy which is purely benchmarked by Western liberal democracy. Most non-Western nations, which are a majority in number and in population, are largely cultural and civilisational in their identities. But their cultural and civilisational democratic orders, despite being genuine electoral democracies, have been discounted by the West. The genuine electoral democratic order of most non-Western countries which are civilisational democracies, will not be entirely compatible with the liberal democratic norms of the West. Because in the Western worldview, individual and human rights overrides society and family, which a civilisational democracy would regard as social capital.

The civilisational consciousness, triggered by China's recent embrace of its past, may also cause a shift in the global order. The shift would be from the purely system-centric model of the West, based on individual rights consciousness without the individual duty element, to a model that is duty conscious, fostering social, cultural and civilisational capital in most non-Western societies. This shift will accommodate the views of the predominantly civilisational rest in remaking the global order. This is where and how what appear as abstract and out-of-date civilisational ideas in the current West-centric paradigm, may emerge as concrete thoughts for the future.

Despite the implicit and explicit reservations of the West, a civilisational element does exist in contemporary geopolitics. The Abrahamic Accord, as the agreements between Jewish Israel and the Islamic Arabic nations brokered by the liberal democratic US, is explicitly a civilisational recall. Abraham is the common ancestor of Jewish, Christian, and Islamic faiths and people. To overcome and transcend their current disputes which has turned them into adversaries, the mythology of their common origin and common civilisational consciousness has been recalled by invoking Abraham, their common forefather, to make the accord acceptable in the minds of warring people on both sides.

China's rise may also provide impetus to other nations which have a civilisational connect to their past but keep underplaying it in the West-centric world order, which sees the past as bad, to assert its existing civilisational character. The danger which the West must recognise here is that China may provide legitimacy, if not leadership, to nations' conscious of their civilisations, to change the current West-led world order, which rejects the idea of civilisation.

Modern West has Discarded Its Civilisational History, but the Rest has Not

The impact and effect of history on the human mind is deep and continuous. There is pride about historical origins and sources in people. That is what has been harnessed to get the Abrahamic Accord through. Historical and civilisational origin defines and distinguishes both people and nations. In countries like India and China, thousands of years of their history are the foundation of the idea of a civilisational nation. The West, by internalising the concept of the Dark Ages, has got the modernisation paradigm distanced and detached from history. Modernity in the West was intended to and has overcome history—the historical continuity. That is not so in most of Asia. The modernisation of Japan from the Meiji Period was debated in Japan post-World War II. Japan, one of the Asian nations which adopted the exteriors of Western modernity and practiced it for over a century, is still ambivalent toward Western modernity. The inherent conflict between traditional Japanese values, principles and sensibilities and Western values of modernity culminated in a symposium on Overcoming Modernity in 1942 in Japan. Despite the Japanese exterior, which seems to be modern in the Western sense, the Japanese sense of modernity is manifest in *Nihon Jinron*, which plainly means Japaneseness.

In recalling its 5000-year history with pride, China has even revived its civilisational symbol—Confucianism, which it discredited for 50 years till the end of the 20th century, as neo-Confucianism. India too recalls its 5000-year history from the Indus Valley and Vedic times. Even Islamic Pakistan traces its origins not to the Arabs, but to the Serpent God Takshaka and recalls Takshashila University that bore his name. It remembers the Mahabharata, Panini, Chandragupta Maurya, Chanakya, Ashoka and Harshavardhana as its predecessors. Whether it is Korea or Taiwan, Malaysia or Indonesia, Sri Lanka or Burma, Thailand or Cambodia, all of them have deep and living memories of their history and civilisation.

Two Different Worlds: A West with Civilisational Disconnect, the Rest with Civilisational Continuity

With Europe disconnected from its civilisation by the Dark Age theory and modern US having no civilisation of its own to recall, the overall Euro West-led world order has never had an ancient civilisational sense. But the rest of the world, with its civilisational continuity, has a high sense of civilisational memory and recall. This contrast makes for two different worlds—one with civilisational consciousness and connect, and the other without it. The Enlightenment emphasised and promoted individualism and that, in its hyper form in the 20th century, has led to the delegitimisation and decimation of society as an entity and even traditional families. Finally, individualism-driven West has lost its collective sense of society, which is a social, cultural and civilisational asset in and for the rest of the world, particularly Asia.

Declaring its past as dark and disconnecting from it, the West firmly linked itself to the Renaissance and the Enlightenment Period as its modern origin. The Renaissance and the Enlightenment proudly dominates contemporary Western minds and resonates in its memory. But despite this labelling of its past as violent and dark and staking a claim to be the origin of modernity, the West, in fact, has generated two world wars and caused the Holocaust. This does not make the dividing line between its 'Dark past' and 'later Enlightenment' too clear. The rest of the world, particularly Asia, and more particularly China, India, Japan and Korea, or most Asian and Arab nations, with no disconnect from its past, have civilisational continuity. China, which experimented with the gift of Communism from the West for a few decades, has now emerged as a neo-Confucian civilisation.

Unlike the Rest and particularly Asia, the West is less civilisationally conscious and dominantly systemic in its reasoning. It has been evangelising the world away from its civilisational moorings through the West-centric world order. As a result, in the post-World War II, West-led global discourse, the delegitimised civilisational paradigm has been dormant if not absent. Therefore, most world nations, particularly in Asia, which have no admitted sense of guilt of a dark past, have a deep civilisational character unlike the West. The rise of Asia, and China in particular, which is asserting its civilisational character as much as, if not more than, its Communist identity, is bound to see the emergence and accentuation of a two-world syndrome—one that is civilisationally connected and the other that is civilisationally disconnected.

No Dark Age in Indian History: Oriental Despotism, a Colonial Interpolation, Says Encyclopaedia Britannica

In order to obliterate the past of all countries and make them accept Western anthropological modernity, the West has even tried to interpolate the histories of the rest of the world with its own version of their Dark Age theory. This was particularly true of countries colonised by the West.

For instance, in Indian history, which largely the colonial West wrote, it invented the equivalent of its own Dark Age by fabricating the theory of Oriental Despotism, thus colouring its interpretation. Karl Marx made it the central idea of his distant study of India, its society and economy. But the theory of Oriental Despotism has been proved false by evidence.

The Encyclopaedia Britannica has concluded that the older notion of oriental despotism was interpolated by colonial scholars as an intellectual justification for colonialism and imperialism. With its deterministic assumptions, the Encyclopaedia concludes that oriental despotism theory clouds the understanding of Indian political forms, economic patterns and social relations—virtually admitting that it is no longer valid. Says the Encyclopaedia:

> A major change in the interpretation of Indian history has been a questioning of an older notion of Oriental despotism as the determining force. Arising out of a traditional European perspective on Asia, this image of despotism grew to vast proportions in the 19th century and provided an intellectual justification for colonialism and imperialism. Its deterministic assumptions clouded the understanding of early interrelationships among Indian political forms, economic patterns, and social structures.

There is substantive and corroborative evidence available to support the conclusions of the encyclopaedia that will establish that India has had no violent dark age like the West to shy away from. During the period declared by the West as the Dark Ages, when mass killings and violence were the order of the day, India alone remained an oasis of peace for 1800 years, from the 5th century BCE to the 13th century CE, when foreign invaders began mass killings in India.

A three-decade-long study by Professor Rudolph J. Rummel of Hawaii University found that in the pre-20th century, mass killings across the world added up to 625 million. The share of mass killing in the West from the 5th century BCE till the 13th century CE was a million, but during the same period, Rummel states India virtually had no record of mass killings except 100,000 killed during the Kalinga War and not more than tens of thousands of Sati and Thuggee crimes.

Rummel's study establishes that, unlike the West, India has really had no Dark Age to disconnect from.

India has had an unbroken civilisational continuity for 5000 years, says Encyclopaedia Britannica.

This explicit and proud civilisational continuity of 5000 years is unknown to any other civilisation on earth. The civilisational continuity of India from the Indus Valley period, when it had a highly sophisticated urban culture, to the present, too has been brought out by the encyclopaedia.

> It is known from archaeological evidence that a highly sophisticated urbanized culture—the Indus civilization—dominated the northwestern part of the subcontinent from about 2600 to 2000 BCE. From that period on, India functioned as a virtually self-contained political and cultural arena, which gave rise to a distinctive tradition that was associated primarily with Hinduism, the roots of which can largely be traced to the Indus civilization.

According to Professor Rummel, India had no dark past of massacre because there was a religious and civilisational tradition, and a science of dialogue and debate known as Tarka Shastra. Scholars used to debate issues in public in a dignified way so that they did not spill onto the streets as violent battles. Therefore, India had, from time to time, evolutionary responses fashioned by unending continuity of spiritual masters and social scientists to correct and undo social, religious, cultural and economic injustices without violence and bloodshed.

Autocratic China and Democratic India Recall their Past with Pride

Now the two largest nations, with a combined population of 2.8 billion out of the world's 7.9 billion, democratic India and autocratic China, are civilisational nation-states. India has always owned its past and civilisation with pride. On the other hand, China has hated its past, but has now begun recalling it with pride. India was under attack by foreign invaders but that did not affect its civilisational continuity or sense of pride. Its freedom movement itself was cultural and civilisational as Pandit Jawaharlal Nehru wrote in the *Foreign Affairs* magazine as far back as 1937.

In contrast, Communism disturbed and drove Chinese civilisation underground, but it re-emerged after its fading, a fact now openly acknowledged by China itself. In his address to the Chinese Communist Party on its 100th anniversary,

President Xi Jinping recalled the greatness of China's ancient history, saying, 'Historical and cultural heritage not only vividly tells the past but also profoundly affects the present and future; it belongs not only to us, but also to future generations. Having gone through over 5,000 years of vicissitudes, the Chinese civilisation has always kept to its original roots. As a symbol of the Chinese nation's unique spirit, it provides the nation with abundant nourishment to grow and prosper.'

All that Communism and colonisation did for China and India, respectively, was to achieve a unified contemporary state after years of struggle. The rest of the world, particularly the Arab and other Asian nations, also have a high sense of civilisational recall.

Need for Dialogue among Civilisations and Religions, Ancient Indian Civilisation Shows the Way

The likely emergence of the civilisational paradigm will have its own consequences which need to be handled. While Huntington's thesis opened the long-suppressed issue, it also misdirected the civilisational discourse because of the provocative term 'clash' he had used. Huntington was perhaps forced to focus on 'clash' because he had come across only those religions which had the propensity to clash and had admittedly not come across Hindu civilisation and religion which had no propensity for clash, but only potential for harmony. Huntington himself confessed in the preface to his book *Clash of Civilisations and the Remaking of the World Order* that, while after his paper was published in the *Foreign Affairs* magazine in 1993, he had travelled across the world and discussed with all civilisations 'except Hinduism'.

Clearly Huntington had no familiarity with Hindu religion or civilisation, which constitutes a sixth of the global civilisational space. He was unaware that in the world of religions where no religion accepts another, Hinduism is the only religion which does not deny any other religion's validity. Swami Vivekananda told the World Parliament of Religions in 1893 that there is in India a religious and civilisational paradigm which not only respects the other view, but also accepts it—an idea that the civilisational and religious history of the Abrahamic knows not.

> I am proud to belong to a religion which has taught the world both tolerance and universal acceptance. We believe not only in universal toleration, but we accept all religions as true. I am proud to belong to a nation which has sheltered the persecuted and the refugees of all religions and all nations of the earth. I am proud to tell you that we have gathered in our bosom the purest remnant of the Israelites, who came to Southern India and took refuge with us in the very year in which their holy temple was shattered to pieces by Roman tyranny. I am proud to belong to the religion which has sheltered and is still fostering the remnant of the grand Zoroastrian nation.

When a century later, after the world was shocked into disbelief by religious fundamentalism and terror, Harvard University started the Religious Pluralism Project in 1994, it recalled the World Parliament of Religions in 1893 and Swami Vivekananda and said:

> The late nineteenth century produced a distinctive solution to the growing awareness of religious diversity and the problems it posed, both in America and the world. That solution was an all-embracing universalism that envisioned a coming together of the great religions of the world. In 1893, a remarkable event took place in Chicago expressing this spirit: the World's Parliament of Religions.
>
> It was the first time that many Americans had ever heard Hindus or Buddhists speak in their own voices on behalf of their own faith. Swami Vivekananda, a Hindu, confirmed the vision of universal convergence that had captured the imagination of the planners. Their self-understanding was confirmed, mirrored back to themselves in the presence of this exotic swami from the East who was one of the most popular speakers at the Parliament.

One journalist wrote of him:

> Vivekananda's address before the Parliament was broad as the heavens above us, embracing the best in all religions, as the ultimate

> universal religion—charity to all mankind, good works for the love of God, not for fear of punishment or hope of reward.

Samuel Huntington missed this core element in the civilisational paradigm that Swami Vivekananda had articulated in 1893, which the Harvard University Pluralism Project recaptured in 1994. In his treatise, Huntington theorised civilisational clashes as inevitable instead of civilisational harmony as possible. With the world shifting to a civilisational paradigm, he said global institutions ought to make efforts to promote civilisational harmony to avoid civilisational clashes. And this is where India will emerge as the principal philosophy and thought giver. Civilisational paradigm does not mean, as Huntington theorised, a clashing paradigm only.

A massive intellectual probe of diverse religions and civilisations pointing to the emergence of a civilisational paradigm and contemporaneous in time to the Harvard University Pluralism Project was the Fundamentalism Project of the American Academy of Arts and Sciences, which published five large volumes or 3500 pages of seminal literature on religious fundamentalism between 1991 and 1995. Martin E. Marty, an Ordained Lutheran Pastor and well-known Christian theologian, and R. Scott Appleby, an acknowledged scholar on Christianity, who had also worked as an academic in India, were the editors of the project. In their concluding essay of the first of the five volumes titled 'Fundamentalism Observed', Marty and Appleby distinguished between (Abrahamic) religions whose beliefs rested on their exclusive texts and their inerrancy and other faiths that were not so and wrote:

> Some traits of fundamentalism examined here are more accurately attributable to the 'People of the Book', Jews, Christians, and Muslims, than to their first or distant cousins in the fundamentalist family: Hindus, Sikhs, Buddhists and Confucians.

Answering why fundamentalist traits of Abrahamic religions are absent in Eastern faiths, the editors answered:

> Sacred texts do not play the same constitutive role in South Asian and Far Eastern traditions as they do in Abrahamic faiths. Both to intensify missionary efforts and to justify extremism.

Samuel Huntington was right in that there is a mix of religion and civilisation and that the civilisational paradigm would also bring in a religious dimension. The only way to find harmony among civilisations is to follow the counsel of Hans Kung, a celebrated Christian scholar of the 20th century, who guided the German church in the 1965 Vatican Council II. In 1992, Kung formulated a three-point religious conflict avoidance formula which said:

- No peace among the nations without peace among the religions.
- No peace among the religions without dialogue between the religions.
- No dialogue between the religions without investigation into the foundations of the religions…

The suggestion of Hans Kung draws from the ancient inter-religious dialogue in India known as *Poorva Paksha*, which legitimises the study and criticism of the fundamentals of the opposing viewpoints by scholars. That culture of dialogue only saved India from bloody religious and civilisational clashes that took place in the Abrahamic world.

Democracy-Compatible vs Democracy-Incompatible Civilisation

All civilisations are not the same. Like any ideology, civilisation may also be either democracy compatible or incompatible. That China, a civilisationally conscious nation, is an autocracy and India, also a civilisational nation, is a democracy, shows that consciousness can be compatible or incompatible with autocracy or democracy depending on what philosophy is driving it. This is true of religions as well as materialist ideologies. There is no dispute about the fact that Communism is democracy incompatible while Free

Market is democracy compatible. Likewise, some religions are compatible with democracy and some are not. The Freedom House Report of 1999 expresses the view that Hinduism is democracy compatible, but, it said, Islam is not. Likewise, some civilisations are democracy compatible, and some are not. Just like the world cannot reject religions, it cannot also reject civilisations. The West, which accepts the fact of autocracies, democracies and religions, should also accept the reality of civilisations. Diversity is not limited to ruling systems only. It also extends to human beliefs, lifestyle and living models.

West as the Only Source of Modernity: A 20th Century View Challenged in the 21st Century

China was openly declared a systemic adversary of the West at the June 2021 NATO Meet. French President Emmanuel Macron went several steps further and said China is 'much larger than just the military issue. It is economic. It is strategic. It is about values. It is technological.'

The critical word in Macron's message is 'values'. The Western values in Macron's mind are obviously liberal democracy, free market, individual and human rights. But those values which define modern Western civilisation are rooted in the claim of the West that it is the sole heir to the history of enlightenment, of which it claims to be the geographical origin. It regards enlightenment as the sole intellectual source of human progress everywhere. The West traces its modernity, individualism, liberal democracy, human rights and even neo-classical economic theories as products of its enlightenment history. Much of the post-World War II geopolitical and geo-economic theories and practices have been, and continue to be, rooted in that assumption. The values Macron speaks of are rooted in enlightenment history.

There was nothing wrong with the West claiming any superior origin. But it became an issue with the Rest when the West began asserting that it was the single geographic origin and the only intellectual source of enlightenment for nations and peoples. It began benchmarking and marketing it as universal values for all on the planet by making them the norms and rules for the world order. This is a fundamental error in the Western understanding of itself and of the Rest which is several times bigger in geographic area and in human population, with a diversity which the West has never known or experienced except outside of it. This founding and continuing error is the cause of misjudgement of the West about the Rest. Universalist views of the West have been intellectually challenged by the Rest over time. This challenge is now resonating in geopolitics with the rise of Asia and China. And China is clearly and cleverly trying to articulate what has been the subterranean struggle of different and diverse civilisations, which do not accept the West claim of being the origin of enlightenment and modernity.

Western Thinkers Now Accept—West is Not the Exclusive Source of Modernity—There are Multiple Enlightenments, Multiple Modernities

Even the emerging opinion in the West itself seems to question its claim as the single source of enlightenment for the whole world. In a seminal essay titled 'Enlightenment in Global History: A Historiographical Critique' (*The American Historical Review*, October 2012), Sebastian Conrad, who holds the Chair in Modern History at Freie Universität Berlin, and is the author of many books, including his latest *What is Global History*—says that the rest of the world does not share the view that the West is the geographical origin and intellectual source of enlightenment and modernity. He also claims there are multiple enlightenments and modernities in different parts of the world. Conrad writes:

> The Enlightenment has long held a pivotal place in narratives of world history. It has served as a sign of the modern and continues to play that role yet today. The standard interpretations, however, have tended to assume, and to perpetuate, a Eurocentric mythology. They have helped entrench a view of global interactions as having essentially been energized by Europe alone. Historians have now

> begun to challenge this view. A global history perspective is emerging in the literature that moves beyond the obsession with the Enlightenment's European origins. The dominant readings are based on narratives of uniqueness and diffusion. The assumption that the Enlightenment was a specifically European phenomenon remains one of the foundational premises of Western modernity, and of the modern West. The Enlightenment appears as an original and autonomous product of Europe, deeply embedded in the cultural traditions of the Occident.
>
> According to this master narrative, the Renaissance, humanism, and the Reformation "gave a new impetus to intellectual and scientific development" that, a little more than three and a half centuries later, flowered in the Scientific Revolution and then in the Enlightenment of the eighteenth century.
>
> The results included the world of the individual, human rights, rationalization, and what Max Weber famously called the "disenchantment of the world". Over the course of the nineteenth century, or so the received wisdom has it, these ingredients of the modern were then exported to the rest of the world. As William McNeill exulted in his *Rise of the West*, "We, and all the world of the twentieth century, are peculiarly the creatures and heirs of a handful of geniuses of early modern Europe."
>
> This interpretation is no longer tenable. Scholars are now challenging the Eurocentric account of the birth of the modern world.

By intensely studying historiographies across the world, Conrad finds no single enlightenment or modernity of which the West is the origin and source as the West would like the Rest to believe. Conrad says that recent interventions provide a welcome reminder that the image of non-Western societies as stagnating and immobile is wide off the mark. The West did not have a monopoly on cultural transformations and intellectual conflicts. Such an archaeology of independent seeds of the modern is frequently connected to the larger project to revise the modernisation theory and to replace it with the paradigm of early, alternative, and multiple modernities. Admitting that the Enlightenment's global impact was not energised solely by the ideas of Parisian philosophies, Conrad says that rather it was the work of historical actors around the world—in places such as Cairo, Calcutta and Shanghai—who invoked the term and what they saw as its most important claims, for their own specific purposes. The challenge of the Rest extended from Egypt to India to China to the Koreas.

Enlightenment and Civilisation—Interchangeable

Enlightenment and civilisation, Conrad says, have been interchangeably used and enlightenment has been equated even to social evolution. In this sense, civilisational continuity means and includes change within continuity, which is an internalised modernisation process. Only when a society is frozen like it happened in the West, which the West itself admits as the Dark Ages, the process of change, that is, enlightenment, looks a distinct and dated event. The social evolution implicit in the civilisational continuity of other nations is the basis of challenge to the claim of the West as the sole geographic origin and exclusive intellectual source of enlightenment and modernity for all peoples on the planet.

Multiple Modernities Challenge Western Social, Economic Theories

The challenge also extended beyond academic and intellectual fields as a brooding provocation in geopolitics. The claim of the West, of it being the origin of enlightenment that modernised the entire world, extended beyond to claim comprehensive superiority and universal validity and acceptance for its own theories of politics, institutions and human social and economic progress. Western theories of politics, economics and institutions celebrated individualism sans relations; individual rights sans individual duties; human rights sans human duties; liberal economics, not just economics; liberal democracy that dismissed civilisational and electoral democracies as second-class democracies. These theories, which evolved from Hegel and Miller to Weber and Marx, are essentially products of Western history, way of life, civilisation and experiences. In equating what is essentially their experience as universal theories is where the West erred, perhaps grievously. By colonisation and exploration, driven by religious and commercial aggression, the West did get the first mover advantage to market and spread its thoughts and institutions to the Rest. Even the contemporary free market and Communist ideologies are both Western. The socialist and capitalist West could consensually conceptualise and construct global institutions after World War II and during the Cold War because both belonged to the same stock. The Western sense of modernity too was common to both.

Capitalism as the West and Communism as the Rest—Fukuyama's fundamental error

Francis Fukuyama and other post-Cold War scholars first saw, wrongly, the success of market capitalism and liberal democracy over Communism within the West as the final victory of the West over the Rest. There was a fundamental error in this formulation, as Communism did not represent the entire Rest of the world. On the contrary, Marxian thought and structures that collapsed were also the conception and construct of Western modernity. The tussle between market capitalism and state socialism is essentially a West vs West affair and not a West vs Rest issue. Both Communism and the free market were Western in origin. Post-Cold War, Western thinkers failed to look at the fundamental fact that Communism was never the civilisational soul of even most former socialist countries.

This was evident from what emerged from the ruins of socialism in ex-socialist nations. When the socialist structures collapsed, what emerged from the remains were indigenous religions, philosophies and values like Orthodox Christianity in Russia, neo-Confucianism in China, Roman Catholicism in Poland, to cite a few, and even ethnic civilisational divisions which turned into civil war among Balkans, and not capitalism. The collapse of the Communist order meant only this: namely that Socialist Universalism of the West was defeated by its Capitalist Universalism—two competing universalisms of the same stock—chips of the same block. When the Cold War order collapsed, socialist countries, or countries which followed neither socialism or market capitalism, did not, at any rate willingly, accept the free market capitalism of the West. Even China, a nation that claimed to be Communist even after the Cold War emerged, and with whom the West had a special engagement, was neither socialist, nor capitalist.

As an Indian thinker, M.S. Golwalkar, said in 1973 that Communism was a passing phase and China would rise with a bit of Confucianism, but with its entire empire building instincts intact. That is precisely what happened.

Later, in 1995, even Francis Fukuyama had to disown his own 1989 theory of the final victory of the West over the Rest and accept that what emerged out of Communist China was Confucian China. That later proved entirely right, as even though Deng Xiaoping disowned feudal Confucius, as he described him in his UNGA address in 1974, his successors began idolising Confucius a quarter of a century later. Now Confucius is a neo-hero in China. China now runs hundreds of neo-Confucian centres the world over as its expression of soft power. The challenge to Western theories and institutions which was subterranean first, slowly began manifesting in the dissenting intellectual discourse of the Rest. That brooding challenge of the Rest to the Western world view has been implicit in the rise of Asia, particularly in Japan and South East Asia following World War II. It is becoming more prominent with the rise of China and partly of India.

The seeds of the change in the world order which is being talked about now were first laid during the great economic crisis of 2008, which was as risky and dangerous as the Great Depression of the 1930s. This was a watershed development in the history of the West and the West-led world order that undermined liberal economic theories and weakened liberal economies and democracies.

2008 Global Crisis: The Watershed Development in the West-led World Order

In a seminal paper titled 'American Power after the Financial Crisis (Sep 2014)', Jonathan Kirshner, Professor at Cornell University, says, 'The global financial crisis of 2007–2008 was both an economic catastrophe and a watershed event in world politics.' Kirshner explains how the crisis altered the international balance of power, affecting the patterns and pulse of world politics. The crisis, Kirshner argues, brought about an end to what he identifies as the 'second post-war American order' because it undermined the legitimacy of the economic ideas that underpinned that order, especially those that encouraged and even insisted upon uninhibited financial deregulation.

The crisis also accelerated two existing trends: the relative erosion of the power and political influence of the United States and the increased political influence of other states, most notably, but not exclusively, China. Looking ahead, Kirshner anticipates a 'New Heterogeneity' in thinking about how best to manage domestic and international money and finance. These divergences—such as varying assessments of and reactions to newly visible vulnerabilities in the American economy and changing attitudes about the long-term appeal of the dollar—will offer a bold challenge to the United States and its essentially unchanged disposition toward financial policy and regulation. This New Heterogeneity will contribute to greater discord among nations about how best to manage the global economy. Kirshner's work, which is a provocative look at how the 2007–2008 economic collapse diminished US dominance in world politics, suggests that the most significant and lasting impact of the crisis and the Great Recession will be the inability of the United States to enforce its political and economic priorities on an increasingly recalcitrant world.

2008 Crisis: A Break Point for the World

Kirshner's analysis, from both financial and economic perspectives, is also about the political and geopolitical impact of the crisis. When Kirshner says that it opens up new heterogeneity in managing the economy, it also means multiple geopolitical centres of influence, if not power, which, in turn, means the resistance to Western social and political ideas also. All this manifests in the way now China is definitely prematurely, if not preposterously, trying to position its civilisational, political and economic world view as an alternative for the world. It is the 2008 crisis that provided this opportunity for a hiding and biding China to push its preposterous alternative to the Western liberal democracy and free market. One needs to understand the depth of the crisis, as admitted by the West itself, to know—one, how it exposed the unsustainability of the US and the liberal democratic and economic theories as of universal value to the world and two, how the crisis encouraged a China, whose autocratic alternative is ex facie unacceptable and unsustainable even for itself, to become so over ambitious as to think of its model as the future alternative for the world.

The 'God of Money', as he was known in his time, Alan Greenspan, himself admitted that the whole intellectual edifice of the financial system of the US he had presided over as its God for 20 years, has collapsed, questioning the entire theoretical foundation of neo-classical economics.

Collapse of 'Whole Intellectual Edifice', Alan Greenspan's Mea Culpa

The liberal West trusted the ultimate invincibility of its system of liberal democratic order and free market as post-Cold War Western geopolitical scholars had assured it. And believing them, without wasting a minute, the West soon built a super structure of one-size-fits-all globalisation, which was founded on a rule-based geo-economic order. Convinced of the durability and invincibility of its own institutional framework, the West was only concerned about how to make rules to manage, discipline, and integrate the non-Western world, particularly Asian nations, which have 60 per cent of the world's population, into that world order—without thinking whether that one-size-fits-all model would suit them. The unbelievably diverse world was too complex to be packed into this utopian hold-all one-size-fits-all idea to make it nearly homogenous. And China, which had decided to 'bide' its time, had pretended to be part of that global order. While other countries, that included India, had tamely accepted the one-size-fits-all rules framed by the West, the West had always perceived China as not a rule-accepter, but as an aspiring rule-setter and treated it with deference. Despite the viability of the one-size-fits-all globalisation project, which included the liberal democracies at one extreme and the autocracies on the other, being questioned, the euphoria of the 'final victory of the West over the Rest' made all counter reasoning against such an approach meaningless.

Despite being a dissenter against the rule-setting West, an autocratic and non-transparent China gate crashed into the rule-based transparent global order and WTO knowing that in market economics, economic actors are individuals and not corporates, that is, it will be a country in the case of China and that would be its huge advantage. It was part of China's game plan to exploit the transparent rule-based world order with its non-transparent political and economic system, which it did with extreme success and unbelievable results. China had gotten deep into the heart of the Western system before the 2008 crisis. Some thinking minds in the West were expecting the crisis, though they were not clear about the date of its coming. When the crisis hit the West, they did not even know what hit them.

The gravity of the watershed crisis to the West was explicitly admitted by Alan Greenspan, who headed the US Federal Reserve for almost two decades and indirectly ruled the capital markets of the world. In his Mea Culpa address to the US Congress on the crisis, Greenspan said:

> This crisis, however, has turned out to be much broader than anything I could have imagined…those of us who have looked to the self-interest of lending institutions to protect shareholder's equity (myself especially) are in a state of shocked

> disbelief...What went wrong with global economic policies that had worked so effectively for nearly four decades?.. A Nobel Prize was awarded for the discovery of the pricing model that underpins much of the advance in derivatives markets. This modern risk management paradigm held sway for decades. The whole intellectual edifice, however, collapsed in the summer of last year.

Greenspan implicitly admitted that the crisis had left financial capitalism operating today bereft of intellectual and theoretical foundations. Six months later, *The Economist* magazine, the most ardent exponent of Western financial capitalism, carried a cover story that said that all modern macroeconomic theories that the guild of economists in the West had developed in the last several decades had collapsed. It actually had carried a cover page cartoon that showed a book of modern economic theory melting away.

Short-Termism, the Cause of the 2008 Crisis

More than thirteen years have passed since the economic crisis hit the West and the world, but there is as yet no inquiry into why theoretical and intellectual foundations had collapsed and what the alternative to that collapse was. The intellectual and theoretical foundations of the West, as stated by Alan Greenspan, rest on the self-interest of economic players, and that assumption is what, he admitted, had collapsed. The short sighted self-interest of economic and market players are essentially short-termism. The main reason for the crisis was the peril of short-termism.

In economics and finance, the perils of short-termism that led to the 2008 crisis were mutely discussed, but never seriously debated or pursued. Sheila Blair, Chairperson of the Federal Deposit Insurance Corporation, spoke on the 'Lessons of the Financial Crisis: The Dangers of Short-Termism' in her remarks to the National Press Club in the US, which was carried in the Harvard Law School Forum on Corporate Governance (4 July 2011). She said:

> There are many causes of this crisis, some of which I will address in my remarks today. But, in my opinion, the overarching lesson of the crisis is the pervasive short-term thinking that helped to bring it about. Short-termism is a serious and growing problem in both business and government.

Despite short-termism being admitted as the cause of the crisis, the West has done nothing to curb it in both its social, economic and political discourse and agenda. Short-termism, which brought about the crisis, continues.

Short-Termism: A Civilisational Peril

In a short, but instructive article in the BBC Online (10 January 2019) on the Perils of Short-termism, Richard Fisher, Managing Editor of the BBC, says that modern society is suffering from 'temporal exhaustion', and brings out the perils of short-termism for a people and their civilisation:

Writing in 1978, sociologist, Elise Boulding, once said:

> If one is mentally out of breath all the time from dealing with the present, there is no energy left for imagining the future.

We can only guess her reaction to the relentless, Twitter-fuelled politics of 2019.

Western Economic Theories Celebrate Self Interest; Self Interest Leads to Short-Termism Macroeconomic Consequences of Short-Termism

How did short termism enter Western civilisation? Richard Fisher, an author, says that 'the longevity of civilisation depends on us extending our frame of reference in time—considering the world and our descendants through a much longer lens. What if we could be altruistic enough to care about people we might never live to see. The time frame of a society is very important. But one needs to go deeper to know why the modern individual doesn't have a longer lens to care about the descendants he may never live to see. The modern West has atomised the traditional society and even families into individuals. An atomised individual has nothing beyond his life to look at—not even his own personal gen-next. Not only has the modern West atomised society and family into the individuals, but it also celebrates individualism as a symbol of a human's rights and liberties un-interfered with by anyone, including the near and dear. An atomised individualist's life vision and mission is limited to him. When he will not think of his own children and grandchildren, why will he think of the next generation world and its descendants? Short-termism is rooted in the unbridled individualist Western lifestyle which impacts on all aspects of their life, including economic behaviour. Short-termism is a product of self-interest. Self-interest is a product of individualist lifestyle to the exclusion of even the naturally near and dear.

Self-interest which forces short-termism is not just legitimised, but it is (also) celebrated in the Western economic theories as the road to success. The celebration of self-interest is the outcome of a more comprehensive disorder, a cultural and lifestyle disorder. Short-termism, which pervades the modern Western way of life, today makes the sovereign political and economic individuals to think only about themselves, not even about their near and dear, much less about future generations. How it affects micro and macroeconomics can be easily seen.'

Analysing the savings behaviour of (society and family centric) Asians and individualist Americans, Barry Bobsworth, a Brookings Institution economist, said while the American savings are personal, for one's own future or retired life, the Asian savings is dynastic, for the grandchild the saver may not even live to see.

Bobsworth said:

> An American might think in terms of saving for their own retirement, but an Asian will think of accumulating resources in terms of saving for their family, for multiple generations in the future.

Asians have kept alive the inter-generational cultural and social link which produces dynastic savings. But individualist

Western theories and lifestyles have undermined that link as a restriction on the individual liberty to live their lives freely and, therefore, illiberally. The macroeconomic impact of the different behaviour of Asians is the high savings and investment rate in that region.

This caused, what Alan Greenspan kept saying, as global 'savings glut' which, in turn, promoted the Western habit of borrowing and spending by governments and consumers in the US. Greenspan even derisively asked, 'What will the saving Asians do with their savings, if Americans do not borrow and spend?', as if borrowing and spending was a favour which the American system did to help Asian savers. No economic theory can be so casual and reckless. And that was precisely the theory that was admitted to have caused the 2008 collapse. But the real and ultimate root cause of the financial crisis is the short-termist lifestyle promoted by Western anthropological modernity and liberalism. With inherent short-termism driving the entirety of modern Western life, self-interested economic players cannot be thinking long term. In brief, short-termism in a self- interest driven lifestyle can't produce long-term economics.

Barry Bobsworth's finding is that the culture of dynastic savings in Asia produces the macroeconomic outcome of higher national and even regional savings and a global savings glut.

Still, the West Shifted the Blame onto the World—'Western Crisis' Labelled as 'Global Crisis'

The Greenspan Mea Culpa clearly indicated that the man who led the US Fed, the institution which the whole world had trusted, had no clue about what happened. The Nobel Prize winning economic theories of the farthest frontiers of financial capitalism had failed. The guild of economists quarrelled about the causes of the collapse using mean language against one another. But after the meltdown, the US Fed and the Western financial system began administering the very same financial steroids which had caused the crisis to lift the economy to demonstrate that it responded and recovered. With the result, the unprecedented 2008 crisis was dismissed once again as a normal, but a bigger crisis, which financial capitalism normally comes across, nothing more. In the end, even after more than a decade, the real cause of the crisis remains unknown and undiscovered. It was necessary for the West to go in depth into what caused the crisis in free markets and that too essentially in the geography of the liberal West. Instead, the West tried to shift the blame for the crisis out of the geographies of the West itself.

In an effort to exculpate itself, the West which was the geographic and causal origin of the crisis, began claiming it was a global and not a Western crisis. This further disabled the West from true course correction. In the review of the book titled *The Consequences of Global Financial Crisis: The Rhetoric of Reform and Regulation* by Wyn Grant, British political scientist and professor of politics at the University of Warwick, Graham K. Wilson, Political Science Faculty of Boston University, Shawn Berslin said, citing Kishore Madhubani's view, that like all earlier financial crises were known by their origin, like the Mexican Peso crisis, East Asian Crisis, etc., Kishore Madhubani argued that the 2008 crisis must be known as the Western financial crisis. It was clear that 'the idea of a 'global crisis' was taken as a means of deflecting attention away from failings of the Western way of doing things.'

The West successfully camouflaged the real cause of the crisis—by underplaying it and not correcting its course, and by trying to shift the blame onto the world for the crisis, when it was clear that the crisis was exported by the West, if not solely by the US.

Alan Greenspan admitted that it was more than a systemic collapse. The collapse of the whole intellectual edifice was enough for a strong and willing competitor like China to see an opportunity to think of itself as a better systemic alternative.

2008 Western Crisis: The Context for China to Give Up Its Hide and Bide Policy

Feeling unchallenged since its self-declared euphoric victory, the liberal and democratic West thoroughly got used to enjoying its ever increasing short-termism. Systemically, its single party dictatorship admirably suited China for long term strategies against the West. While the democratic West, facing elections and change of rule every five years, was inherently incapable of matching the length of China's long term strategic play. Leveraging on its huge population, its autocratic control over them, its nuclear assets and its capacity to break the Communist bloc and end the Cold War—its unique strategic assets—China decided to play a long-term game to secure the recognition of the West, replacing Taiwan in the 1970s and getting close enough with the West to make it start engaging with Beijing.

In 2001, the West admitted China into the World Trade Organisation (WTO), which gave the non-transparent Communist regime an unprecedented opportunity to overawe the rule-based global system. In its engagement with China, the only long-term aspiration of the West—not the goal—was that, by making it economically liberal and prosperous, China would become politically liberal too. The other strategy of the West was to prove that the Western system was superior to China's and make China move away from autocracy. Both were benevolent approaches.

In contrast was the parallel and malevolent Star Wars of the US in the 1980s, with the intent to force the USSR to get into a competitive arms race, which led to the eventual collapse of the Soviet Union and Communism. The West intentionally did not pursue the benevolent alternative strategy of helping the Soviet Union to show the Communists that theirs was an inferior system. While the West played a benevolent game with the China and was malevolent to the USSR, China responded with its own malevolent strategy of hiding and biding its time to hit back at the US. The advent of the 2008 crisis seems to have signalled to China that the hiding and biding time would end soon. China also seemed to have got convinced that the Western model or order would no longer work for the world and it was time that China prepared itself to market its model as being better not only for itself, but also for the world.

This is the background to an emboldened China challenging explicitly, and also perhaps crudely, the Western view as the universal worldview for all. The China challenge has questioned the euphoric claim of the West from the 1990s that the cocktail of liberal democracy and free market constitutes the contours of the perfect (modern) society Hegel had conceptualised centuries ago.

China Began Asserting After the Crisis

It was not till after the crisis of 2008 that China began talking of its 'core interests' consisting of 'state system and national security', 'sovereignty and territorial integrity', and 'the continued stable development of China's economy and society'. In 2011, the State Council of the Republic of China defined the country's core interests as including 'state sovereignty, national security, territorial integrity and national reunification, China's political system established by the Constitution and overall social stability, and the basic safeguards for ensuring sustainable economic and social development'.

China has claimed that its security interests include specifically Tibet, Xinjiang, Inner Mongolia, Taiwan, its maritime rights and its environmental sustainability. China's core interests were a mix of civilisation, politics and nationalism in which Communist ideology did not seem to play a constitutive role. Whether it was Hong Kong or Taiwan or Xijniang, the core interests of China clashed with liberal democracy, rule-based trade and geopolitics and the human rights ideological paradigm of the West—not market capitalism.

Graham K Wilson and Shawn Berslin (see para 35) said that the (2008) crisis did not mark the start of the rise of Chinese power, but it certainly accelerated it in some areas, and helped undermine the legitimacy of the neo-liberal model that China stands as an alternative to, in some minds at least.

As Alan Greenspan said, the 2008 crisis had questioned the very intellectual fundamentals of the Western system. The crisis also played a similar 'catalyst' role in China's domestic sphere. The authors say that in some respects, China seems to be the latest in a line of Asian challenges to the dominance of a 'Western' world order.

China Used the Opportunity to Claim—Preposterously—Its Model as Superior and Global Alternative

China also did not accept the West escaping the responsibility for the crisis, giving technical explanations for its cause, nor was it impressed even with the claim of the West about its recovery from it. Looking at more basic fundamentals, it began perceiving the Western financial system as basically defective, seeing in it an opportunity to claim its own model as the better alternative not only for itself, but for the world as a whole!

Wilson and Berslin went on to say that 'China's top leaders, including Wen Jiabao (2009), were also quick to assert that the origins of the crisis were not just Western, but specifically rooted in the failure of American economic regulation and the "blind pursuit of profit"'.

The authors said that 'as it began to appear that China's response to the crisis seemed to be working, there was an upsurge in interest within China to the idea of a "China model", that might act as an alternative to Western modes of development.'

Qian Gang (2010) has traced the phenomenal rise in what he calls 'the discourse of greatness' in 2008 and 2009, reflecting a growing national pride in China's apparent increase in global economic power vis-à-vis the existing (crisis hit) powers.

Undoubtedly, an autocratic China's claim that its model is superior, and it is a global alternative, is preposterous as it has no rational basis. In fact, China's model is a home grown mix of Marxian autocracy that pretended to be a market economy and co-opted the West to promote and partner it. This is no model for anyone else who did not and could not pass through the mix of Confucian philosophy and Communist Revolution. China's own reasoning that the Western model cannot be imported and fitted into another country with a different history, culture and values is equally applicable to the Chinese model as well.

China's preposterous claim that its model can be global is the outcome of the stress that the West had been undergoing since the 2008 global crisis and the former's relatively faster recovery and growth after the crisis. But the rebound from the 2008 crisis is not China specific, as all Asian economies rebounded which made *The Economist* magazine wonder at the 'astonishing rebound of Asia' when the West was still providing stimulus to overcome the crisis.

Short-Termism Inherent in Liberal Democracy; Long-Termism Inherent Autocracy

Short-term economics aside, the short-termism of Western political liberal ideas has made the West vulnerable against the long-termism of the Marxist ideological China. In an article titled 'Why Democracy Cannot Deliver' and subtitled 'Endless elections, unqualified leaders, uninformed voters, and short-term thinking are impeding economic growth', the *Foreign Policy* magazine says:

> At the root of the problem is a predilection for short-termism that has become embedded in the political and business culture of modern democracies. By design, Western politicians have relatively short political horizons; they are often in office for terms of less than five years. So, they find their duties regularly interrupted by elections that distract from the job of addressing long-term policy challenges. As a result, politicians are naturally and rationally drawn to focus their efforts on seducing their electorates with short-term sweeteners—including economic policies designed to quickly produce favorable monthly inflation, unemployment, and GDP numbers. Voters generally favor policies that enhance their own well-being with little consideration for that of future generations or for long-term outcomes. Politicians are rewarded for pandering to voters' immediate demands and desires, to the detriment of growth over the long term. Because democratic systems encourage such short-termism, it will be difficult to solve many of the seemingly

intractable structural problems slowing global growth without an overhaul of democracy.

A China that does not have to worry about the next elections in its politics and next quarter results of its companies seems to have had the better of the Western liberal democracies which was afflicted by both. This is not to say that liberal democracy is no good and autocracy is all good. But as the world stands at present, within the West, overtaken by the euphoria of its superiority, hit by the 2008 crisis and its aftermath and now by the Pandemic, the Chinese autocracy does seem to hold an advantage against Western liberal democracies. The Western world, convinced that liberal democracy alone will sustain in the long run, had hoped that, when allowed into the global market, even a Marxist China, which had to liberalise its economics, would finally liberalise its politics. But not only that hope has not been realised, what has happened was the other way round—Chinese autocracy has stood undiluted against both free market and liberal democracy. With the result, at least in China's perception, today the liberal West looks weaker and vulnerable against the autocratic China.

A Telling Comparison: Chinese Autocracy, a Long-term Project; Liberal Democracy, a Short-term Project

The real advantage China has over the West is the stability which the autocratic political system provides. That autocratic stability enables China to take an extraordinarily long-term view, which democracies, more particularly liberal democracies, cannot afford. Here is a telling picture of the changes in the leadership of single party Chinese autocracy since 1949, as compared to the two-party democracies in the US and the UK.

From 1949 till Xi Jinping became the paramount leader in 2013, China has had just five paramount leaders—Mao Zedong from 1949 to 1974 (twenty-five years); Deng Xiaoping 1974 to 1989 (fifteen years); Ziang Jemin from 1991 to 2004 (thirteen years) and Hu Jintao from 2004 to 2013 (nine years)—all under a single Communist Party dictatorship. Just four minds ruled

China for sixty-four years (1949–2013), while the fifth mind (Xi Jinping) continues to rule since then.

In the same period, the US has had fifteen Presidents and power has changed hands between Republican and Democratic parties eleven times. If the incumbent person and party changes are added, the number of times power has changed from one ruling mind to another is twenty-six times in seventy-two years.

In the same period, the UK has had seventeen Prime Ministers and power has changed hands between the Labour and Conservative parties eight times. If the incumbent person and party changes are added, the number of times power has changed from one ruling mind to another is twenty-five times in seventy-two years.

The telling comparison shows how autocracy is inherently a long-term project and democracy is inherently a short-term project.

Autocratic Stability: China's Long-Term Advantage

Deng Xiaoping, who ruled China unquestioned for fifteen years, could tell the Chinese to bide their time and hide their capacities because China decided to be a long-term player domestically and geopolitically. No leader of a democratic nation could have had nor could afford that long-term vision as his term of office and his party was subject to elections itself and would be short-term. Chinese rulers had no worry that their people, except through a remote possibility of a counter revolution, would remove them from power and put someone in place which naturally and casually happens in a democracy. This was the reason why China chose to remain isolated from the West and the world till 1970, building aggressive domestic power, including nuclear capability, despite being abysmally poor. Had China not built nuclear capability, no one, and certainly not the US, would have bothered about it.

The West began disputing China as a market economy after fifteen years and eventually got the WTO to declare it as not one at all. China outsmarted the West with its long-term mission and built itself into a huge real techno-economic power.

Chapter 9, titled 'A 50 year Chronology: How The US Raised its Own Frankenstein Monster, Bhasmasur China—A Lesson for Itself and for all Free Nations', brings out the chronology of China-US engagement which shows how China outsmarted the US. China bided its time, while the West looked for short-term advantages. The West has been a victim of short-termism for so long, that now it has lost its sense of what is long-term.

Ideology-free Short-termist West; Ideological Long-term Player China

The 2008 economic crisis has shown that while the West had no time to spare for the long-term view, China had no time to waste on short-term things. The short termism of the West seems to be up against the long-term mission of China. The capitalist order is inherently short-termist. Lester Thurow, the MIT Sloan School economist, wrote in the 1990s that capitalism 'is too individualist, short-termist and self-indulgent, and a capitalist society produces imprudent and uncoordinated economic creatures'.

The short-termism of the West got accelerated by its post-Cold War sense of the final victory of the West over the Rest. Once its future was guaranteed by the final victory it had got, all problems became short-term. This is where, in euphoria, the US even declared that with its dollar becoming the global medium of exchange by choice and acceptance, the US Federal Reserve could officially discard the Nobel Prize winning monetary theory of Milton Friedman, which had rescued the US from deep recession, hyperinflation and high unemployment in early 1980s, as no longer valid.

Subsequently, the West regarded every crisis as a short-term one and applied short-term solutions. Each short-term solution hid and made it difficult to probe the deeper and long-term causes of the crisis. Repeated crises are an indication of a hidden long-term cause, but repeated short-term solutions hide and defer knowing what the long- term cause is. Market economists who had solved this long-term-short-term riddle, convinced themselves, and also the world, that repeated crises are a part of liberal market economics and one must deal with them as they emerge and not bother too much about the long-term, as in the long-term all are dead! This justification might be justifiable where there was no challenge to the free market economy, but not when a non-market economy and long-term strategist like China, which incidentally the West itself had created, could take advantage of the crisis and claim to be a challenger, which it did post the 2008 crisis.

Normal crisis resolution and management tools which the West has been employing might not work when a hostile challenger of the market system is keen to exploit the crisis. Since the end of the Cold War, the short-term rule of market economics has shaped ideology-free Western approach geopolitics as trade and economics. This seems to be facing the greatest challenge from long-term ideological China. The ideology-free Western system is market centric, with the State acting as a watchdog, while the ideological Marxist Chinese system is State centric with the market treated as its pet dog.

With the West still licking wounds from the 2008 crisis and not being able to diagnose or address the fundamental weaknesses of its own system, the Covid-19 pandemic that has emerged from China has hit the world hard, leaving China virtually unharmed. It is the post-2008 crisis weaknesses of the West and the Covid-19 challenge to it, which has emboldened China to openly challenge it.

The liberal West needs to introspect on where or what liberal democracies lack that makes them vulnerable against an autocratic China. Where did the liberal West err for China to take advantage of it?

Euphoric West Erred in Projecting Free Market and Liberal Democracy as Icons of Final Victory

When the liberal West had set out on the paradigm of globalisation after the collapse of the socialist world, the premise was final victory of liberal democracy and free market capitalism over all ideas, ideologies and institutions. But, within a quarter of the century, liberal democracies and rule-based market economics stand challenged by China with its strange mix of a Marxist state and market economics. It did not need a seer to tell that this mix of a Marxist state and market economy is an oxymoron. But, a euphoric liberal West saw harmony between oxymoronic contras. The liberal West-centric globalisation, which allowed Marxist and autocratic China to operate on par with and even preferred over democratic nations, has done the West and the world in. The liberal West's euphoria at the fall of the Communist Bloc was a fatal error of judgement that failed to distinguish between long-term players and short-term actors in geopolitics. An overconfident US which declared a policy of 'positive engagement' with China from 1993, and the European Union joining it, enabled China to enter the world market (World Trade Organisation) in 2001. The West did this primarily to gain access to a stable Chinese market for their own growth. But very soon, in 2016, both the US and the EU began pleading in the WTO that China was not a market economy at all, and China retorted that the very fact that it was admitted to the WTO meant that it was a market economy. Just a couple of years before China was admitted into the global market, in 1999, the West had awarded the Nobel Prize for Economics to Amartya Sen who had made a comparison between an autocratic China and a democratic India and found that the free market operated in a democracy and not in an autocracy. Against this background, even a blind man would have known in 2001, when the US admitted China into the WTO for its own short-term gains, that the new entrant, a Marxist autocracy, could never operate a market economy.

The strategy of the US/West to gain short-term economic advantage by engaging and promoting China has now destabilised the geopolitical world order forever. This is the sorry state of the liberal West-led rule-based contemporary world order. The lesson that emerges from post-World War II and post-Cold War history is that no one should make far reaching decisions when one is euphoric, just as one should not make decisions when in extreme distress. But the misjudgement caused by its euphoric victory in the 1990s was not the only cause of the liberal West under threat of loss of its lead over China. The West must recognise the fundamental weakness in liberal Western democracies, that is, the erosion of the civilisational element by the promotion of unbridled individualism at all levels, including private and family life.

Political liberalism transforming into social liberalism has undermined natural human relations and de-legitimised all norms and sense of moral duties and obligations of human beings inter se. This has made a people who were once interdependent among themselves through relations, into dependents of, and on, state support and largesse. Studies show that more than half of the population of the US is state supported today. Thus, post the 2008 crisis, the US came out of recession by interdependent people helping each other. The interdependence of the people had been undermined and destroyed by the intervening state to turn the market economy into a market society.

Having seen where the euphoric US and West erred on China, is not China, which has far less reasons to be euphoric now as compared to the West in 1990s, committing the very same blunder by claiming its model as an alternative to the Western model?

Is China Repeating the Errors of the West?

Today China, under President Xi Jinping, seems to be committing the same historic error that the West committed when claiming final victory for liberal democracy. The 2008 crisis and its aftermath has definitely landed the Western market economy-turned market society in a mess, and the short-termism approach spread over decades has greatly contributed to this mess. But does that not mean that China, with its autocratic model, is a success and can win global acceptance, or think of emerging as the winner, as no country, including Soviet Russia of the past, can afford the scale of violence needed to work the Chinese model in the long run? It needs no seer to say that autocratic China's success is a largesse from the US/West, which had wrongly judged China and thought of moderating Chinese politics with economic prosperity. If in its euphoria, which is more due to the perceived weakness of the West than its own standalone strength, China thinks or claims its model as a global alternative to the US/West, it will be committing the same error as the West. Also unlike today's China, the West had historic, real and original strength in every sense to think it had succeeded. In the absence of continued Western engagement, whether China's model is durable for itself in the long run, is itself a question.

The assumptions underlying China's challenge to the West are highly questionable. With the economy of the West and China deeply intertwined, decoupling between them is no easy affair. In any event, China needs the West much more than the West needs China. And yet, China's aggressiveness outside and repressiveness inside seems to have forced it to decouple from the West. What is its end game?

Can China Afford to Decouple from the West? Marx vs Market Tension Within, Geopolitical Issues Outside

The signals from Xi Jinping show that China has decided to decouple from the West. Commenting on the crackdown on tech companies by the Chinese government, the South China Morning Post (SCMP), which is China's window to the world, hinted at China decoupling from the US.

The very title of the SCMP article written by a former editor-turned editorial adviser, postulates as follows: 'Will China learn its US$1 trillion lesson from the stock rout and be more transparent? The signs are still unclear'.

It brings out the tension and contradictions within China, between Marx and Market. The contents of the article, which is, by Chinese standards, a severe indictment of the Chinese government, and is summarised for a better understanding of how Deng Xiaoping-led reform is being reversed by Xi Jinping.

Behind closed doors, Chinese regulators appear to have been shocked by the scale and extent of the market reactions that saw the nation's best tech stocks lose about US$1 trillion in market value by some estimates.

SoftBank Group, a leading investor in Chinese tech companies, including e-commerce giant Alibaba and ride-hailing company Didi Global, indicated that it would hold off new investments in China and wait.

They are more worried about international reactions than domestic ones, but publicly, have kept mum.

There is little indication that the Chinese will learn from the costly lessons and be willing to mend their ways and become more transparent with future policies.

The domestic grumbling over the way in which the regulators launched a spate of investigations into China's leading tech companies has been equally strong, even though hardly anyone can speak publicly.

Chinese officials appear to have given scant regard to how the policy changes would go down with investors and their wider political implications before they were announced.

The unintended consequences are not just financial losses suffered by investors. They have geopolitical implications, particularly for China's fraught relations with the United States.

For instance, most of China's leading private education companies are listed on Wall Street as Variable Interest Entities (VIEs), a legally uncertain structure. The Chinese government's crackdown on those companies included a warning that they could be banned from using this structure and this has raised considerable concerns about other US-listed Chinese companies that are also VIEs, including Alibaba, the parent company of the South China Morning Post, and Pinduoduo, another e-commerce giant.

According to reports, as of late April 2021, about sixty Chinese companies were still planning to go public in the US this year. A growing crackdown by Beijing threatens to touch every part of the Chinese tech industry. Things are looking pretty dire for Chinese tech right now, especially firms that have been considering overseas listings as a way to raise money. The chill created by tensions, both within China's borders and with its greatest rival, could bring overseas investment in Chinese tech to a grinding halt.

Xi Jinping Risking Killing the Golden Goose That Made China Prosperous?

Since 2014, when Xi Jinping began turning aggressive outside and regressive inside, a debate has been going on about whether he intended to kill the golden goose that made China prosperous. In an article titled 'Why suddenly this aggressive behaviour by China?', Gary Schmitt, Director of the Marilyn Ware Center for Security Studies at the American Enterprise Institute, wrote in the *Los Angeles Times* (2014) a farsighted article, in which he asked, will China kill the golden goose of globalisation which transformed it from being land of poverty into the second largest economy, and answered it thus:

> China's remarkable leap from impoverished nation to the second-largest economy in the world has been made possible by an international economic order that it has taken full advantage of Beijing has every reason not to kill the golden goose of globalization by turning the attention of the region's other powers from trade and business to matters of security and armaments. Nor would one think that China would want to challenge the United States now since, arguably, it is American power and leadership that has largely kept the world's trading system humming by keeping both the great commons free and cataclysmic wars among the great powers from happening.

Saying so, and searching for China's aggressive behaviour, Schmitt said that an argument offered to explain recent Chinese behavior was linked to American weakness.

In 2009, with the great recession underway, the Obama administration's grand strategic outreach to Beijing was seen by the Chinese as a sign of US retreat. Talk at the time from senior American officials of a possible G-2, and President Obama's statement that 'the relationship between the United States and China will shape the 21st century,' making 'it as important as any bilateral relationship in the world', appeared to convince the Chinese that its rise to the top might be occurring faster than anticipated because of a more precipitous US decline.

This narrative has only increased as the administration's planned 'pivot' to Asia has been undercut by declining defence budgets and doubt that the Trans-Pacific Partnership free-trade agreement will be concluded anytime soon. However, perceived US weakness cannot be the whole story, even if it's an important part. What is also at play are Chinese ambitions. China's leaders want their nation to be a great power; they want China, as in its imperial past, to have a predominant say in the region. Xi's earliest speeches and appearances were to stoke the 'Chinese Dream', and it was on his watch that Chinese passports were issued with watermark maps that included territories claimed by Japan, Vietnam, the Philippines and India. In 2014 again, Steve Tsang of *Times* UK wrote that Beijing wouldn't hesitate to crush the Hong Kong protests if it meant preventing democracy infecting the mainland, even though Hong Kong is the goose that lays the golden egg for China. He wrote:

> The ruling Communist party allows Britain's former colony a degree of freedom denied to other parts of China because of its status as a financial centre. No less importantly, the families of many leading Communists have luxurious properties and huge investments in Hong Kong. This is why the party has no wish to repeat the brutal military crackdown of Tiananmen Square in 1989. I will not, however, rule it out. Killing the goose is costly and regrettable but the party believes China is now wealthy and powerful enough to forsake the golden eggs and withstand the international backlash

> that would follow. Beijing does not depend on Hong Kong in anything like the way.

In December 2017, the *Huffington Post* wrote 'Tightening Its Grip on Hong Kong, China Could Kill Its **Golden Goose**.'

In June 2019, award-winning journalist and author William Pesek wrote that China risks killing the **Hong Kong golden goose**.

In July 2019, the *Telegraph* UK wrote asking 'Is the Chinese dragon about to **kill its golden goose**?'

In November 2019, The *New York Post* editorial board wrote Why Beijing's likely to **kill the Hong Kong golden goose**.

In June 2020, *Fortune* Magazine wrote that it was often argued that the 'Chinese would not risk killing the golden goose' whose shiny eggs enriched Chinese and foreigners alike; but Hong Kong's golden goose has lost its former luster—at least in the eyes of Chinese President Xi Jinping. As with the new security law, China's current leadership is determined to rein in Hong Kong's independence even if it jeopardises the city's role as a global financial capital.'

It further said that 'Xi and his allies seem far more willing than any Chinese leader since Mao Zedong to trade away growth for the sake of greater stability and control,' and concluded, 'That for now, Xi and his allies seem less intent on preserving the golden goose than on keeping their ducks in line.'

When China cracked down on technology firms that targeted the huge investments of SoftBank in July 2021, *Japan Times, Project Syndicate, South China Morning Post, Fox Business, Taipei Times, Forbes*—all of them again asked almost the same question, Is Xi's China killing the golden goose of tech firms?

On China destabilising globalisation, or of it disturbing the status quo in Hong Kong, or in its crackdown on tech firms, while Western media keeps asking whether China is killing the golden goose, the analysis of Gary Schmitt in the *LA Times* in 2014 suggests that China's superpower ambitions are at play. This takes us to the next issue, has China decided to enter a do or die game with no retreat option?

Xi Jinping Can Neither Step Forward nor Step Back: Is China in a Do or Die Game Without a Retreat Option?

When Trump threatened China in 2018, China buckled. China was keen not to decouple from either the US or the EU. The *South China Morning Post* wrote in a recent article (13 August 2021) that soon after then US president Donald Trump launched a trade war against China in 2018, Chinese leaders decided to open up to foreign investment in greater breadth and depth at home, making it harder for businesses to leave the country with a further key strategy to encourage Chinese companies to trade on Wall Street. Xi personally pushed and China went the farthest to sign the Comprehensive Agreement on Investment with the EU in December 2020–March 2021 to open up its market to EU products in return for China to make strategic investments in the EU, in a desperate bid to divide the Trans-Atlantic Alliance.

But when the US and G-7 raised the issue of human rights in Xinjiang and took strong positions against China in March 2021, Beijing seems to have sensed the emergence of Trans-Atlantic Alliance unity and the collapse of the EU-China Comprehensive Agreement on Investment (CAI) with the EU Parliament withholding its consent for it. China's unprecedented and hostile reaction against the US and EU has put it on an irreversible collision course with the US and G-7. After Trump's defeat in the US Presidential elections and with the Covid-19 sparing China and devastating the West and the rest of the world, China seems to have decided that its moment has come. It is clear that China has decided to decouple from the West without the long-term preparation needed for that. The steps that Xi has taken to assert Chinese superiority and to project its own model as a better alternative to the Western one, which has been holding both the mind and geographic space of the world, seems to indicate China's arrogance rather than its confidence. The sequence of events has made disengagement between the West and China beyond the capacity of both to recall or undo without serious loss of face and compromises by both of their core interests. As the *Foreign Affairs* magazine wrote (July 2021) that Xi seems to have taken a move and reached a stage from where he cannot step back nor move forward. Xi, who is keen to secure his second term of ten years in 2022, has obviously taken huge external risks for China to overcome the internal challenges to him. China's military might seem to have also influenced Xi Jinping to go overboard. But neither is China fully mature for—nor contemporary geopolitics will permit—a military option for China, or for that matter for any country in the world which may lead to a World War. Having taken a belligerent position which may lead to a military standoff in Taiwan or the South China Sea or Hong Kong or even a war beyond borders with India, Xi can neither move forward nor go back. The consequences of this confidence which borders on arrogance are more likely to put China on the back foot than help it to move forward.

Like the US and its allies were overconfident about their own superiority in the post-Cold War period, underestimating China as an underdog, promoting it for its own benefit and getting into a mess, now China too seems to be overestimating its own strengths and underestimating the strengths of the US and its allies. It perhaps thought that with Trump's defeat, Trumpism will die out and with the wolf warriors dividing the US into pro and anti-China, the US will continue its one-sided engagement, which will continue to benefit China.

China thought that it had successfully divided the Atlantic Alliance through the EU-China Comprehensive Agreement on Investment (CAI), which Xi Jinping personally pushed, but finally all this came to nought.

Evergrande Crisis: Is the Chinese Economy Facing the Lehman Brothers moment of the US?

The most relevant question now, as the latest development in China's economy—the housing giant Evergrande debt crisis—unfolds, is whether it will be the Lehman Brothers moment of China in 2021 and what will China do with it? Whether it will follow the US, namely let it fall like the US did first in 2008, but when the contagion spreads threatening a total collapse, it had to do a massive rescue act later which made the US weaker as an economy and as the geopolitical power, or do what the US did with Lehman Brothers and wait to see whether the Evergrande spreads beyond control and act later or never act at all. The Evergrande crisis is the biggest test for the strange three-decade old Marx-Market mix of China with the potential of its turning into a Marx vs Market issue.

Just to get an overview of the problem, according to a 2020 US National Bureau of Economic Research (NBER) paper, housing accounts for 29 per cent of the Chinese Economy—higher than the previous estimates of 24 per cent. Undoubtedly, this is the principal domestic driver of China's growth. Evergrande is the second largest housing company in China. With more than 1.6 million undelivered homes, and with a debt of $300 billion—making it the world's most indebted—Evergrande is on the brink of bankruptcy, according to Lina Batarags, Managing Editor, *Business Insider* Singapore. She says, citing China Household Finance Survey, that one-fifth of the homes in China—at least sixty-five million housing units, enough to house the entire population of France—accounting for 21 per cent of the total are empty. The massive housing problem, as many issues in China, has been kept secret. While the fraudulent market practices had kept the Lehman Brothers crisis suppressed, the non-transparent Marx-Market mix in China had kept the Evergrande crisis under the carpet—finally the market exposing both. The most telling facts about Evergrande are:

- More than 90 per cent of Chinese households are homeowners
- With more than 20 per cent of homeowners in China having more than one home, housing is real estate investment rather than residence
- 70 per cent of the household wealth in China is real estate holdings
- The total debt of home developers in China is $5.2 trillions
- The debt, 46 per cent of which is from banks, has doubled since 2016

- It is almost ⅗ of global housing debt—the US' being ⅙—and is more than the total GDP of Japan
- Added to this, Evergrande has 700 projects under construction, covering 132 million square meters of total floor area
- Total sale of housing is down by 36 per cent for most developers and 44 per cent for ten top developers as compared to September 2020
- Housing prices have hit the roof—the median apartment in Beijing or Shenzhen costs more than forty times the median family annual disposable income
- Ten of the sixteen soccer clubs in the Chinese Super League are wholly or partly owned by developers.
- Chinese government budget deficit to GDP ratio which is 4.2 per cent will shoot up to 7.0 per cent by 2025—excluding issues like Evergrande
- China's banks loans to private sector to GDP is over 182 per cent in 2020—as compared to Japan 110 per cent, US 54 per cent, India's 55 per cent
- Chinese banks have exposures ranging from 6 per cent over 10 per cent in housing sector
- China's local government debt tops 50 per cent of the nation's GDP.

In a brilliant analysis titled 'The Economic and Geopolitical Implications of the Evergrande' published in the VIF India Site (14 October 2021), Dr Anantha Nageswaran has unveiled the implications of Evergrande debt issue. Dr Anantha Nageswaran says that it is difficult to say objectively whether Evergrande will or will not be Lehman Brothers for China, but Evergrande definitely makes a good match for Lehman Bros.

Here is the summarised version of the author's views:

The issue is not Evergrande but the Chinese housing sector. Regardless of whether Evergrande was China's Lehman Brothers, China's property sector was indeed way too big to fail or, 'to be allowed to fail'. The Catch-22 situation is this. With median home prices already topping forty times the annual disposable income, unless the prices fall, house sales which are falling—and have fallen by over one-third—cannot stop or pick up. If the prices fall, then the Chinese household wealth will shrink. If the prices fall then there has to be a bail out of the housing companies and also the banks which have lent to them. And no one is sure how the Chinese authorities will manage the situation without destabilising the larger economy. Also, if the government were not to let Evergrande fail, then it would take a lot more government money than China's budget can afford, to shore up the household wealth, local government revenues which are under stress even without providing support to the housing sector.

In avoiding others' mistakes, is China making its own?

The last quarter century of unprecedented growth of China has been driven by private capital. According to McKinsey & Company,

> just in the past 20 to 25 years, the share of Chinese urban employment supported by the private sector including foreign enterprises more than quadrupled from just 18 per cent in 1995 to 87 per cent in 2018. Exports created by the private sector also more than doubled from 34 per cent to 88 per cent. Private influence on fixed asset investment is still lower at 65 per cent in 2018, up from 42 per cent in 1995.

Clearly economic power has shifted from the state to private capital which has emerged as the principal driver of the national economy. It is at this point that the Chinese President Xi Jinping, who had already positioned himself as the leader without limit on his term, seems to have decided on a huge domestic politico-economic course correction—almost a U-turn—which has geo-political ramifications. The course correction is clearly to ensure that the private capital which has been in the driver's seat serves the state power and not think of a share in it and never think of overawing it, like in the US, for instance.

Referring to the reports of why and what is happening in China from close watchers of China, Dr Anantha points to three lessons which China may have drawn from—one, how after the 6 Jan 2021 Capitol Hill attack, the social media companies banned Trump, which shocked the world leaders and demonstrated the power of the capital over the power of the state; two, from how corruption brought down the Russian communist state that did not centralise its authority; and third, how the Japanese economy collapsed, wilting under the pressure of the US to strengthen the yen against the US dollar. Xi Jinping's action against the Capitalists, his purges against corruption, and the Chinese government's efforts to prevent the yuan from appreciating may have been the result of the lessons drawn from other's experiences.

But in trying to avoid the errors of others, China has paid such a high price that Dr Anantha rightly says, 'In short, China is failing not because it emulated the West but it sought to avoid the mistakes of the West and committed its own, in the process.' When a small power makes mistakes, it affects only itself, but when a big power makes mistakes, it affects the whole world. This is how what may be the mistakes born out of China's actions are likely to affect the whole world's economic and political order.

Marx-Market bonhomie turning into Market hate Marx? Common prosperity idea not to share wealth but to bring down the wealthy?

Deng Xiaoping declared in the 1980s, 'China will let some people get rich first.' A *New York Times* report (7 September 2021) says that China's top 1 per cent own nearly 31 per cent of the country's wealth, according to Credit Suisse Research Institute, up from 21 per cent in 2000. The same study says that the top 1 per cent in the United States own about 35 per cent. Deng's vision has been more than realised. What next? One doesn't know what Deng had in mind after his vision was realised. Now China and the US on par on both the power of private capital and income inequality. Xi Jinping, who ought to have felt threatened by both income inequality and the power of private capital, seems to feel more threatened by the latter, given what is happening in the US. Jinping obviously sees wealth and the wealthy as no more the assets of China, but as a threat to the Chinese communist state. Evidently he has decided to put an end to any remote possibility of something similar happening in China. He seems to have decided to hit the wealthy to create the perception that he is acting against income inequality. Many may tend to think that the Jinping idea of 'common prosperity' is the next chapter in Deng's mission first to create the wealth and then distribute the wealth created. But Jinping's idea will rather bring down the wealth created as testified to by the destruction of Chinese private wealth in the market and not distribute the prosperity among the common people.

The point that Dr Anantha makes is that, with Xi Jinping's extension in 2022, he cannot be seen to be in the company of, or allowing the likes of Jack Ma around, matches with the need to destroy the wealthy more than distribute the wealth. Jinping sees the possibility of his political goal impeded by the rise of private wealth almost equal to the capitalist US. Here Dr Anantha cites Richard McGregor who writes in the *Foreign Affairs* magazine, 'The timing is touchy for Xi, as he would be demanding a third five-year term as head of the CCP, following his alteration of term limit rules in 2018 to allow him to stay on past a decade. That move bought anger and angst from many of his colleagues—expressed privately, for the moment, but with the possibility of more open dissent in the lead-up to the party congress. It's no wonder he is looking for rich villains and greater loyalty. He will need both.' The result is back to the basics of communism, to destroy the wealth of the rich as the first step to distribute the wealth—contrary to Deng's idea of creating the wealth for distribution later. In the process, what is happening is that instead of the traditional communist theory of a clash between the proletariat and the rich, the contemporary Chinese model is to promote ideological clash between Marx and Market—between the Marxist state and Market, both local and global. The result is that the three decades of bonhomie between Marx and Market in China has U-turned to reinstate

Marx's hate for Market. The consequences of this shift can be unimaginable for China and the world.

Why Aggressive China Cannot Be a Soft Power

From the global perspective, the wide acceptability gap between China and the West, which China can never manage to bridge, is that the West is democratic and, therefore, transparent. China, on the other hand, is autocratic and non-transparent. The world would find it difficult to trust a non-transparent autocracy like it would trust a transparent democracy. Again, democracy is itself soft power, and autocracy, by nature, is hard power. In the contemporary world, hard power is not a substitute for soft power and can only be a supplement and support for the latter. During a part of the Cold War and for most of the post-Cold War period when hard power mattered, the West had an advantage over the Communist Bloc because its democratic identity made its hard power softer and naturally acceptable to the public. At that time, the idea of soft power was not in global discourse. After geopolitics grew beyond raw and hard power, global discourse began to place emphasis on soft power.

In an essay titled 'Constraints on the Soft Power Effects of Authoritarian States: The Case of the 2015 Military Parade in Beijing', Camilla Sorensen of the Institute for Strategy at the Royal College for Defence Studies at Copenhagen, Denmark, asks: 'Is it possible for authoritarian states such as China, Russia and Iran to combine the soft power narratives directed primarily towards an international audience with the narratives directed primarily towards a domestic audience that are aimed at maintaining regime security?'

To investigate that question, she analyses, 'the 2015 military parade in Beijing', using this case to highlight and discuss the constraints on Chinese leaders' efforts to project soft power. Her key finding is that 'soft power will continue to be the weak link in China's pursuit of a great power position and status as long as what continues to count as "Chinese" is defined in opposition to hostile "others" and the humiliation narrative continues to function as the central identity marker in the party-led construction of national identity (the "us").'

She concludes: 'Soft power is about the non-coercive ability to change the preferences of others, to make them want what you want purely by the force of attraction and persuasion. This is not an easy task for authoritarian states. The analysis of the 2015 military parade in Beijing shows the complex, contingent domestic/international dynamics at play when authoritarian states engage in the promotion and management of their international image and attempt to project soft power.'

If the 2015 military parade was a constraint on China's claim to soft power, the 2021 Communist Party centenary speech of Xi Jinping improved upon the 2015 parade speech by miles, as it vowed to maintain iron grip over Hong Kong, to unite Taiwan with the mainland and assert its rights over the South China Sea—each one of them provocative and aggressive, and none of which was mentioned in the 2015 speech. Xi Jinping took the aggressive agenda forward, saying:

> We Chinese are a people who uphold justice and are not intimidated by threats of force. As a nation, we have a strong sense of pride and confidence. We have never bullied, oppressed, or subjugated the people of any other country and we never will. By the same token, we will never allow any foreign force to bully, oppress, or subjugate us. Anyone who would attempt to do so will find themselves on a collision course with a great wall of steel forged by over 1.4 billion Chinese people.

The geopolitical aggression of China, which is coercive, undermines all its cultural soft power narratives.

Autocracies are basically insecure. The primary concern of an autocracy is its own security. Camilla Sorensen says that meeting and managing the challenges to regime security takes first priority for the Chinese leaders, and the Chinese leaders' efforts to boost both the party's legitimacy and national cohesion has strong negative consequences for China's international image and its soft power efforts.

Camilla says soft power will continue to be the weak link in China's pursuit of a great power position and status. Soft power is not an easy task for authoritarian states.

This being so with China, the West has its own issues to settle. The West needs to understand that its ultraliberalism is in crisis in politics, sociology and economics, and is exhausting its civilisational assets. That is one of the reasons for China to fast forward the time scale of its global ambitions. Along with ultra-liberalism, the West has to address a host of other issues, particularly linked to its liberal polity and liberal market, which has turned Western nations from market economies into market societies.

Liberal Democracies Need Introspection

The China challenge ought to make liberal democracies introspect on what went wrong with their sense of nation and national identity, their social and economic theories for choosing to promote first and now suffer an autocratic Chinese challenge. There is something fundamentally and seriously wrong for the West to have landed itself in this unenviable situation where an underdog raised by it challenges not only it, but also the very world order created and led by the West for its sustenance in the post-Cold War liberal order.

The West needs to rethink their social, democratic, and economic theories and structures on which they stand, in the context of how they have worked within the West and how suitable they are for the rest of the world. An observation, which a commentator made in Fox News as the Taliban seized Kabul, was that the US was wrong in imposing its gender perspectives and policies which it thought were progressive for Afghanistan. The latter, however, saw it as repulsive to them. This matched with what China had said about the US failure in Afghanistan. China said it has been once again proved that 'mechanically copying an imported foreign model cannot readily be fitted to the use in a country with completely different history, culture and national conditions.'

Of course, China specifically pointed out, consistent with its own addiction to single party dictatorship, that the US was wrong in imposing multi-party democracy on Afghanistan. But what it meant was that things which cannot fit into domestic culture or national conditions should not be exported. This is something the liberal West should not ignore in a world of increasing diversity consciousness.

There are two aspects on which the West needs introspection—one, on how its fad for ultra-liberalism is weakening their liberal democracies, and two, how their export of liberal democratic ideas and structures to countries with different history, culture and values is repulsive to them. On top of it, the West is ever improving its liberal version of liberal democracies and insisting on those to whom it exports it to accept it.

Unbridled Liberalism, Internal Risk of Liberal Democracies

An important thing the West must introspect on is how and why liberal democracies are fatiguing and weakening in their home of birth because of the very theory and practice of ultra-liberalism.

The global satisfaction with the Democracy Report 2020 by the Centre for the Future of Democracy at the Bennett Institute for Public Policy, Cambridge, finds that dissatisfaction with democracy has risen over time, reaching an all-time global high, particularly in developed democracies. It is no small survey. It covers a period of fifty years taken from twenty-five data sources, 3500 country surveys and four million respondents from 1973 to 2020. The report finds an acute crisis of democratic faith in Anglo-Saxon countries—the US, Australia, Canada, New Zealand and the UK—and says that the proportion of citizens dissatisfied with democracy in those countries has doubled from a quarter in 1990s to half of all individuals. In the US, those dissatisfied have risen from a quarter in 2010 to more than half in 2020. The twenty-seven EU member states also show the same trend. In contrast, the report says that Asia, where 2.52 billion people are under electoral democracies, including the world's largest democracy, is a notable exception, with more than two-thirds of the people satisfied with democracy. In world democracies excluding Asia, 58.4 per cent of people are dissatisfied with democracy, but in Asia, which has a population of 2.52 billion, only 35.7 per cent of people are dissatisfied with democracy. In developed countries—read liberal democracies—the dissatisfaction levels rose steeply after the economic meltdown of 2008.

Why are liberal democracies weakening? A study by the Institute for Democracy and Electoral Assistance (IDEA) shows that in free democracies, the voter turnout has fallen from over 75 per cent in the 1970s to less than 65 per cent in 2010. In established Europe, it has declined from 85 to 65 per cent. In post Communist countries, it has fallen from 75 to 60 per cent. In Asia, it has risen from 60 to 70 per cent. The IDEA data also shows that only 43 per cent of voters under the age of twenty-five vote, 33 per cent of them never vote at all and 23 per cent of them vote at times. It means that 57 per cent of the youth are seriously not interested in political affairs. The strength of a system is also its weakness—like the speed of an aircraft which is its strength, is also its weakness in a crisis. Likewise, liberalism, which is the strength of liberal democracies, is also becoming its weakness.

A research paper titled 'The Democratic Paradigm: A Vanishing Act' published in *Glocalism: Journal of Culture, Politics and Innovation* and written by Qasir Shah of the UCL Institute of Education, with a focus on the UK, explains why liberal Western democracies are fatiguing, if not declining.

An important reason it cites for the decline is the neo-liberal vision of the world which sees the individual possessed of superior rights, unencumbered by state interference. The paper cites the Audit of Political Engagement Report, whose 54 per cent respondents state 'they are too busy for political involvement' and say that 'many citizens no longer see politics as being central to their identity due to their many social and economic interests'. Only a minority (38 per cent) desired to participate at the national level.

Based on his finding that liberalism makes the society heterogeneous, Shah strikingly concludes,

> I believe the heterogeneity argument, in its extreme form, can lead to the neo-liberal idea of the primacy of the individual and the prioritisation of individual liberties. This is because individuals are unique and have different wishes, desires and needs. Since the 1980s, with the rise of Thatcher and Reagan, politically the individual has been held at the heart of society, with a radical rollback of the state, with laissez-faire economic policies leading to deregulation of markets, privatisation and radical tax cuts – citizens have been encouraged to become more self-sufficient and self-interested.

The very liberties which the democratic polity guarantees to the individual makes the individual so self-centred that nothing, including the very system of which the individual is the beneficiary, is more important for the individual than himself and his self-interest. Liberalism seems to be the death knell of liberal democracies.

A 2020 Chatham House research paper on The Future of Democracy in Europe, says: 'A number of indicators point to a state of dysfunction in democracy in Europe. Satisfaction with democracy has been declining. The party system has changed dramatically with the rise of radical political parties, which has increased the overall number of parties in many European legislatures and may diminish the effectiveness and ideological coherence of governments.

Over the past few decades, there has been a general decline in voter turnout in many European countries, particularly, among groups such as younger or less well-educated voters. There has also been a decline in the membership of political parties – and a rise in electoral volatility as voters have become more likely to change affiliation. As a result of these trends, some fear that Europe may be part of a worldwide "democratic recession".'

Liberal Democracy, Ideology and Illiberalism

Many, including proponents and exponents of the post-Cold War order, speak of the impending change in the world order 'forever' post the Covid-19 pandemic. The post-Cold War order was projected as founded on rule-based political, economic, trade, finance, and climate pacts. But in its true sense, this order was intended to be ideology free. But the core Western values of liberal democracy, free market, and human rights, have been implicitly turned into ideological mode. What was supposed to be the symbol of freedom from ideologies itself, has turned into symbols of ideology. Had liberal democracy, free market, and human rights been merely philosophic in their conception, they would not have turned ideologies. For understanding this phenomenon, one needs to understand the difference between philosophy and ideology. There is a world of difference between the two.

Ideology is powered by a certain dogma akin to religious dogma. But philosophy is sans dogma. But surprisingly, this apparent distinction is not in the intellectual or global discourse on either or both. It was not a philosopher, but a political leader, the former US President, Bill Clinton, who spoke of the distinction between philosophy and ideology—although in the context of politics. Citing too much dogma and too little philosophy as the reason why it is so hard to achieve political consensus, Clinton said: 'If you have a philosophy, it generally pushes you in a certain direction or another; but, like all philosophers, you want to engage in discussion and argument. You are open to evidence, to new learning. And, you are certainly open to debate the practical applications of your philosophy. Therefore, you might wind up making a principled agreement with someone with a different philosophy. The problem with ideology is, if you have got an ideology, you have already got your mind made up; you know all the answers. And, that makes evidence irrelevant and argument a waste of time. So, you (use) assertion and attack. If you have a philosophy, it means you're generally inclined one way or the other, but you're open to evidence. If you have an ideology, it means everything is determined by dogma and you're impervious to evidence. Evidence is irrelevant.'

It is surprising that the mainline discourse on either philosophy or ideology does not bring out this vital difference between the two paradigms of thought. This may be because global discourse today is dominated by ideological groups and anti-ideological groups sans philosophy. Anti-Ideology too is not philosophy. That in itself is another ideology. The exclusiveness of different ideologies, religious, social, economic, or political, ensured that there is no space for philosophy, as each one of the ideologies claimed to be the only truth. The global discourse has become a prisoner of 'either this or that' approach—thanks to the dominance of ideological attitudes in all aspects of life. Unfortunately, even liberal democracy which looks like philosophy, has also become another ideology which is far more exclusive than any other. Liberal democracy thinks that it is only right and perfect, and any other form of democracy is inferior and imperfect. Once liberal democracy became ideological, it ceased to be liberal also. There is implicit illiberalism in (a) liberal democracy.

Liberal Democracy is as Intolerant as an Autocracy, It Considers What it Cannot Accept as Unacceptable

As a system, liberal democracy has ceased to be a philosophy and has just become another ideology, which not only does not accept another view, but is also intolerant of a differing view. Liberal democracy is intolerant of electoral democracies—which are not, according to it, liberal—as much as it is intolerant of autocracies. It does not accept any other view which it regards as less liberal or illiberal. Therefore, democracy which started off as a philosophy has ended up as an ideology when it became liberal democracy. This ideological orientation is endangering liberal democracies themselves and weakening electoral democracies. For Western liberal democracies, India's genuine electoral democracy is illberal because it does not conform to norms set by liberal democracies.

'If you do not conform to my norms, you are no good' is not a norm of democracy but the rule of autocracy. This is how liberal democracy has become an ideology and an intolerant one, like autocracies. This impedes the alliance of democracies so necessary to resist the growing influence of autocracies.

One has to understand how liberal democratic ideology evolved in the post-World War II world order.

Ideological Origins of Liberal Democracy and Economics: Contrasting Paradigms of H.G. Wells and Mahatma Gandhi

To understand how the philosophy of liberal democracy became ideological, it is necessary to recall why Mahatma Gandhi refused to sign the Human Rights Declaration formulated by H.G. Wells. Gandhi refused to sign it unless Wells renamed it as the Human Duties Declaration. That was Gandhi's huge warning to the world that was getting mesmerised by the ideology of unbridled individual and human rights and by the institution of democratic governments coordinated by international bodies like the UN. The result of this contextually powerful fad with the unrestrained rights paradigm was the atomisation of society, community, and now even families. Unbridled individualism has freed human beings from elementary duties even to families and made it an individual choice, rather than a moral obligation. The result has been greedy competition for gain—sometimes even boasted as arousing animal spirits in man—which delegitimised the philosophical underpinning of the duty-centric as distinct from the rights-centric ideological way of life. The ideas of contentment and humility, which the unbridled and animal spirit-driven competition destroys, are an anathema to neo-classical economics which regards such virtues as impediments for growth. Modern economics celebrates greed and competition that build egotistic individuals, nations and institutions, on unbridled rights sans duties.

The substitution of basic human duties by unbridled human rights, of contentment by greedy competition, and of humility by egotism, has led to the substitution of a normative life by a formal rule-based and rights-centric way of life. This has disturbed and displaced families, communities and societies which were sustained by the trade-off between rights and duties. Modernity, as developed by Western anthropology, abhors the very idea of society which is the source and support for normative life based on a rights-duties trade-off. It was society and social norms in the past that ensured the unity and integrity of families, and the stability of community life. With society and non-formal normative life ceasing to be legitimate and, therefore, dysfunctional in the modern West, families which are basic institutions that socialise an individual into the larger human social capital, are collapsing. In the US, for example, one half of first marriages, two thirds of second and three-fourths of the third marriages end in divorce. Less than 30 per cent of families consist of couples with children. The durability of families and marriages are crashing because of the change from a relation-based traditional lifestyle to a contract-based modern life model. The very notion of a normative life has become anachronistic, even barbaric. Normative institutions of families which became households are turning into live-in affairs.

With the rising longevity of human life, coupled with the erosion of the institution of families, the burden of taking care of the unemployed, infirm and elderly has been ceded by failing families to the government. Governments taking over a vast range of family functions virtually meant nationalisation, even destruction of the age-old normative institution of families. On the other hand, modern economics advocated the privatisation of what was, in human history, always regarded as the functions of governments. This inverted economics is what has converted market economics into market society. Briefly put, market economics works with society, but market society destroys and replaces the society itself. Before we examine in detail what is market economics and what is market society, it is necessary to understand how liberal democracies' economic policies could destroy societies and families.

Underlying Ideology Identical for Liberal Democracy and Liberal Economics

At the time of the emergence of the liberal economic order for the world, Justin Stein of the Department of Political Science, University of North Carolina-Asheville, wrote how liberal economics and liberal democracy are founded on the same ideological ground. He emphasised the need for a global political authority to regulate the global market.

Stein wrote:

> Classic liberal economic theory, also known as the market system, claims that individuals have the right to choose their own ends... It is this competition among individuals, and their desires for the accumulation of wealth and resources, which gives the marketplace its robust nature. Like economic liberalism, liberal democratic theorists, such as Locke, Kant, Jefferson, and Mill, exalt the rights of the individual above any desired ends of the community or the state.

John Stuart Mill wrote:

> The only freedom which deserves the name is that of pursuing our own good in our own way...

Likewise, John Rawls argues,

> Each person possesses an inviolability founded on justice that even the welfare of society as a whole cannot override...The rights secured by justice are not subject to political bargaining or to the calculus of social interests.

This twin idea of ultra-liberal democracy and ultra-liberal economic free market which were seen as the final victorious symbol of the West over the Rest, became the two pillars of the global order post the Cold War.

Unbridled Liberalism, Long Term Vulnerability for Liberal Democracies—Francis Fukuyama

As the liberalism of the post-World War II West began to undermine society and families, it resulted in the government assuming household obligations. There was a protest against this wrong trend, surprisingly from the guild of economists itself. In 1980, many economists, including Milton Friedman, the Nobel Prize winner for Economics, warned the political system about civilisational and social debilitations such policies would cause.

The US National Bureau of Economic Research (NBER), which had compiled their views, said: 'In more subtle ways, government programmes that substitute the state for the family, cause behaviour that weakens the development of future population; fewer births, more unmarried individuals, more unmarried couples and more divorced parents; that medicare and medicaid introduced to help the elderly and poor might lead to an explosion in health care costs.'

Milton Friedman declared that 'as children stopped contributing voluntarily to the support of their parents and began contributing through a system of government fiat, a serious erosion of family values became inevitable and saw the social security system as a detrimental influence on social patterns.'

The NBER compilation pointed out that 'family functions such as production of food, clothing and fuel and some other staple items were taken over by business firms, and responsibilities such as education, childcare and social insurance have been assumed by the state.' What the NBER meant here is that business firms and the state had, together, robbed the families of their functions, leaving them functionless, therefore, dysfunctional. While conceding that 'the market system is the most efficient, and most conducive to individual freedom yet devised,' the NBER pointed out that the market itself 'doesn't provide for the organisation of the society' but its 'success during the last 200 years is attributable in good part to the existence of strong non-market institutions such as the family'; adding that the 'decline of the family and the growth of the government will jeopardise the market system and associated social, political and cultural freedoms.'

It concluded:

> In the long run, a healthy economy requires a healthy society.

This sagely advice was rejected by the political system which had set out to destroy society through political and social liberalism. Francis Fukuyama, who in his first work, *End of History*, in 1989, celebrated the final victory of Western liberal democracy and free market over the rest, said a decade later, in his book, *The Great Disruption*, 'The tendency of contemporary liberal democracies to fall prey to excessive individualism is perhaps their greatest long-term vulnerability and is particularly visible in the most individualistic of all democracies, the United States.'

This is a clear enough warning from a scholar who celebrated liberal democracy as the culmination of the perfect society that Hegel had postulated, that ultra-liberalism is a long-term vulnerability for liberal democracies themselves.

Economic Philosophy of India's Bahuka: Economic Practices of America's Greenspan

The short-termism of politicians to win elections cast aside the sagely advice of NBER experts and moved even further to replace the families by government. Alan Greenspan, who was called the God of Money, ruled the US economic policy making for two decades. He proudly upheld the replacement of family responsibilities by the state social security as a virtue of liberal economics to promote purchasing power beyond one's income, by borrowing money. In his famous book, *The Age of Turbulence*, published in 2007, he said that households in developing countries are forced to save whilst households in liberal democracies need not and they can even borrow and spend beyond their means. Why? He said: '"the developing countries" households seek buffer against feared destitution and since few of these countries have government safety nets adequate to protect against adversity, the only way for the households to do so, is to set money aside. People are forced to save for a rainy day and retirement.' Nationalisation of families meant that the most basic fundamental tenet of economic development, that is savings, was unnecessary for an economy. Within a year of his proud declaration, occurred the 2008 financial meltdown for which he could not even understand what the reason was. In his Mea Culpa before the US Congress, Greenspan admitted he did not know how and why the crisis occurred. And, even now, many economists try to bury the crisis as a systemic failure and nothing else. But a deeper analysis is needed to know, as NBER experts had counselled in 1980, that the free market and liberal democracy taken to the extreme of destruction of families and society, will destroy the market economy itself.

How the destruction of society and families can be caused by the politics of power and populism has been explained in the ancient Indian text *Bhagavad Purana*. In a story which is believed to be over 5000 years old, Bahuka, a towering intellectual of the time, was the advisor of King Kamsa of Mathura. Kamsa, who was hated by his subjects for his barbaric autocracy, sought Bahuka's advice as to how to persuade the people to accept him. Bahuka advised Kamsa, 'Open your treasury to the people. Make the people eat, drink, and enjoy themselves. Bring up children to look upon parents as old and useless. That will make them laugh at those who talk of duty, love and compassion. Like well-fed cattle at the mercy of the cowherd, the people will be completely dependent on you.' This was the Indian equivalent of Greenspan's economics—the economics of Bahuka. But fortunately, what Bahuka advised was rejected by the people of India. That is perhaps why Indian society and families have survived. Though the Bahuka brand of economics was rejected in India, it was adopted in the US without crediting intellectual property rights to Bahuka. That led to the destruction of families and societies, resulting in the creation of market society out of market economics.

Market Economics, not the same as Market Society; Market Society, the Product of Unbridled Liberalism

Debate on what is market economics and what is market society in contemporary economics began as a fall out of the 2008 crisis from which market economies in Asia (Japan for example) recovered faster, while market societies in the liberal West did not. What is market economy and what is market society? When everything—from family, relations and even the human body—is made an economic good and exchangeable for money, it is market society. It is beautifully, yet shockingly brought out in an article written in 2012 by Michael J Sandel, who teaches political philosophy in Harvard University. Simply stated, the difference between market economy and market society is that in the latter everything is up for sale, while in the former, certain things are not. Sandel's article brings out the difference between both and also explains how market society evolved out of market economy after the Cold War. To make the difference between the two understandable, Sandel gives live examples.

Sandel says that we live in a time when everything can be bought and sold. There were certain things which money couldn't buy—but these days, not many. Almost everything is up for sale and buy. That has opened up lots of new ways to make money. If you need to earn some extra cash, here are some novel possibilities:

Sell space on your forehead to display commercial advertising: $10,000. A single mother in Utah, who needed money for her son's education, was paid $10,000 by an online casino to install a permanent tattoo of the casino's web address on her forehead. Temporary tattoo ads earn less.

Serve as a human guinea pig in a drug safety trial for a pharmaceutical company: $7,500. The pay can be higher or lower, depending on the invasiveness of the procedure used to test the drug's effect and the discomfort involved.

Fight in Somalia or Afghanistan for a private military contractor: up to $1,000 a day. The pay varies according to qualifications, experience and nationality.

Stand in line overnight on Capitol Hill to hold a place for a lobbyist who wants to attend a congressional hearing: $15–$20 an hour. Lobbyists pay line-standing companies, who hire homeless people and others to queue up.

If you are a second-grader in an underachieving Dallas school, read a book: $2. To encourage reading, schools pay kids for each book they read.

There are other kinds of deals like:

The services of an Indian surrogate mother: $8,000. Western couples seeking surrogates increasingly outsource the job to India and the price is less than one-third the going rate in the United States.

The right to shoot an endangered black rhino: $250,000. South Africa has begun letting some ranchers sell hunters the right to kill a limited number of rhinos, to give the ranchers an incentive to raise and protect the endangered species.

Your doctor's cell phone number: $1,500 and up per year. A growing number of 'concierge' doctors offer cell phone access and same-day appointments for patients willing to pay annual fees ranging from $1,500 to $25,000.

A prison-cell upgrade: $90 a night. In Santa Ana, California, and some other cities, non-violent offenders can pay for a clean and quiet jail cell without any non-paying prisoners to disturb them.

The right to emit a metric ton of carbon dioxide into the atmosphere: $10.50. The European Union runs a carbon-dioxide-emissions market that enables companies to buy and sell the right to pollute.

The right to immigrate to the United States: $500,000. Foreigners who invest $500,000 and create at least 10 full-time jobs in an area of high unemployment are eligible for a green card that entitles them to permanent residency.

This new economic architecture evolved after the Cold War. Sandel says:

> As the Cold War ended, markets and market thinking enjoyed unrivaled prestige, and understandably so. No other mechanism for organizing the production and distribution of goods had proved as successful at generating affluence and prosperity. And yet even as growing numbers of countries around the world embraced market mechanisms in the operation of their economies, something else was happening. Market values were coming to play a greater and greater role in social life. Economics was becoming an imperial domain. Today, the logic of buying and selling no longer applies to material goods alone. It increasingly governs the whole of life.....Over the past three decades, markets and market values have come to govern our lives as never before. We did not arrive at this condition through any deliberate choice. It is almost as if it came upon us.

Sandel then says we have to decide what is the role of the market:

> These examples illustrate a broader point: some of the good things in life are degraded if turned into commodities. So to decide where the market belongs, and where it should be kept at a distance, we have to decide how to value the goods in question—health, education, family life, nature, art, civic duties and so on. These are moral and political questions, not merely economic ones. To resolve them, we have to debate, case by case, the moral meaning of these goods and the proper way of valuing them.

Sandel says that there was no such debate, with the result that the market economy turned into a market society and he explains the difference between the two:

> This is a debate we didn't have during the era of market triumphalism. As a result, without quite realizing it, without ever deciding to do so, we drifted from having a market economy to being a market society The difference is this: A market economy is a tool, a valuable and effective tool, for organizing productive activity. A market society is a way of life in which market values seep into every aspect of human endeavor. It's a place where social relations are made over in the image of the market. The great missing debate in contemporary politics is about the role and reach of markets. Do we want a market economy, or a market society? What role should markets play in public life and personal relations? How can we decide which goods should be bought and sold and which should be governed by non-market values? Where should money's writ not run?

The most important question that Sandel raises is what role should the market play in public and private relations. When the market enters the domain of relations, it turns society into a market.

Market Economics vs Market Society Debate in Mainline Economics

The distinction between market economics and market society is now recognised in mainline economics too. After the 2008 crisis, when Asia recovered and the West did not, it became a matter of debate. In an editorial titled: 'Astonishing Rebound', *The Economist* magazine (15 August 2009) wrote that even as the West was struggling to overcome the 2008 financial crisis, the Asian economies had turned around astonishingly.

Saying that the Asian economies increasingly decoupled from the Western shopping habits, *The Economist* distinguished between Japan, which worked on market economic principles, and the US, which functioned as a market society. It is the shopping habit and the economic behaviour, like leveraged buying, risky savings habits it brings along, which makes a market economics, a market society. It is not just about behavioural differences. The mainline education system began teaching that consumption was integral to modernity, and how for that purpose, it is necessary to make consumption the goal of life. Shopping as the goal of life is the very soul of a market society.

Disintegration of Traditional Society as a Precondition for Economic Take-off

It is about the goal and aim of life and the lifestyle changes it brings about. Rooted in unbridled individualism, buying becomes an end itself, as indeed theorised by Walter Rostow, whose thoughts were for long taught in business schools in the West and those in the Rest, like India, carbon copying the West.

Rostow's theory is shockingly common to both capitalism and socialism. In a paper titled: 'On the Anthropology of Modernity' (June 2011), Marshall Shalins, a prominent American anthropologist, shows how capitalism and socialism converge their goals. Shalins aligned the seemingly conflicting and incompatible capitalism and socialism by citing Walter Rostow, who theorised how the modern Western anthropological development model works in developmental economics.

Says Shalins: 'A late classic of the genre was Walt Rostow's Stages of Economic Growth (1957), with its unilinear sequence of five developmental stages from "traditional societies" to "the age of high mass consumption". (Rostow must have been among the first to perceive that the culmination of human social evolution was shopping.) Explicitly argued as an alternative to Marxist stages of progress, Rostow's thesis appeared as a mirror image, with the added advantage of turning left into right twice over. Common to many theories of development was a cheerful sense of cultural tragedy: the necessary disintegration of traditional societies that functioned, in Rostow's scheme, as a precondition for "economic take-off". Foreign domination was needed to accomplish this salutary destruction, since otherwise the customary relations of traditional production would set a ceiling on economic growth. By its own providential history, Europe had been able to develop itself, but according to Rostow, other peoples would have to be shocked out of their backwardness by an intrusive alien force. No revolutionary himself, Rostow could agree with Marx that in order to make an omelette one must first crack the eggs.'

Socialist Karl Marx and capitalist Walter Rostow had agreed that if traditional societies have to develop, they have to necessarily give up their cultural values and way of life.

In sum, shopping as the goal of life is the underlying essence of a modern market society.

Market Economics Works in Relation-based Societies, Market Society Does Not

There is a structural and sociological difference between market economy and market society. Market economics works in a relation-based, family-based lifestyle, while market society is individualistic and contract-based. In the former, the society and family works with the market, while in the latter the society and family too are replaced by the market. In brief, market society abhors family and community and rests on contract-based human life. In a market society, there are only three legitimate institutions—the state, the individual, and the market. The family and society are just options to keep or to drop.

In market economics, in addition to the three institutions of market society, the family and the society are also legitimate contributors and participants. Modern economists tend to view Asia as basically market economies, as nations in this region have largely retained their normative civilisational assets, i.e., families, communities and societies, aligned to market economics. This social evolution of adjustment by traditional society with market economics has happened because of a trade-off between individual rights and duties to the collective civilisational assets of families and society. In contrast to the Asian, the guild of economists regards continental European and Anglo-Saxon economies, which are driven by unbridled individualism, as market societies.

Civilisational Democracies like India Preserve Diversity, Culture and Relations, Abhor Homogeneity

A civilisational democracy like India legitimises and preserves diversity, culture, and relations, and abhors homogeneity. It is different from a liberal democracy and is more liberal in the global arena than liberal democracies. In a seminal essay titled: 'India's Civilisational Identity and the World Order', Zorawar Daulet Singh, a Fellow at the Centre for Policy Research, and the author of *Power and Diplomacy: India's Foreign Policies during the Cold War* (2018), brings out the distinct civilisational character of Indian democracy. He contextualises his thoughts on the decline of the liberal order and says that India's civilisational ethos of reconciling different ideas will be of immense value in navigating the uncertainty and turmoil at a critical juncture of world history.

Zorawar Singh says the Indian Constitution, along with a largely uninterrupted period of liberal democratic practice, has laid a normative framework that has been difficult to challenge by any serious political force. Therefore, he says, on human rights, freedom of speech, equality of opportunity, private property rights, political participation and peaceful transfer of power between competing parties or groups, and the rule of law and access to justice, India is very much part of a liberal political tradition. But, thereafter, Indian democracy differs from Western liberal democracy.

Zorawar Singh says the biggest difference between India and the West is that the Western mind assigns little value to nationalism, culture and civilisation. These are usually seen as anachronisms and obstacles in the path of homogenisation of political communities. Civilisation is seen as regressive and antithetical to the order and modernity that democracy and neo-liberalism are intended to bring. But, for India, it is a core value that enables rather than hinders its domestic order, social stability, and development.

He goes on to say

> This difference in approaches can only be explained by the absence of a historical determinism in Indian strategic and philosophical thought, which, unlike Western liberal or radical Marxist ideas, has never had a proselytising historical tradition nor an ideological vision of the world that insists on universality as a necessary prerequisite for a world order and geopolitical cooperation. It is no accident that India's democracy has managed to survive in a region with diverse regimes and political systems. It is also instructive that India was among the first to embrace non-alignment and carve out its own path when confronted with rival ideologies, neither of

> which were entirely appealing to India's identity, culture and ethos. Prime Minister Narendra Modi's multi-alignment is another version of that same philosophy, that India can find common ground and derive stable and mutually beneficial ties with a variety of different civilisational states and political systems.

The Indian civilisational democracy legitimises diversities and abhors homogeneity based on liberalism. When India interacts with the rest of the world, these other values and beliefs also come into play.

Zorawar Singh says: 'This is because Indian thought is constituted by a variety of ideas, and being a liberal democracy, is merely one of those identities. The Indian worldview is a hybrid one, shaped by a combination of liberalism, a belief in a plural multi-civilisational world order, a unique colonial experience and post-colonial identity, an aspiration for regional leadership with a corresponding geopolitical identity and Westphalian values of sovereignty and non-interference. Collectively, these have created a distinct world view and a prism through which India perceives and interacts with the world.'

Innate Illiberalism in American Liberalism, Absent in Indian Civilisational Democracy

Zorawar Singh points out that 'there is an innate illiberalism in American liberalism that does not prevail in Indian culture, which, by historical tradition and experience, is not so easily threatened or overwhelmed by rival "others".'

The absence of 'Them vs Us' tussle in Indian civilisation makes it less prone to violence. In contrast, Western liberal democracies are prone to violence because of their ideological character. Saying that Western tradition could not be more different, Zorawar Singh quotes American historian, Eric McKittrick, who said (in the 1950s) 'With nothing to push against it, (liberalism) thinks in absolutes; the occasional shadows which cross its path quickly lengthen into monsters; every enemy is painted in Satanic terms and it has no idea how it would behave if the enemy were either bigger or different.'

To show how this approach leads to war and violence, Zorawar cites a study which found that between 1871 and 1965, 'Liberal states waged 65 per cent of non-major power wars (which almost always are against weaker states).'

Another study found a similar pattern, with 'Liberal states starting 100 per cent of these wars of choice'.

Saying that, 'extending this pattern to the last three decades would reveal a similar conclusion, Zorawar Singh concludes 'there was, and still is, an ideological hubris and an ambition to change opposing systems in the Western mind. None of these facets are part of the Indian psyche and world view.'

This leads to a contrarian approach to foreign policy and foreign assistance. Zorawar Singh points out.

One key distinction between India and Western approaches is that the latter promotes democracy by providing moral, diplomatic and financial support to individuals and organisations that are openly resisting or challenging the political status quo in a state.

India, on the other hand, rarely enters into such interference that might defy the ruling regime and undermine the sovereignty of a state. India works with the legitimate government of the day to offer different types of assistance. India's interventions are in concert with the recipient—to strengthen the recipient state and its people—while the Western approach is fundamentally one of changing the target state and its institutions in concert with a section of the polity. It is about creating or exploiting a divide between the state and the people.

In this sense, a civilisational democracy does not see or practice democracy as an ideology which a liberal democracy does. Civilisational democracy can work with any kind of rule, democracy or autocracy. In this sense, civilisational democracy is internally different from liberal democracies and is seen as illiberal by liberal democracies, and, therefore, is externally more liberal than liberal democracies.

Liberal Democracy, Compatible with Market Society; Civilisational Democracy, Incompatible with It

Liberal democracy in the West was founded on Western anthropology of modernity, based on unbridled individualism, which necessarily undermines families, communities and societies. The Anglo-Saxon West introduced liberal democratic principles into normal and normative societies and turned them into liberal societies that eventually destroyed traditional society and families. The mix and identification of liberal democracy with liberal society has turned Anglo-Saxon economies into market societies. Anglo-Saxon market societies began setting the very rules of market society for the rest of the world in the era of globalisation. But fortunately, in Asia, liberal political ideas have not penetrated deep enough to undermine the civilisational assets of family, community, and society. And the West does not regard the world's largest democracy, India, as a liberal democracy because Indian society has not yet become the carbon copy of the atomised individualistic and liberal West. (It is only after the West saw China emerging as a threat to the democratic world post Covid-19 pandemic, that recently the G-7 has begun working on the Democratic 10 nation collective that included India).

India's political ideas have not de-legitimised her normative civilisational assets to turn it into a market society. India is a liberal civilisational democracy, not a liberal social democracy, which the West alone accepts as liberal democracy. What is the difference between liberal civilisational democracy and liberal social democracy? In a liberal civilisational democracy, the government works without affecting the cultural unity of a society of diversities. In a liberal social democracy, the government disturbs and destroys society and replaces it with itself. A liberal social democracy is more appropriate for a homogenous society and least suited for a society of diversities. It cannot work in a highly diverse society like India which is far more socially variegated than the rest of the world put together.

A liberal civilisation like India operates its electoral democracy without destroying its traditional assets of families, communities and society. Asian democracies are largely and broadly civilisational. In the field of economics, market economics works in and with civilisational democracies. But a market society, a product of liberal democracy, is sans the civilisational element. As Walter Rostow found a commonality between Marxism and liberal economics, market society evolves in a liberal democracy and in an environment of liberal economics, but it is ideologically mandated in Marxism.

Unbridled Liberalism Mothers Market Society just as Autocratic Marxism Produces Market Society

The seemingly competing Marxist and Market society theories have actually no conflict when it comes to undermining society and atomising the individual. Hegel's theory is common to both Marx and Market. The social contract theory, which is the foundation of the modern Western state, is also common to both Marxist states and Free states. The theories underlying both, delegitimise all non-formal institutions, including families, and deny them their due place. For example, while market society left to the individual the choice to live or leave marriages and families, in his Commmunist Manifesto, Das Kapital, Karl Marx wanted its total destruction. He even advocated women as common property, and said, 'Bourgeois marriage is in reality a system of wives in common and thus, at the most, what the Communists might possibly be reproached with is that they desire to introduce, in substitution for a hypocritically concealed, an openly legalised community of women.'

Karl Marx drew his inspiration for proletarian revolution from the Anabaptist Christian Revolt in Munster in Westphalia in 1534–35, which abolished all books other than the Bible, nationalised all properties and also women into common property and made promiscuity obligatory.

What Marxism wanted to do by force, the market society system endeavours to do by the very opposite model of ultra-individualism and liberalism. In the final analysis, the only difference between the Marxist vision of perfect society of Hegel and the goal of free market in alliance with liberal democracy as Francis Fukuyama would see it, is power and property dispute, namely whether that should be in the hands of the individuals or the collective state. Both the Marxist social engineering model and the free market-liberal model of the Western sociology have thus wrecked the civilisational assets of different nations. Unbridled liberalism mothers market society, while autocratic Marxism mandates market society. The two Western ideologies have also ruined global environmental assets, the consequences of which are far more serious.

'One-Size-Fits-All Model' 1951 West-led UN Advisory to turn all Nations into Market Societies

The homogenising approach of converging Marxian and liberal ideologies instituted an impractical one-size-fits-all model, which was the ideological origin of market society for the hugely diverse world. This intellectually arrogant and politically autocratic approach held ground for almost 60 years when the very institution, the UN, which mandated it in 1951, completely negated it in 2010. This interesting history is instructive too.

Much earlier than Walter Rostow, who had theorised on the need to destroy culture and traditions as a precondition for economic take off and development, the UN did precisely what he said later. In an advisory titled, 'Measures for the Development of the Underdeveloped Societies', the United Nations Department of Social and Economic Affairs had said precisely the same thing. It said:

> There is a sense in which rapid economic progress is impossible without painful adjustments. Ancient philosophies have to be scrapped; old social institutions have to disintegrate; bonds of caste, creed and race have to burst; and large numbers of persons who cannot keep up with progress have to have their expectations of a comfortable life frustrated. Very few communities are willing to pay the full price of economic progress.

The UN was clear that unless underdeveloped societies gave up their culture and way of life, they could not hope to develop and would be condemned to have their expectations of a comfortable life frustrated.

The one-size-fits-all model was the agenda to destroy traditional societies and turn them into market societies. And that was precisely what Walter Rostow also later theorised. He said, to recall, that

> Foreign domination was needed to accomplish this salutary destruction (of traditional society) since otherwise the customary relations of traditional production would set a ceiling on economic growth.

By its own providential history, Europe had been able to develop itself, but according to Rostow, other peoples would have to be shocked out of their backwardness by an intrusive alien force. Shockingly, the UN chose to be the intrusive alien force to accomplish a market society out of the ruins of a traditional society.

From 2005, the West gradually gave up the one-size-fits-all model market society

But with the rise of Asia in the last couple of decades, the West began insisting less on the one-size-fits-all market society models, which meant destruction of local cultures as a precondition for development. First, the finance ministers and central bank governors of G20 countries announced on 15–16 October, 2005:

> We recognise there is no uniform development approach that fits all countries. Each country should be able to choose the development approaches and policies that suit its specific characteristics, while benefiting from the accumulated experiences in policy making over decades, including strong macroeconomic policies for sustained growth.

Later the World Bank, in its letter of May 2008, months ahead of the global meltdown, conceded:

> In our work across the world, the World Bank has learned the hard way that there is no one model that fits all. Development is all about transformation. It means taking the best ideas, testing them in new situations, and throwing away what does not work.

Soon, the UN, which officially endorsed the modern Western anthropology of development and called for the destruction of indigenous philosophies and values in 1951, officially joined the bandwagon of 'no one-size-fits-all' paradigm, but, a bit late, in 2010.

'Development must be nationally driven' Deputy Secretary-General Asha-Rose Migiro stressed, rejecting the "one-size-fits-all" approach to eradicate poverty and foster economic growth.'

And finally, on 12 June 2013, during the General Assembly debates, Secretary General Ban Ki-moon again stressed the need to recognise that there is no 'one-size-fits-all' development model, adding that, 'many well intended development programmes have failed, because they did not take cultural settings into account. This must be an overarching principle for all development efforts.' He further said: 'Development has not always focused enough on people', adding, 'To mobilise people, we need to understand and embrace their culture.'

It is now clear that the one-size-fits-all model theory founded on Western anthropology of modernity, which demanded, as a condition for development, that societies wishing to develop should give up their culture and way of life and adopt the Western way, that is to become a market society, has failed and is now gone. While liberal market economic theory founded on Western anthropology of modernity has been given up in economics, liberalism is still insisted by the West as the index of a democracy. As we saw, liberal democracy produces, and is compatible with, liberal market society. Market economics is compatible with civilisational democracy.

Threat to India's Civilisational Democracy: From the Unbridled Liberal West, Also from Autocratic China

Unbridled individualism and ultra-liberalism are an evolution of the Western history of violent tussle and even wars between the state and the church, people and autocracies, and countries and countries. The West has had largely a homogenous anthropological development model through Christian religion and church first and through politics later. The anthropological development of the West into liberal democracies is a homegrown model through the internal struggles of the West. Prescribing its homegrown liberal democracy as a universal idea, besides undermining cultural and civilisational assets, including families and communities, erodes the very idea of nation in the non-Western countries, peoples and democracies which had not undergone the traumatic experience of conflicts like in Western history. And more so, even electoral democracy is no democracy from the perspective of liberal democracies which hold their liberal ideals and ideas as the benchmark for other democracies. The liberal West does not accept civilisational and electoral democracies unless they become like the Western ultra-individualistic and lose their civilisational sense, which is a great risk for them as their people have not undergone the Western historical process. Western liberal democratic norms are undoubtedly a civilisational threat to electoral and civilisational democracies. On the other hand, autocratic China, which is against all kinds of democracies, is also a threat to both civilisational and electoral democracies.

Ultra-Liberal Media Threat to All Democracies Including Liberal Ones

The most serious and dangerous development in the years preceding, and even now, has been the ever-intensifying liberal ideological drive of the Western media. They began deciding the direction of social and political discourse in the US and Europe since Donald Trump entered the US presidential race in June 2015. As the Western media originates and peddles the ideologies, ideas, narratives and storyline to the democratic world, particularly the English media in the other democracies, it turned on and against any leader who had exhibited a sense of nationalism in their respective countries. While the white race was demonised in the West by the liberal media, the majority communities in other democracies too were demonised. With the advent of Trump in politics and in the establishment, the US media ceased to be a fair news media and has become a virtual ideological campaigner for ultra-liberals and against those who were not.

The media began playing the role of opposition to the Trump establishment in the US and against the Trump-US in the EU and in most democracies around the world. The philosophy and purpose underlying the idea of media freedom is that mutually hostile media sources and views will bring out the truth and that is what media freedom is celebrated for.

If the entire media gangs up for any one view, it will become agenda-driven and the truth will never get revealed, as it would expose that agenda. That is precisely why liberal media suppressed or decided to overlook, or did not take seriously, the prima facie facts supporting the lab leak theory of the Covid-19 virus. Pursuing the truth was likely to be to the advantage of Trump, whom the media had decided to oppose at any cost. Another significant factor that misdirected and distorted the media, and made biased coverage look acceptable and normal, is the Chinese influence in the media in the West and elsewhere—driven by the popular Wolf Warriors. Never in history has global politics influenced national politics like in the case of the Wuhan Virus discourse.

Finally, once the liberal ideology of the media begins to determine what facts are to be probed and informed to the public, the media becomes the unchallenged dictator that will irretrievably conquer, command, and freeze public opinion. This most serious, even disastrous, development, unless corrected, is likely to distort and even destroy democracies.

Liberal West Needs to Recall Emile Durkheim and Rebuild Social Capital

Civilisational values that continue from generation to generation guide even ordinary humans to think of future generations of one's own families, of even communities and villages. It is ordinary humans who planted trees to yield for future generations and they even worshipped them in ancient societies, which modernity has scorned as backward.

Contemporary liberal Western theories have undermined the legitimacy of traditional societies and the civilisational sense of human beings and atomised into contractual individuals. This has reduced their vision of their own little life that does not even extend to their children, or family.

Western theories tend to leave the future of humanity exclusively to individualism-centric modern institutions with no role for ordinary humans except to vote and elect those who man and run institutions. But pampered by excessive individualism, having become so narrow in their own vision of life, they do not even vote. The atomised individuals, leaders, and institutions elected and manned by them, have no vision of the future beyond the next elections.

The monopoly formal institutional mechanism stuck in elections is challenged from outside by China. From within as well, it is facing a challenge as in liberal democracies, less than 45 per cent of youth only vote, and some 30 per cent never. The unchecked rights granted by liberalism have made the people in liberal democracies so self-centred that they tend to enjoy their lives more and do not even go to the polling booths to vote to strengthen the roots and ensure continuity of the very liberal democracy that grants them the rights. In a sense, liberal democratic institutions have really no real and durable continuity beyond the term of the political rule. Will the next administration follow or not the previous administration's policy is the kind of question which liberal democracies face, election after election. Liberal democratic institutions actually symbolise more discontinuity than continuity. The

West has substituted unreliable institutional continuity for durable civilisational continuity, instead of aligning both, as Emile Durkheim recommended.

It needs no seer to say that liberalism and liberal democracy have begun yielding diminishing, even negative, returns. Emile Durkheim dissented against celebrating a purely contractual society as modern, saying that even for contracts to work, a stable society is needed. Durkhiem's theory of voluntary association by way of professional guilds outside the formal law as an alternative to traditional society, too, has been undermined and dismissed by hyper individualism. This has sequenced into the contemporary modern society, which is sans kinship, even family relations.

The delegitimisation of relations has eroded the civilisational assets of society, including family in the West; the long-term consequences, not even recognised then, have begun visiting upon the West.

Liberal democracies will need to recall Emile Durkheim who had theorised the idea of what is now known as social capital in Western conditions. Social capital is a social virtue, not individuals' asset or state asset.

The non-formal institutions to interface with the individual and to intermediate between the state and society conceptualised by Durkheim is very much needed for Western liberal democracies.

Francis Fukuyama, who wrote the *End of History and the Last Man*, to announce the victory of liberal democracy and free market in 1989, quickly stepped back in 1994 to recall Durkheim to say that there is a need to foster social capital. Social capital is formed by families and societies and not by the state or market. Market society destroys social capital. The assertion of market society over market economy is complete negation of the very idea of social capital. It is time that the West recalled Durkheim, who it has neglected for over a century and negated him in the last half a century.

Short-Termism Causing Crashing Lifespan of Ideas

History shows that when short-term vision began driving the world, the lifespan of ideas that dominated the world too progressively shortened, even though each one of them, in their times, was presumed to last forever. To start with, colonialism founded on the goal of the white man's burden to civilise the world seemed once as the future of the world. But it just lived an exuberant life for a couple of centuries. Then came mercantile capitalism in economics whose life got exhausted in under a century. It turned into free market capitalism which soon transformed into financial and agency capitalism. Both of them destabilised businesses and further eroded and reduced the time span in the world of commerce from decades thirty years ago to hours now. In the interregnum, came Communism, that seemed to upset the applecart with revolution to overawe and overthrow all existing orders and take over the world. But its life too was snuffed out in half-a-century. In the end, came globalisation with a bang, as the final, unalterable and unimprovable future tense of the world, signalling the end of all conflicts and the dawn of global peace forever to achieve the perfect society Hegel envisioned.

But in less than a quarter of a century, the euphoric globalisation, which promised a conflict-free world, has had a premature demise and the world is now back to its ways of conflicts in trade and geopolitics. Globalisation has been formally pronounced dead by its very proponents like *The Economist* magazine. But why does the lifespan of ideas that dominated the world keep getting dwarfed and progressively reduced? The answer is self-evident. As human objectives are increasingly defined by ever shortening short time goals, the lifespan of ideas that govern human lives are bound to shorten even more, not lengthen.

Climate Change: Need for Shift from Anthropocentrism to Ecocentrism

The Western world was running for tens of centuries on anthropocentric ideologies, lifestyle habits and laws and rules which were founded on man—not woman—as the centre of creation, which is drawn from the Genesis in the Bible. Cartesian-Newtonian science extended that to position man as the master of creation. Following religion and science, political, social and economic theories of the modern West too internalised the unquestioned ideology of humans—women included—as the master of the entire animate and inanimate worlds.

The inhuman invasion of the animal and plant world by humans over centuries,which devastated nature and environment, led to the revival of environmental consciousness in the later decades of the 20th century. A couple of decades earlier, some Western thinkers began questioning anthropocentric ideas.

The process of rethink began with Lyn White's introspective writing in the *Science* Magazine in 1967, that the anthropocentric beliefs of the Abrahamic were incompatible with nature, while pagan faiths—that included Hinduism in their eyes—which worshipped trees, animals and rivers were environment-compatible.

With the rise in environmental consciousness, climate issues have emerged as the greatest challenge to human life on the planet. That seeded the birth of bio-centric philosophy in the West that included all living beings, not just humans—an improvement over anthropocentrism. That has now improved in scope to become ecocentrism. Ecocentrism, distinct from biocentrism, uses the study of ecology to demonstrate the importance of non-living elements of the environment.

A body of thinking has since begun to realise that environmental destruction cannot be stopped by state and global regulations. There is a call for deeper ecological consciousness to save the environment. Deeper ecological consciousness is built on an environmentally compatible philosophy and way of life along with allied habits. Animism, which was once regarded by Western theologians as an inferior pagan faith, is now seen by environmentalists as a high philosophy.

Ancient Indian philosophy was totally environment centric. It regarded the entire creation as divine. The ancient Hindu religious text, Isavasya Upanishad, which proclaimed, as translated by Mahatma Gandhi, that 'everything in creation down to the tiniest atom is divine', emphasised the ecocentric philosophy.

Speaking on the importance of Isavasya Upanishad, Gandhi said, 'If all the Upanishads and all the other scriptures happened all of a sudden to be reduced to ashes, and if only the first verse in the Ishopanishad were left in the memory of the Hindus, Hinduism would live forever.'

It is this ancient wisdom that—everything down to the tiniest atom is divine—is the core ancient Indian philosophy defining the ecocentric perspective. Contemporary civilisation that rests on anthropocentric ideologies, which were the foundation for short-termism of the West, has now come to a dead end. This is now forcing the world to look at the past, distant and deep past, for ideas to align humans and nature, for the survival of humans.

For Avoidance of Conflicts, Need for Universal Education in Astronomy 'Humbling and Character-Building Experience'

The world desperately needs to avoid conflicts before they arise and not attempt at resolution after the conflicts arise. A paradigm shift in education is needed which will make humans humble, not philosophically, but physically. The world needs contentment and humility, the two virtues necessary for conflict avoidance. It is said that education in astronomy will make the billions of humans dwelling on the planet realise how small, just tiny speck their own planet is, and how much smaller they are in it. The humbling and character-building knowledge of astronomy has great potential for conflict avoidance. The world is an aggregate of people of different countries, religions, ways of economic and political life, each believing not just in the greatness of its own model but prescribing and even forcing it as a solution to the problems of all. Other than the Indic ones, which believe that all religions are valid, each religion thinks that it is the only true one, and unless it conquers the world, there is no salvation for its own followers. This leads to conversion, religious clashes, and even terrorism.

Like such a religion, liberal nations think that liberal democracy is the sole best and the only solution for all nations and peoples, including half liberal, illiberal democracies, and autocracies. Likewise, free market nations think that the free market is the best and that answers all economic problems. This made the victorious West prescribe a global order that was founded on its own model as the global model. This started with aggressive attempts like colonial conquest, took the form of two World Wars and ended in the Cold War. With the West presenting its model as the final victory over the rest, globalisation became the final effort. And each one of them has been an increasingly short-lived model.

There is something seriously wrong with the entire discourse and the education on which it is founded. The most critical issues of today, environment, ecology and climate, were not in the horizon of human consciousness when the United Nations advised underdeveloped nations to give up their ancient philosophy and way of life to get on to the Western model and vehicle for development. Environment now connects the world not only within, but with the universe. Knowledge and understanding about the universe has to be internalised and integrated into education to fill the gaps in the understanding about the world and humanity. In comparison with the universe, Planet Earth is just a speck of dust. This knowledge provided by astronomy is the most humbling and character-building experience, said famous American astronomer Carl Sagan in his equally famous video of just 210 seconds titled 'Pale Blue Dot'. It explains profoundly and beautifully how our planet, Earth, is just a tiny dot, a speck in the cosmic darkness as compared to the ever expanding and vast universe. Sagan's view is not an arguable and disputable philosophy, but indisputable science, astronomy. It contains the seeds for future education by all nations for conflict avoidance. Here is that instructive transcript of Carl Sagan's video.

> From this distant vantage point that does not seem to be of any particular interest. But for us, it's different. Consider again that dot. That's here. That's home. That's us. On it everyone you love, everyone you know, everyone you ever heard of, every human being who ever has lived out their lives. The aggregate of our joy and suffering; thousands of confident religions; ideologies and economic doctrines; every hunter and forager, every hero and coward; every creator and destroyer of civilisation, every king and peasant; every young couple, in love. Every mother and father, and hopeful child; every inventor and explorer; every teacher of morals; every corrupt politician, every superstar, every supreme leader. Every saint and sinner in the history of our species—lived there, on the mote of dust suspended in a Sunbeam. The Earth is a very small stage, in a vast Cosmic Arena. Think of the rivers of blood spilled by all those generals and emperors. So that in glory and triumph, they could become the momentary masters of the fraction of a dot. Think of the endless cruelties visited by the inhabitants of one corner of this pixel, on the scarcely distinguishable inhabitants of some other corner. How frequent their misunderstandings, how eager they are to kill one another, how fervent their hatred. Our posturings, our imagined self-importance, the delusion that we have some privileged position in the universe are challenged by this point of pale light. Our planet is a lonely speck in the great enveloping, cosmic dark. In our obscurity, in all this vastness, there is no hint that help will come from elsewhere to save us from ourselves. The earth is the only world known so far to harbor life. There is nowhere else at least in the near future to which our species could migrate. Visit, yes. Settle not yet. Like it or not, the moment the girth is where we make our stand. It has been said that astronomy is a humbling and character-building experience. There is perhaps no better demonstration than the folly of human conceits than this distant image of our tiny world. To me, it underscores our responsibility to deal more kindly with one another and to preserve and cherish the pale blue dot, the only home we've ever known.

The cosmic phenomenon, which reduces the earth to just a mote of dust suspended in a sunbeam, a tiny dot in the whole universe, is not a static one, but a ceaselessly dynamic phenomenon, which constantly undergoes changes. This is where the modern cosmos and ancient Indian philosophy coalesce. Hindu philosophy says that both creation and destruction are an integrated process. Speaking about the relation between the ancient Indian philosophy measured time on a cosmic scale—in billions of years—and modern astronomy, Sagan says

> The Hindu religion is the only one of the world's great faiths dedicated to the idea that the Cosmos itself undergoes an immense, indeed an infinite, number of deaths and rebirths. It is the only religion in which the time scales correspond to those of modern scientific cosmology. Its cycles run from our ordinary day and night to a day and night of Brahma, 8.64 billion years long. Longer than the age of the Earth or the Sun and about half the time since the Big Bang.

The Sankalpa Mantra, which is recited for any function in any traditional Indian home, connects the present day and time of the Sankalpa and say that the first half of Brahma's day, which 4.32 billion years, is over and we are in the beginning of the second half of Brahma's day, which will go for another 4.32 billion years. Carl Sagan calculates 8.64 billion years as a day of Brahma. If in terms of space we are a speck in a speck, in terms of time, how small our lifetime of 100 years can well be imagined.

Like the United Nations mandated in 1951 measures for the development of underdeveloped nations, it should mandate an agenda for education of all nations in astronomy and cosmology which will scientifically introduce in the curriculum at all levels, a humbling and character-building experience in humans. It is a science but it is regarded as philosophical, even religious, since it conflicts with origin and life of the world in the Abrahamic religious texts and, therefore, not encouraged in our education system.

2

A Helicopter View: The World Today and Its Future Look

A helicopter view of the world as the year 2020–21 ended presents a very complicated and largely negative picture. Here are some important headlines and, more importantly, questions emerging from the picture.

'Engaging' West Disengaging with 'Biding' China Makes it Belligerent: The Greatest U-turn After 1970

The year 2021 will go down in history as the greatest turning, or U-turning point in geopolitics after the turn of events in the early 1970s, which led to the evaporation of the Cold War. The West is now tending to disengage itself from China, decades after it began chasing it with one-sided initiatives that turned into one-sided love and admiration later.

China, which was advised by Deng Xiaoping to bide its time, is now turning belligerent to the West after acquiring a strategic position and an almost equal superpower status with the US/West.

Not Just a Superpower Struggle, But a Challenge to the West-led World Order

This disengagement on the one side and belligerence on the other is not just a struggle for superpower status, it portends far more. The *Foreign Affairs* magazine (June 2021) wrote, 'China earlier believed that it must continue to bide its time by overseeing rapid economic growth and the steady expansion of China's influence through tactical integration into the existing global order, but it is now impatient and seems to feel a pronounced sense of urgency in challenging the post-World War II international order.'

The National Bureau of Asian Research Special Report (13 Jan 2020) said that the post-war international order is the creation of Western civilisation which rests on values and institutions that pose risks to the Chinese system.

But Beijing's effort at changing the world order is partly defensive and partly defensively offensive, and that is where it conflicts with the contemporary order. China's vision for a new world order, which is strikingly narrow and parochial, is mostly about inveighing against a Western-dominated world order that is deemed threatening to the Communist Party of China's survival and about altering the world and making it safe for Beijing's unimpeded rise under the party's continuous rule.

China's Shift—From Deng Xiaoping's UNGA Address in 1974 to Xi Jinping's Message on 100th Anniversary of CPC in 2021

Deng Xiaoping, who advised the Chinese to hide their talents and bide their time, told the United Nations General Assembly in 1974 that 'China was not a superpower nor will she ever seek to be.' Saying that a superpower strives for global hegemony, he declared that 'if one day China should turn into a superpower, subjecting others to her bullying and aggression and exploitation, the people of the world should expose it, oppose it and work together with the Chinese people to overthrow it.'

Moving from there to the informal Open-Collar Summit in Sunnylands in 2013, Xi Jinping proposed 'A new type of great power relations' between the US and China. After the pandemic spared China and hit the West and the Rest, Xi declared 'East is rising and West is declining' in March 2021, and thereafter, viciously took on the G-7 and NATO in June 2021. Finally, in July 2021, on the 100th anniversary of the million-strong CPC parade in Tiananmen Square, he turned ballistic and said China would not allow sanctimonious preaching on Xinjiang and Hong

Kong, and declared his country's unshakeable commitment to the unification of Taiwan. He also said that anyone who dares to bully China will have their heads bashed bloody against the Great Wall of Steel forged by over 1.4 billion Chinese people. It was a clear and pronounced shift over a period of six decades.

Ideology Back in World Affairs After Long Holiday

As the socialist world collapsed, Francis Fukuyama declared in his 1989 essay 'End of History?' that the great ideological battles between East and West was over and that Western liberal democracy had triumphed.

Three years later when he turned that essay into a book, the qualifying question mark was gone and the book was titled as 'End of History and the Last Man'. Fukuyama became the court philosopher of global capitalism.

The 2001 terror attack in the US and the rise of Islamic fundamentalism did remind the world about smouldering ideologies. The rise of far right ideologies and deepening of liberal left ideologies in the US and West on the one hand, and the rise of China challenging the Western liberal worldview on the other, seemed to suggest that ideologies were back in world affairs.

World Order Turning Back—To Undeclared Cold War?

The return of ideologies in Western polity and in geopolitics with the advent of China, the disengagement of China and China's belligerence, portend a return to Cold War ideological rivalries. Independently, even without ideological fault lines, the post-Covid-19 world seems conducive to the return of the Cold War.

When the Covid-19 virus began devastating the world last year, leading geopolitical thinkers began perceiving a change in the post-World War II and post-Cold War world order forever. The global developments that unfolded through 2020 and during the first half of 2021 seem to be threatening to move the world back to recall the Cold War order as the future world order.

The complete U-turn of Western powers who, for three decades, had improved from positive engagement with China to equal superpower relations, seem to have realised all too suddenly that their experiment of engaging with and promoting China in the hope of moderating its autocracy and making it a responsible global player have failed. That realisation has obviously led to an open and unprecedented declaration by G-7 and NATO that China is a systemic challenge to the West.

This development which was unthinkable even as late as last year, testifies to the emerging change in the post-Cold War world order back to where it stood decades back.

The three summits of the G-7, NATO and EU-27 between June 11–15 constituted the biggest and most far reaching geopolitical turn after the end of the Cold War in early 1990s, even though US President Joe Biden, or NATO Secretary General Jens Stoltenberg, or US Secretary of State Antony Blinken explicitly rule out going back to a new Cold War.

If the trend of G7 vs China persists and deepens, as it is mostly likely to, it may even lead to a new Cold War founded not on post-World War II ideological divisions between socialism and capitalism, but on a divide between democracies and autocracies.

World of Diversity Asserts over Post-World War II Agenda of Homogenous World?

The agenda of the post-World War II world order was founded on the worldview of a victorious West, which, in the civilisational sense, included even Russia. It divided the world into developed and underdeveloped, and prescribed how the underdeveloped world could develop. The Western worldview was rooted in the Western anthropology of modernity (WAM). The WAM was common to both the free world and the Marxian world. The WAM manifested itself in the United Nations advisory to Underdeveloped Countries in 1951, which counselled the underdeveloped countries to give up their philosophy and their social institutions if they wanted to develop. The advisory further stated, development cannot be achieved without paying a price.

This was the Euro-centric worldview. Its short prescription was for the one-size-fits-all (OSFA) model for the overall development of the world of diversity—an impractical idea that proved to be so as the post-World War II world moved ahead. Yet, this principle which informed the global establishment discourse, peaked with the advent of globalisation in the 1990s. But later, with the rise of Asia, from 2005, the OSFA principle began to be explicitly doubted by G-20 itself and the World Bank in 2008. From 2010 onward, the UNGA itself turned against OSFA. Aided by the perceived withdrawal of the US from global leadership and the rise and challenge of China to the West, the world of diversity that was lying low seems to be asserting itself over the post-World War II agenda to homogenise the world. This seems to be the underlying drive for massive and multiple changes, including the change in the world order that is being talked about by many today.

The world had a West-led, West-formulated and sustained institutional order for the world order, partially from the post-World War II period, and totally from the post-Cold War period. The common drive behind the post-World War II and post-Cold War period global order was, and continues to be, the Western development model as the OSFA model for all. This was founded on the ambitious Western agenda of a homogenous world. As the third millennium AD opened, international organisations from the G20 to the UN, all started realising that this would not work for all and declared as much.

The social, cultural, and political diversity of the world began to impact on and disturb the OSFA mindset. Post-2008, with the Western model losing its sheen, the world of diversity seems to have begun asserting itself over efforts of uniformity and homogeneity of the West-led economic model through neo-classical economics and West-centric social model, through West-generated institutionalised thoughts like rights sans duties at the level of the non-formal individual and human collectives.

Will China Lead the World of Diversities Against the West-Centric OSFA Model?

From North Korea to Iran to Taliban, China seeks to support global diversities which the West thinks is against the world order led by it. The agenda of China, which is like an opposition party trying to leverage on anti-establishment views and unite disgruntled elements to challenge the established world order, is comparatively easier. The ruling West has been trying to export its own values as global values, which in many cases do not fit with the domestic situation of different nations. The world of diversity cannot be homogenised on the lines that the West has been attempting to do in various fields, including politics, economics, and culture. While the democratic Western hegemony is cultural, political, and economic, Chinese hegemony will be political and economic and will perhaps not interfere with different nations' cultural models through human rights and similar issues.

This may help China garner the support of the world of diversity which the West has been attempting to homogenise through different elements of the world order designed by it.

End of Geopolitics of Engagement Across Divides?

The developments during the year under review and in the months after that, clearly and unmistakably bring out the virtual end of three decades of engagement of the US with China that began with the collapse of the Soviet Union, with outgoing US Secretary of State Mike Pompeo saying in mid-2020 that engagement with China had ended.

Covid Origins Probe to Unsettle Global Relations?

The Covid-19 virus origin issue has emerged as a contentious issue in a world that is already getting divided as pre and post-covid. The Biden regime's order to US intelligence officials to 'redouble' efforts to investigate the origins of Covid-19, including the theory that it came from a laboratory in Wuhan, China has mainstreamed the lab leak theory which was dismissed as a conspiracy last year.

China's hostile reaction to Biden's action citing the dark history of US intelligence has only added fuel to fire. In recent times, Donald Trump's claim that he was right that the virus had its origin in the Wuhan lab and his demand that China pay a reparation of $10 trillion to the world, has added a new dimension to the Covid-19 issue in and outside the US. The reparation talk has gone mainstream in the media via a column by Lewis Libby and Michael R Pompeo (Washington Post 7 June 2021) titled 'China's COVID wrong doing warrants punishment by a Biden-led coalition'. China has surprisingly been silent on the issue.

Post-Trump, US has Become Trumpist US

Despite the change of regime in the US, the deep divisions in the polity in America, which seemed to have peaked with the riots in Capitol Hill and ebbed after that, shows no sign of abating even after Biden's call and efforts for unity, and even after a large part of Trumpism lasting beyond Trump having been accepted and subsumed by the Biden administration.

End of Mutual Attraction Between EU and China?

The EU–China relation, which scaled new heights and led to the Comprehensive Agreement on Investment (CAI), has hit rock bottom with 'alleged' human rights abuses in Xinjiang, leading to mutual sanctions against individuals and institutions belonging to each other—the most notable being the sanction against a key member of the Green Party, which is likely to participate in the coalition in Germany in place of the coalition headed by Angela Merkel, who single-handedly pushed the CAI.

The weakening of the US–EU Transatlantic Alliance under the Trump administration, which compelled the EU to sew up the Comprehensive Investment Agreement with China, appeared to have been addressed by the Biden regime and that, coupled with the human rights conflict between China and EU and the emerging issues around the origin of the Coronavirus, seems to have caused the perceived collapse of the CAI, which was the much trusted bait of China to lure EU away from US and the Transatlantic Alliance.

The Three June Summits Set the Pace for Rapid Changes in Geopolitics

Three rapid developments in June 2021—the G7 (11–13 June), the NATO meeting (14 June) and the US–EU Summit (15 June)—seem to mark this huge change in geopolitics, i.e., the official policy of the US, NATO and EU.

The quick revival and powerful reassertion of the Transatlantic Alliance at the 2021 G7 meet, was seen as a counter to Chinese assertiveness in the world and even over the EU and the US.

The G7 Communiqué released at the end of the meet clearly targeted China on issues like human rights, Xinjiang, Hong Kong, Taiwan, South China Sea and China's relations with others in the region in a language and manner unseen in recent times, and revived the memories of the Cold War. Despite the reported moderate views of Angela Merkel, there appears to be no substantial divergence within the G7, and mood of all, including France and Italy, appeared to be 'over how hard to criticise China' and the differences within the G7 were not over the content of the message to China but about its intensity.

The next big, and in a way surprising, development was the NATO meet, where member nations who had never mentioned China till mid-2019, clearly targeted an ambitious and assertive Beijing as a systemic challenge and threat to a rule-based world order and to areas relevant to NATO security.

The third meet, the US–EU meet, which appeared to be overcoming conflicts to achieve harmony within the group, seem to have persuaded the EU to go soft and put a break on the Comprehensive Investment Agreement it had entered into with China towards the end of 2020, beginning of 2021.

The announcement in the US–EU Summit that the 17-year-old aircraft subsidies dispute further aggravated by Trump era tariffs, has been resolved is more than a 'major confidence boost for US–EU relations'.

It was a part of measures to counter investment in the aircraft business by 'non-market actors' and to confront Chinese ambitions to build an aircraft sector on non-market practices as the US and EU kept busy fighting each other. It strikes at the root of the EU seeking Chinese capital under the ill-fated CAI.

The powerful tone of the G7 Communiqué emerging from the resurgent Transatlantic Alliance and the belligerent response of China, belittling it as a small group of nations whose rule over the world is nearly gone. It alleged the G7 of having a Cold War mentality.

Will G7 B3W (Build Back Better World) Act as Counter to China's BRI?

The G7 accepting the US-inspired B3W global infrastructure initiative to counter the BRI platform of China is a strategic and positive move to undermine the growing influence of the latter and extend the former's influence over developing and least developed nations which are in need of infrastructure.

The recent decision to allocate an additional $650 billion as Special Drawing Rights (SDRs) to enhance the International Monetary Fund's (IMF's) liquidity needs to be seen in this context. The faltering BRI overseas investments by China, as its own economic woes mount, only adds to the significance of the addition to the IMF liquidity.

Democratic Alliance as the Fulcrum of an Alternative World Order?

The issue before the G7 and other democratic nations is, having allowed an autocratic China to exploit the global market with its opaque Marxist practices, whether allowing it to continue to exploit the global market without weakening the competitiveness of the democratic order and turn the world towards autocracies rather than democracies. This is contrary to the very premise for including China in the global market, to make it democratise, and not the world to turn autocratic.

This development is likely to lead to the broadening and widening of the paradigm of democracy from being limited to merely liberal democracies as it is in the West now, to include civilisational democracies of modern nations with ancient history and culture—the indication for which was evident in the inclusion of India in the G7 summit as a Guest Nation, which is in contrast to the consistent Western attempt to classify Indian democracy as a second-rate democracy.

This inclusive approach is evident from the fact that the Western media had been proclaiming that leaders attending the G7 represent over 60 per cent, or 2.2 billion people living in democracies around the world. Without India, this figure would be a mere 900 million, or less than 12 per cent of the global population.

Global Supply Chains: To Move from Cheap to Safe and Cheap Sources?

Undoubtedly the post-Cold War world order led by the US and Europe, and founded on global cooperation, multilateralism, emergence of powerful and binding global institutions like the WTO, climate agreements which came under pressure because of the Covid-19 phenomenon, has come under more severe stress with the UN and the WTO virtually in intensive care.

On global trade, which is haunted by diverse issues of a failing WTO and even regional trade agreements, the WTO forecasted a rebound and growth of 8 per cent in 2021, as against a fall of 5.3 per cent in 2020, but slowing down to 4 per cent in 2022.

But all this is based on assumptions which can go wrong in the context of fluid situations emerging from issues on the origin of Covid-19 and their direct consequences on relations between major economic nations.

Unsettled Russia-EU-US Relations

Just a month prior to the human rights conflict between EU and China, in February 2021, Russia and EU clashed over the arrest, detention and trial of Russian opposition leader Alexei Navalny, which has unsettled two decades of durable and comprehensive co-operation on issues ranging from trade to security to culture.

The extra traction which Russia has gained with Iran with the collapse of the nuclear deal may lead to a positive outcome with the participation of Britain, China, France and Germany working on an agreement that might get the US on board and lead to the US lifting sanctions on Iran.

There is considerable opposition to the Joint Comprehensive Plan of Action (JCPOA) within Iran itself.

The MENA (Middle East and North Africa) Region: Russia Scores in Syria, Saudi Arabia Continues to Moderate Wahhabi Islam

In the MENA region, the bloodiest clash between Israel and Palestine which made the Middle East hot and tense for over a month, has ended in a ceasefire. The Syrian Civil War has considerably abated with the steep decline in the scale of violence and the re-election of Basher Al-Assad, though rejected by the US and the EU as illegitimate, was overseen by delegations that included legislators and dignitaries of 30 countries, including Iran, Russia and Venezuela.

Saudi Wahhabi Islam, which was the root cause of Islamic terror in the world, continues to moderate under Crown Prince Mohammed Bin Salman who promised in 2017 that Saudi Arabia would go back to moderate Islam; the Boko Haram terror in Nigeria and around has not abated; the death of its leader, Abubaker Shekau, in May, could affect the dynamics of this situation, but more time is needed before the picture becomes clearer.

Asia, Indo-Pacific Region: Emerging New Hotspot of Geopolitics

In Asia, the divide between China and the ASEAN as well as the Iran issue, continue to be played out between the US (whose backing of Saudi Arabia being an element of its Iran policy) and Russia aided by China.

The full withdrawal of US forces from Afghanistan by end-August 2021 has exposed that country to a takeover by the Taliban which has huge consequences for the region and particularly India.

The conflict in Ladakh between India and China, which is implicitly linked to the issues of China's fears over the worsening situation in Tibet and Xinjiang, has drawn India closer to the US, West, Japan, Taiwan and also its participation in the QUAD. China's strategy is to keep India's mind and resources occupied, while the Tibet and Xinjiang questions remain unsettled.

Chinese claims of control over the succession of His Holiness, The Dalai Lama, are without foundation and need to be publicly negated. Taiwan, Hong Kong and South China Sea issues too are becoming prominent in the light of relations between China and US–EU coming unstuck.

China's efforts to reach out to ASEAN by hosting a meeting of the region's foreign ministers in June 2021, was done with the hope of undermining the Biden regime's Free and Open Indo-Pacific strategy.

After months of silence, the bellicose statement of Kim Yo Jong, the powerful sister of North Korea's leader, Kim Jong Un, that 'We take this opportunity to warn the new US administration trying hard to give off the (gun) powder smell in our land', threatened to tear up the fragile military agreements with South Korea, reviving US concerns about North Korea.

Threats to Vulnerable India: Delicate Economy, Two Converging Adversaries at the Border, and Now, the Taliban in Afghanistan

In comparison to China, its main regional competitor, India, remains highly challenged in terms of the Covid-19 impact, and because of its direct and indirect impact on the Indian economy which was not doing well even before the advent of Covid, with the added disadvantage of important supply chains linked and dependent on China.

With the PLA at the border, the threat of a two-front war cannot be dismissed because of India's traditional enemy Pakistan willing to support the Chinese agenda to spite India.

And, the latest addition to the security risks is the re-emergence of Taliban rule in Afghanistan, with Pakistan and China having a greater leverage over Taliban 2.0. The consequence of the advent of Taliban 2.0, which is a serious development for the world and for India, is captured in Chapter 3.

Added to these high external risks is the simultaneously growing political heat in India because of a divided polity obfuscating all national issues and disturbing national consensus evolving on any issue, including unity against the external threat. The divided polity threatens national security more than the anti-national forces at work over a long time against India.

Environment Issue: Shifting Goal Posts, Yet No Clear Way Forward

On the environment, even though the Trump administration's rejection of the Paris Climate Treaty has been undone by the Biden regime, the West, particularly the EU, fears that without the greatest polluter of the planet, China, the issue can never be clinched.

China, in a way, is in a position to implicitly blackmail the rest of the world and make a deal out of even the Covid-19 virus issue. The story line has been changing over the decades with the title of the concept shifting from 'global cooling' in the 1970's to 'global warming' to 'climate change' to simply 'climate' or 'climate crisis', whatever that means.

The major missing element in the climate-related discourse is population growth: the planet cannot sustain a seven billion-plus without causing resource depletion and the destruction of biodiversity.

India, in particular, needs to pay greater attention to its demography. It is also high time to hold another world population conference, the last one having been held in 1994. Even the IPCC recognises the importance of population control for addressing climate change.

These are just illustrations and do not exhaust the issues confronting the world today.

3

Afghanistan: The Re-emergence of Taliban Ominous for the Entire World

After the Afghanistan President Mohammed Ashraf Ghani abdicated and left Afghanistan, the Taliban seized power in August 2021 the way rulers changed by invasion and conquest in medieval and colonial times, and unlike change of rulers in civilised democracies today.

They have ended up installing a cabinet, half of whose members are either on the global list of terrorists, or drug peddlers, rapists and kidnappers, with a medieval agenda to establish Islamic Sharia rule over the Afghan people. The Taliban, which was sacked by Western forces in 2001 in their first step in the war against terror for having abetted the Al Qaeda attack on the US, is back in its new avatar as Taliban 2.0.

Shocking events between mid-August and mid-September that installed the terror outfit Haqqani network-led Taliban influence in parts of Pakistan, are now having an impact and effect in Kabul.

Here is a brief summary of the dramatic changes in Afghanistan: Though the US had been planning the withdrawal of its troops from Afghanistan from former president Barack Obama's time, in February 2020, Zalmay Mamozy Khalilzad, US Special Representative for Afghanistan, made a deal with the Taliban that left the Ghani-led government in the cold. Though surprised by Ghani's sudden abdication, the US putting the entire blame on him for the situation prevailing in Afghanistan after his exit, sounds disingenuous.

The refusal of the US to delay its withdrawal from Afghanistan as its allies had pleaded, is regarded by some experts as more strategic in intent than spontaneous in content.

President Ghani's exit created a vacuum that shocked the Taliban itself and denied to it all scope for deliberations needed for government formation, and provided an ideal opportunity for a swift coup within the triumvirate—Taliban, the Haqqanis, and Al Qaeda. The coup turned the entire peace pact between the Taliban and the US on its head.

The coup seemed contrived by Pakistan Inter Service Intelligence's (ISI's) direct intervention on September 5, clearly tilting the balance of power in favour of the Haqqanis, which was not part of the Taliban-US peace talks.

The coup-triggered Islamic Emirate, powered by the Haqqanis and formed by the Taliban, is viewed by the international community as neither inclusive nor gender or human rights compliant.

Far from the Taliban complying with its commitment to abhor its terror-linked agenda and to keep away from other terrorist groups like the Haqqanis and Al Qaeda, the new regime has handed half of its authority to the Haqqanis.

The originally conceived new regime, negotiated in Doha by Abdul Ghani Baradar, who was projected as Afghanistan's Prime Minister in waiting, seemed to have been aborted by ISI Chief Lt. General Faiz Hameed's visit to Kabul on September 5, which facilitated the coup. The coup reduced Baradar to being one of three deputies instead of the head of government.

The total breach of the Doha pact by the Taliban in the manner of its surge towards Kabul and further accentuated by the composition of the government post the coup, set recognition for it by the US/West and others back.

The rise of Haqqanis, who are regarded by the National Counter Terrorism Centre as 'the most lethal and sophisticated terror group', has led to a high risk ideological tussle between the Doha branch of the Taliban and the Taliban Afghanistan/ Pakistan combine backed by the Haqqanis.

The ideological tussle between the two Talibans was whether Afghan Taliban's Jihad won, or Taliban's Doha peace pact won, Afghanistan for the Taliban. The government was formed by those who proclaimed it is the Jihad, and not the peace pact, which won Afghanistan.

The truth, however, is that the US withdrew voluntarily from Afghanistan after signing a one-sided deal with the Taliban that was meant to extricate the former from the country sans any long-term strategic thinking. Even during the Obama presidency, Vice President Joe Biden was opposed to any nation building project in Afghanistan. He was for withdrawal and a 'pivot to Asia'. Not surprisingly, the Taliban and the global jihadi groups see it as a great 'victory' over the West.

The Jihadi groups' conclusion that it is the Jihad which won Afghanistan, and not the peace treaty, is consistent with the Islamic psyche rooted in the Badr War (CE 626) which was turning point in the history of Islam. In this war, the prophet with an army that was less than a third of the army of Meccans, led the Jihad on Mecca, massacred the Meccans and won—the Quran regarded that as a divine-ordained victory.

Two years later, the victorious prophet signed a peace treaty with the Meccans called the Pact of Al-Hudaybiyah (CE 628), that gave Muslims religious rights in Mecca, finally leading to all Meccans getting converted to Islam.

But it is not the Al-Hudaybiyah Pact, but the Badr Jihad which is etched in the psyche and consciousness of Muslims as the turning point in Islamic history.

The perceived success of the ideological supremacy of the Afghan war (Jihad) over the Doha peace treaty, which is manifest in a government that has 14 hardened terrorists who are on the international most wanted list, has the potential to lead to fratricidal killings and a civil war in Afghanistan, besides promoting global terror on a large scale.

The reported physical clash between Khalil-ur-Rehman Haqqani and Abdul Ghani Baradar who was upset with the Haqqani-dominated composition of the new government, (Khalil-ur-Rehman seemed to have punched Baradar—first reported in the Indian media, and later by the BBC and Bloomberg), that forced Baradar to leave for Kandahar to meet with Supreme Leader Hibatullah Akhundzada, is ominous and a productive for unimaginable consequences.

The reported clash between the ISI chief and the Pakistan Army chief on the former's secret visit to Kabul without informing the latter, and the humiliation meted out to the army chief by the ISI chief on his return and his belated apology to the army chief, bring out the contrived information gaps in the high risk national and international assignment of Taliban government formation, and the tensions within the ruling establishment in Pakistan over Afghanistan.

This signalled the Pakistan Army Chief–ISI Chief tussle which commenced then, has sequenced into a major issue between the Prime Minister, and the Army, insisting and getting his way through in the removal of ISI chief, Lt Gen Hameed who was posted as the Peshawar Corps Command, and Lt Gen Nadeem Ahmed Anjum who was the choice of the Army Chief being appointed in his place, contrary to the decision of the Prime Minister. This seems partly the fall out of the Af–Pak issues and partly the preparation for the succession to the office of Army Chief next year.

The reported move of the Pakistan Army chief to make a Shia Muslim his successor to ensure the army's uncompromising fight against the Tehreek-e-Taliban Pakistan (TTP), which has close ties with the Taliban in Afghanistan, not only reiterates the Pakistan Army's continuing hostility to the TPP, but also points to what can become an explosive dispute between Pakistan and the Taliban.

The testimony of US Secretary of State, Antony Blinken, to the House Foreign Affairs Committee in response to lawmaker charges that Pakistan was 'hedging its bets', and that in the coming days and weeks, the US will be looking into 'the role that Pakistan has played over the last 20 years, as also the role that the US would want to see it play in the coming years, and what it will take for Pakistan to do in the days and weeks ahead', suggests a possible shift in US relations with Pakistan, which is regarded as a major non-NATO ally.

Finally, against the three possible scenarios post the US withdrawal developed by global analysts, including the United States Institute of Peace in August 2021, namely one, negotiated settlement with Taliban; two, a civil war; and three, a Taliban takeover—a totally unexpected, complicated and dangerous fourth scenario, which is a cocktail of high risk problems, is developing in Afghanistan.

This unfolding fourth scenario includes the Haqqani being dominant and exclusive in an openly split Taliban government; Pakistan's direct intervention in Afghanistan through the ISI and its pincers, the Haqqanis; the unsettled Afghanistan situation creating issues ranging from influx of refugees into Pakistan from Afghanistan, and unbearable forseeable financial costs for Islamabad which is already broke; the possible escalation of terror attacks by the TTP, making the Pakistan Army react vengefully and the impact of its spills into Afghanistan and a non-inclusive new government imposing obligations on Pakistan to answer world opinion on issues ranging from breaches of human rights to minority and gender rights, and finally, the possibility of a protracted civil war in Afghanistan.

The emergence of this unforeseen fourth scenario, which seems to have upset the calculations of all nations, including China, Iran and Russia—the initial enthusiasts of the reemergence of the Taliban rule in Kabul—is making it difficult if not impossible for any of them to take the lead in recognising the new regime. This is because with the Haqqanis controlling Kabul, no one can guarantee how the regime will behave in the future.

In this background, with Western powers closing the tap of financial flows into an economically broken Afghanistan, and a human crisis looming large, the problem is getting more and more complicated.

And finally, if the Taliban fails, as they probably will, it will be a disaster. What will replace them? Obviously, anarchy. Afghanistan will become the unruled, unsupervised, unruly geography of hundreds of global outfits establishing Jihadi ideological and terror schools. It will become a hot bed of terrorism targeting all nations—islamic and non-Islamic.

And the story continues without break at this point.

Before the reemergence of the Taliban is discussed in detail, it is necessary to answer an intriguing question on whether the US left Afghanistan without a government in place.

Did the US Leave Afghans Without a Government and in Disorder, Recklessly or Strategically?

The way the US vacated Afghanistan, when the Taliban mounted its thrust from April onwards towards Kabul, indicated one of two opposites. Either as an accused within and outside, the Biden administration was reckless in not planning and executing an orderly withdrawal from Afghanistan—like handing the baton in a relay race, which is the norm—and fully knowing that President Ashraf Ghani's abdication would leave the Afghans without a government. Or it wanted to withdraw intentionally in a disorderly manner so that it did not seamlessly hand over Afghanistan to the Taliban 2.0. Answers to these questions will indicate the many developments that are likely to follow in the coming weeks and months. But here are a few critical dates and pointers.

- On 11 August, 2021, President Ashraf Ghani appeals to the warlords and people to rise against the Taliban.
- On the same day, US Intelligence says that the Taliban could isolate Kabul in thirty days and take over in ninety days.
- On 14 August, Ghani vows to regroup the army and fight the Taliban.
- On 15 August, Ghani abdicates and flees.
- On the same day, the Taliban proclaims victory.
- On 17 August, Reuters reports that the gains surprised even the Taliban. Mullah Abdul Ghani Baradar, one of the main architects of victory, said it was an unrivalled triumph but one that had come unexpectedly swiftly. 'We have reached a situation that was never expected', he said.

- On 2 September, the Taliban announces the formation of the new government.
- On 3 September, the Taliban defers government formation as there were reports of differences between it and the Haqqanis.
- On 5 September, General Mark Milley, Chairman of the US Joint Chiefs of Staff, questions whether the Taliban would be able to transition from an insurgent force to a government and says there is a good possibility of a civil war taking place.

A single event—Ashraf Ghani's abdication twenty-four hours after he had called upon the people to resist the Taliban—forced the Taliban itself into a situation it had never expected. Because of that single development, it never had, or it was denied, the time needed to deliberate with its allies to form a government plan for a smooth and seamless takeover. Whether the Taliban could transition from insurgency to governance, as General Milley had asked, was made more difficult by the suddenness of the developments.

And, the swiftness of events has been the cause of the confusion and chaos that portends a possible civil war. A recall and closer look at the happenings in August seem to indicate that the sudden withdrawal by the US in April was no accident, but a deliberate strategic move.

A Brookings research (15 April 2021) titled 'The US decision to withdraw from Afghanistan is the right one' almost said that Washington's decision was taken intentionally after it clearly foresaw a civil war situation emerging. The Brookings study said

> (T)he Biden administration's decision to withdraw all U.S. troops from Afghanistan by September 11, 2021 is a wise strategic choice that took significant political courage. The administration correctly assessed that perpetuating U.S. military engagement in Afghanistan has become a strategic liability and a futile investment that lost the capacity to alter the basic political and military dynamics in Afghanistan. That does not mean that desirable political and security developments will follow in Afghanistan after the U.S. military withdrawal. Unfortunately, the possibility of an intensified and potentially highly fragmented and bloody civil war is real, and at minimum, the Taliban's ascendance to formal power will bring painful changes to the country's political dispensation.

Did the US Create the Vacuum to Suck Russia and China in?

Reports published on the website of The Hill TV foresaw that China planned to 'swoop in' and 'fill the vacuum' left by the withdrawal of US troops and that China will be the 'next empire to enter the Afghan graveyard'.

Responding to that report, a less known Indian commentator and political analyst, Farooq Vani, wrote profoundly that even if The Hill report didn't come true, can Russia and China prevent the 'graveyard' itself expanding to areas where their interest lies, is a real question. Vani came surprisingly close to saying that the US strategy was to create a security vacuum for Russia and China to get sucked into. Writing in the *Financial Express* online, Vani said,

> (The) sudden decision by the US to withdraw forces from Afghanistan is not a decision taken in jiffy; it is part of a well thought strategy to get out the "graveyard" creating a vacuum for China and Russia to get sucked into. The all weather friend Pakistan may also, at one point of time decide to stay out of it as it has enough problems to handle. Moreover, Russia and China may not be in a position to pay Pakistan to the magnitude which the US did in the 1980s and 2000s. Pakistan's economy, the internal situation, the situation at borders and the internal political turmoil may force it to recoil and re-join US camp. In a scenario like this, the "graveyard" will engulf XUAR and some Central Asian countries.

A profound assessment indeed! This seemed to reflect the difference between the enthusiastic first reaction of Russia and China to the Taliban's seizure of Kabul, and their late realised reaction to Taliban rule in Afghanistan.

After Spending $9 trillion, Loss of Thousands of lives, War on Terror Back to Where It Was on 11.9.2001

This marked the return of the Taliban and the West shockingly back to where it was in 2001—wiping out the effect and impact of a twenty-year war on terror which, according to the Cost of War Project at Brown University, has cost Washington $9 trillion. If lifetime care of the war veterans is included, 3000 direct American deaths and 900,000 deaths world over, and drove thirty-seven million, may be even fifty-nine million people, out of homes in different countries.

August 2021 Conquest of Kabul Will Recall Battle of Badr in Extremist Islamist Mind?

The fact that the twenty-year effort by the West at huge financial and human cost seems to have come to nothing will be projected by the terrorists as the victory of true Islam. Extremist theologians will equate this to the Battle of Badr. The prestige of the battle in Islamic consciousness is marked by the fact that it is the only battle mentioned by name in the Quran.

According to the Encyclopaedia Britannica 'The victory at Badr was a watershed so momentous for the nascent Muslim community that it was believed to be miraculous. Not only did it confirm to the Ummah divine sanction of the new religion of Islam—for the Qur'ān attributed the success to divine intervention (3:123)—but it confirmed the vitality of the Ummah in challenging the hegemony of the Quraysh.'

Extremist theologians will tend to draw a parallel between the Battle of Badr and the Battle for Kabul, as everything in Islamist perspective finally lands in religion as the real and only guide.

The perceived victory of the Islamists in Kabul will greatly add to the capacity of the diverse Islamic movements to find more enthusiastic recruits. It is bound to stir up global Islamist terror which has been fatiguing in the last six years.

The presence of proclaimed terrorists in the Taliban government will only enhance the value of the Battle of Badr parallel in the minds of terror groups. An inclusive government at Kabul would not have had the same impact.

With 14 Terrorists as Ministers in Taliban 2.0 Government, it is Anything but Inclusive

The new Taliban avatar has broken every promise it had made to sew up the February 2020 deal with the West, namely that it would give up terror; disconnect from Al Qaeda and Haqqani terror outfits; prevent use of Afghan geography for terror against others; respect human rights; permit press freedom; protect gender rights, safeguard minorities and form an all-inclusive government. Instead, it has formed the most exclusive, Islamic Sharia and extremist government, in which fourteen out of thirty-three ministers, including the Prime Minister and his two deputies, are declared as terrorists by the UN Security Council, and its interior minister is the leader of Haqqani terrorists who carries a US reward of $5 million, dead or alive.

Besides, it has arrested and beaten-up journalists, censored news of women's protests, killed a protesting pregnant woman to show and threaten to what extent it could go to, even killing people outside Kabul to keep the crime beyond global notice. It has targeted the minority Tajiks in Panjshir, cut off their water, electricity and fuel supplies to force them to surrender, and even shot and killed the brother of Vice President Amrullah Saleh. It has qualified all its commitments made by it under the February 2020 pact but subject to Islamic Sharia law—a declaration that destroys the very premise of the pact, as Sharia law is contrary to all principles of human, gender, and minority rights.

As Friends Turn Away, Taliban Cancels Inaugural

Many liberal analysts and thinkers in the West had certified the Taliban as a mellowed and moderate force, and that influenced different nations to initially view the new rule in Afghanistan positively. But the words and deeds of the Taliban seem to have convinced them that it is as bad as it was during its original incarnation. The most notable example is Russia, which had good words for the Taliban to start with, but ended up taking the same position as India. Of the five other nations—Pakistan, China, Turkey, Qatar and Iran—invited by the Taliban to its swearing-in ceremony, China and Pakistan remained silent. This seemed to have forced the Taliban, which planned for the inaugural to coincide with the 9/11 attack on the US, to cancel the inauguration to avoid wasting money. It said the government has started functioning, implying that no inauguration is needed. This major setback to the Taliban and its promoters—China and Pakistan—seem to have not been properly noticed in the discourse on the Taliban. The trend shows the isolation of Taliban which seems to have frightened its promoters.

Global Discourse on Taliban Confused and Compromised

And yet, many liberal-minded global citizens would like to see Taliban 2.0 as a moderate version of Taliban 1.0 and have turned its apologists, if not, its advocates. This is, perhaps, only to be expected as most countries, with the exception of India, have been in talks with it and have not been averse to it being allowed to assume control of Afghanistan.

Having committed the original sin of, so to speak, supping with the devil, it takes courage to express Mea Culpa and to break with it. Accordingly, a totally false narrative is now being developed which seeks to paint the Taliban in a favourable light with calls for economic assistance to it. Not only is a shroud sought to be cast on human rights atrocities being committed by the Taliban, but it is simultaneously being painted as ten feet tall, by asserting that it has defeated the US—a palpable falsehood as there was no fighting at all between the two, and the US left Afghanistan of its own volition after a year's notice due to domestic considerations.

The narrative further goes on to perversely suggest that the Taliban is more popular than the US in Afghanistan due to the cruelties perpetrated by the latter in that country. The underlying truth is that the global discourse on the Taliban is confused, compromised, and overtaken by the shocking developments in Afghanistan.

Friends as Much Confused and Distanced as Others

Nations which had first warmed up to the Taliban take-over, seem to be confused and some are even distancing themselves from the Taliban. Keeping behind its proclamation that the

Taliban is a terrorist outfit, Russia, which was its admirer when it seized Kabul, later refused its invite for the inaugural and even began NSA-to-NSA discussions with India on the regional security risks of the fall out of Taliban rule in Kabul.

Iran, another friend, has started condemning the Taliban and its friend, Pakistan, for the violent Panjshir thrust and is also upset with it for forming an exclusive government by not including anyone from Panjshir. China, also a friend invited for the Taliban swearing in, kept silent on attending till the inaugural itself was cancelled and has begun saying that the Taliban should form a broad-based, inclusive government.

Pakistan ISI Army Divide Over Haqqani Dominated Taliban Rule?

And Pakistan, which the Taliban calls as its second home, seems to be facing a greater problem in the wake of domestic divide over not only happenings in Kabul but also how Pakistan should deal with it. The Army chief and the ISI chief seem to have reportedly clashed over the role of the latter's visit to Kabul to facilitate the installation of a Haqqani-dominant Taliban government. The army chief had reportedly humiliated the ISI chief by removing the official flag from his vehicle for going to Kabul without informing him. It was seen as a violation of military discipline and protocol. The tussle led the ISI chief to plead guilty and tend an apology. The issue seems to have been closed for the time being. However, did things stop at this? The installation of a Haqqani-dominated Taliban seems to have led to Pakistan Army Chief General Bajwa, a Shia himself, appointing Lt. Gen. Azar Abbas, also a Shia officer, as the 35th Chief of General Staff of the Pakistan Army. This has indicated that General Bajwa is considering having a Shia as the next chief of army staff. so that it can guarantee an uncompromising fight with Pakistan's Tehreek-e-Taliban (TTP) which sustains close ties with the Haqqani network.

The Taliban-Haqqani alliance in Kabul may lead to a TTP-Haqqani alliance in Islamabad, which can be dangerous for both Pakistan and Afghanistan. This is also leading to a power struggle between different claimants, the humiliated ISI being one of them, which is bound to weaken the unity of Pakistan security apparatus.

Taliban Doha vs Taliban Afghanistan

The Taliban Doha office, which carried out the negotiations with the US, is reportedly angry that most ministers now in Afghanistan are UNSC-listed global terrorists and most of them are wanted by the US for drug trafficking, rape, murder and extortion and kidnapping for ransom.

The Doha office, run by Mohammed Abbas Stanikzai, is also reportedly angry over the inclusion of the Haqqani group in the Taliban ministry, with its leader as Afghanistan's interior minister.

Analysts think this could lead to bloody clashes within the Taliban.

Afghan Jihad or Doha Peace Pact: Which is the Winner?

The tussle within the Taliban between the diplomatic group that negotiated the February 2020 peace pact and the jihadi group which seized Kabul seemed to be focused only on which of the two was responsible for the victory.

The Jihadi group, which fought the war along with Haqqanis, seems to have asserted it was the twenty-year battle which was responsible for the victory, while the Doha group claims it was the peace pact that ensured the win.

Obviously, the Jihadi group seems to have won and the peace pact group seems to have lost. This is evident from the fact that Baradar, who negotiated the peace deal, was physically assaulted by the Haqqanis and his position was reduced from being the head of the Taliban government as first reported, to being one of three deputies.

The two groups fired at each other in the presidential Palace in which one person was reportedly killed. Indian media reported this incident in the first week of September, and much later, the BBC and Bloomberg confirmed the incident quoting Taliban sources.

The fight and its conclusion that jihad group only won is an explosive development with far reaching consequences.

Badr War Psyche Prevails Over Al-Hudaybiyah Peace Psyche?

In Islamic religion, the two important turning points were the Badr War (CE 626) and the Pact of Al-Hudaybiyah (CE 628).

In the Badr War fought against the Meccans, Prophet Mohammed's outnumbered Jihadi army outnumbered by Meccans by 1:3, massacred the Meccans.

The Pact of Al-Hudaybiyah by which the Meccans granted Muslims equal rights to practice their religion and even agreed to empty the city to allow Muslims to practice their rituals, was a big victory for Islam and Mohammed.

But it is not the Pact of Al-Hudaybiyah which occupies pride of place in Islamic consciousness, it is the Badr War. The Badr Jihad is the only war which the Quran, the word of Allah, mentions and attributes to divine intervention, and thus, occupies the highest place in Islamic religion and history.

The word Badr became popular in Islamic military and Jihadi tradition. Egypt launched 'Operation Badr' during the fourth war against Israel in 1973; Pakistan's offensive against India during the Kargil War of 1999 was also called 'Operation Badr'. Iran's offensive against Iraq in the 1980s and the Libyan rebel attack on Tripoli chose the Badr war anniversary to launch their respective attacks.

This psyche of placing the Badr War above the Pact of Al-Hudaybiyah seems to have influenced the Taliban to place the Afghan Jihad above the Doha Pact.

Against this background, it is necessary to understand how the rise of the Taliban will impact the security of Afghanistan, South and Central Asia, and the world as a whole.

Rise of Taliban 2.0 Ominous and Dangerous

The rise of a reincarnated Taliban, now popularly known as Taliban 2.0, in Afghanistan is one of the most ominous, destabilising and dangerous developments for the entire world. We postulate that—

- The advent of Taliban 2.0 as the Afghan ruler is the deadliest blow to the West, which is bound to affect the global war on terror
- The impact of the Taliban's success will not be, as most analysts seem to think, limited to spreading terror in South and Central Asia.
- It will be the most potent steroid to activate and empower global terrorist forces.
- It is most likely to land Afghanistan in a protracted civil war.
- The Taliban cannot unite to rule Afghanistan as Jihadis can fight brutally but cannot rule peacefully.
- The ISIS and the Haqqanis, which had helped the Taliban conquer Afghanistan, will seek rewards, which the Taliban cannot grant and, if it does, it will be undoing itself.
- Any nation, whether it is Pakistan, China or Iran, which seeks to derive advantage from the exit of the US and the entry of the Taliban in Afghanistan, may be in for a disappointment and even face the risk of terror against its interests.

The reappearance of the Taliban should be seen in the background of the rise of global Islamist terror in the 1990s, culminating in the 9/11 attack on the US by the Al Qaeda.

The Taliban was not only an ideological partner, but also an infrastructure provider for the attack, besides protecting and giving asylum to the perpetrators of the carnage. It led to the global war on terror and on the Taliban by the US and the NATO, which sought to extinguish Taliban 1.0, but failed.

Having failed, they negotiated a peace treaty with the Taliban which was founded on the assumption that Taliban 2.0 is a saintly version of Taliban 1.0, the original sinner. The basis of the deal was that Taliban 2.0 has given up terror for which it was born and had become a moderate outfit.

We shall see how this completely ignores the reality of seeing Jihadi Islamic terror as a self-motivating and self-propelling phenomenon rooted in Islamic apocalyptic theology and the political ideology founded on it and therefore, no terror outfit, be it the Taliban or any other, can bargain that core theology.

At this point and before going deeper into current happenings in Afghanistan, it is necessary to get an idea about the social and anthropological soul of that nation.

Anthropological Soul of Afghanistan—Read Taliban

Not much currently valid anthropological studies on Afghanistan is available and what is available are only colonial writings on the subject. One needs to understand how these tribal affinities work, to understand and to make policies on Afghanistan.

More anthropological studies on Pashtun tribes and on Pashtunwali are needed, but visits to those areas are difficult. The essence of anthropology in foreign policy analysis is a long-neglected subject.

Yet, from the available information, it is necessary to understand the anthropological and social soul of Afghanistan to know how far Taliban 2.0 is compliant or contrary to it. This understanding will reveal the internal dynamics of different social and tribal groups for policy approaches to contain the toxic effect of the present regime.

There are four main historic confederacies of Afghanistan which are relevant to understanding the present Taliban government. The Pashtuns claim to be descendants from Qais Abdul Rashid who had three sons, named Bet, Gharghasht and Sarban, and one adopted son, named Karlan. The four confederacies—Bettani, Gharghashti, Sarbani and Karlani emerged from them. From within these individual confederacies emerged the more widely-known divisions of Pashtun tribes. The Ghilzais are prominent in the Bettani confederacy; the Durrani among the Sarbani; the Haqqanis are Zadran, dominant among the Karlani; the Kakars are prominent among the Gharghashti. There are, of course, sub-divisions among the ruling Pashtun dynasties of Afghanistan—the Abdalis, the

Sadozais, the Barakzais and the Mohammedzais to which Zahir Shah, the last King, deposed in 1973, belonged. Pakistanis prefer all confederacies over the Sarbani Durranis, the Pashtun nationalists who had very aggressively pressed the case for the right of self-determination for the Pashtuns of Pakistan. The Soviets and the Americans, each in their turn, foisted a Ghilzai Pashtun on the country when they felt the need to sweeten the Pakistani mood.

The Soviets switched to Najibullah, an Ahmedzai Ghilzai, in 1986. The Americans foisted Ashraf Ghani, another Ahmedzai Ghilzai, in 2014. Did he remember the cruel fate suffered by his fellow-Ahmedzai at the hands of the Taliban in 1996 as he fled from Kabul?

This background provides an insight into the formation of the current government. The ISI chief was in Kabul to finalise the government formation.

Anthropological Composition and Social Diversity of the Present Government

Afghanistan's Prime Minister, Hassan Akhund, is a Kakar from the Ghaghashti segment, chosen, probably because the Pakistanis refusal to have a Durrani at the top, because the invisible and inaudible spiritual leader of the Taliban, Hibatullah Akhundzada, is a Durrani anyway.

The First Deputy Prime Minister, Mullah Baradar, is a Durrani. He is a Poplazai like Hamid Karzai. In fact, Baradar was imprisoned by Pakistan because he had had unauthorised meetings with Karzai in 2010. Clearly, he was the US choice, because they had him released in 2018 from Pakistani detention so as to lead the Taliban talks with US Special Representative Zalmay Khalilzad. Both Akhundzada and Khalilzad are Noorzai Durranis. This would explain why the ISI would not have Baradar as Prime Minister. Abdul Salam Hanafi, the Second Deputy Prime Minister, is an Uzbek from Jowzjan Province. Like Akhund, he is neither a fighter nor a political figure, but a cleric. His duties and role are not clear.

Mohammed Yaqub, the son of Omar, regarded as the founder of the Taliban (the actual founder is Gen Nasirullah Babar, then the Interior Minister in the Benazir government), is a Hotak Ghilzai of the Bettani confederacy. Obviously acceptable to the Pakistan Army and ISI, who took his father under their protection after 2001. He is the Defence Minister.

Sirajuddin Haqqani, the Interior Minister, is a Zadran from the Karlani confederacy. The Haqqani family is the closest in terms of the ideology and activities of the ISI. The father of the current leader, Jamaluddin, was the first to declare a jihad against Afghanistan in 1973, after King Zahir Shah was overthrown by his cousin, Mohammed Daud Khan. The clan remains close to the ISI, though it does maintain links with the Tehrik-e-Taliban Pakistan, who are openly anti-Pakistan and anti-China now.

The final figure of interest is Army Chief Qari Fasihuddin, an ethnic Tajik, who is said to have played an active role in capturing the Panjshir region.

Thus, in their own twisted way, the Pakistanis have provided some diversity in the new Afghan government, but with some clear principles. The first is that the Durranis are to be kept down, but not out. The second is loyalty to the ISI. Linked to this is the importance of keeping the coercive arms of state—the Defence Ministry and the Interior Ministry—in the hands of persons trusted by the ISI.

Taliban 2.0—Varying Degrees of Risk for All

Taliban 2.0 rule cannot, by its nature, be an undiluted advantage for anyone—be it Afghanistan itself or Pakistan, or even China, which seems to be enthusiastic about the exit of the US from Afghanistan and the entry of the Taliban. While all consequences of the rise of Taliban 2.0 cannot be predicted with precision now, the likely consequences as we see are:

- The Taliban 2.0 is bound to be more aggressive and anarchic.
- Afghanistan may become safe haven for global terror groups.
- It may encourage and promote terror groups in Pakistan.
- It will persecute the Shias and pose risks to Iran.

- It may also provoke extremism and terror in Xinjiang.
- It may be pose risk to Central Asian nations and Russia.
- It may revive terrorism in Jammu and Kashmir.
- It may land Afghanistan in a perpetual state of civil strife.
- Afghanistan, which is already insolvent, will be at the mercy of nations with divergent interests—China, Pakistan and the West.
- It will even land Russia and China in the alleged 'graveyard of empires'.
- It may lead to a repeat of the 9/11 attack.
- It may set the entire Islamic world on the boil by attracting new recruits to Islamic terror the world over.

The West, however, seems to be trying to whitewash the danger posed by the Taliban. Pakistan is in the lead in this project. It has unleashed a propaganda barrage to project the Taliban as amenable—that they should be given time, or so goes the refrain.

A New Taliban 1.0 within the Old Taliban 2.0?

Taliban 2.0, which some see as different from Taliban 1.0, has, despite its assurances to the contrary, confirmed that it is the same by its actions.

According to a UN press release, since mid-April when the Taliban began its thrust toward Kabul along with different terror groups, it launched more than 5,500 attacks in thirty-one of Afghanistan's thirty-four provinces. Despite this explicit evidence which confirms that Taliban 2.0 is little different from Taliban 1.0—being no more than a bunch of terrorists aided and abetted by Pakistan—the horde of apologists tend to overlook a crucial but uncomfortable truth. And that is, even if Taliban 2.0 intends to reform itself, the transformation of its psychology of terror against perceived enemies rooted in the Jihadi ideology which is its DNA, to governance of all that includes the very enemies they fought, needs a different and positive state of mind—which is a near impossibility.

Jihadis can fight brutally, but they cannot rule peacefully. The only reason why there is a perception that Taliban 2.0 would be a reformed version of Taliban 1.0, is the massive hope and wish some in the West have got, which the Taliban 2.0 media strategy has successfully created in them. The reasons for that hope are that, one, the Taliban 2.0 has given assurances, and two, Pakistan has trained it to be so media savvy that it has created such hopes. But its actions since April on the ground belie these hopes and yet there is hope against hope.

The apologists of Taliban 2.0 are likely to prove gravely wrong given that the DNA of the Taliban is Islamic Text-based terror. While the old order of Taliban 1.0, who had perpetrated barbarity in the 1990s, may have matured beyond barbaric mind and acts and may have acquired some aspects of running an orderly state, the new recruits to Taliban 2.0 would have the same mentality as the older one had in the 1990s. Without the same violent jihadi spirit of the Taliban 1.0, they would not have joined the Taliban 2.0 to fight for Islam. That is, within the old Taliban 2.0, there is a new Taliban 1.0.

In a blog in Brookings Edu titled 'Will the Taliban Regime Survive?' Vanda Felbab-Brown, Director, Initiative on Non-State Armed Actors, Co-Director of the Africa Security Initiative and Senior Fellow Center for 21st Century Security and Intelligence in the Foreign Policy program at the Brookings Institution, a Washington-based think tank, thematically captures this brooding dichotomy of the new Taliban 1.0 with the old Taliban 2.0. She says:

> The most significant threat to the Taliban regime could come from within. The Taliban's success as an insurgency rested on its ability to remain cohesive despite NATO efforts to fragment the group. But the group's challenge of maintaining cohesiveness across its many different factions of varied ideological intensity and material interests is tougher now that it is in power. The factions have disparate views about how the new regime should rule across just about all dimensions of governance: inclusiveness, dealing with foreign fighters, the economy, and external relations. Many middle-level battlefield commanders—younger, more plugged into global

> jihadi networks, and without personal experience of the Taliban's mismanaged 1990s rule—are more hardline than key older national and provincial leaders. (emphasis added)

In short, the beast Taliban 2.0 contains the seed of its own destruction—a new Taliban 1.0.

Is it Taliban 2.0 at All?

In a highly informative article in *The Atlantic* titled 'This Is Not the Taliban 2.0', Graeme Wood, a staff writer and author of 'The Way of the Strangers: Encounters with the Islamic State', says that the group's claims of having changed are probably more reassuring to those unfamiliar with its history. Referring to the assurance of Taliban 1.0 when it sacked Kabul 25 years ago, that it was not for revenge, no personal rancour, it offered general amnesty to those who worked for the previous government, Wood wrote that it 'castrated the former President Mohammed Najibulla and, according to some reports, stuffed his severed genitals in his mouth, and soon after, he was strung up from a lamppost'.

Saying that the reports from Kabul are probably more reassuring to those unfamiliar with this history, Wood says the Taliban declaration of a general amnesty, asking everyone to show up for work in the morning and unite behind a Taliban government that will rule according to Islamic law, is not in the harsh manner that made it infamous during its rule from 1996 to 2001. Wood says in harsh language that 'those who wish to avoid being force-fed their own testicles should probably not read too much into the kinder, gentler Taliban initiatives currently being implemented in Kabul'. Saying that the Taliban are cruel, but not fools, and magnanimity early in their rule does not mean that they will be any less vengeful than they were at the height of their power.

Wood points out that outside Kabul—away from the eyes of the world, there are reports of summary executions. And saying that Taliban leaders are showing no signs of mellowing and accusing them of being dishonest in negotiations to secure the US exit, Wood makes the most important and dangerous point that 'the current generation of leaders is simply meaner than its predecessors, and in some cases hardened by time in Guantánamo Bay', citing an Afghan in Kabul, who knows senior Taliban, who told Wood they are 'much more strict, much more hardline'.

Asking 'Have the Taliban changed themselves in the last twenty years', Aqil Shah, a scholar in the South Asia Program at the Carnegie Endowment for International Peace, writes:

'The Taliban have sought to rebrand themselves as a moderate political movement. Even though this so-called new Taliban or Taliban 2.0 has won the approval of some Western officials and analysts, there are no indications that the militant group is willing to make significant political concessions, moderate its extremist ideology, or change its harsh social policies with respect to women's mobility, education, or right to work.

The Taliban do appear eager to engage the international community, presumably out of the need for international recognition and future economic assistance. They have made positive overtures to religious minorities and have even offered a general amnesty to opponents. But actions speak louder than words. Despite promising to form an inclusive government, the Taliban have monopolised power in their hands since assuming power in Kabul. Amnesty International alleges the Taliban brutally murdered nine ethnic Hazara men in July. The Hazaras are one of the largest ethnic groups in Afghanistan who faced severe repression from the last Taliban regime because they practiced Shia Islam in a Sunni-majority country. Media reports suggest Taliban fighters are searching door-to-door for Afghans who worked for the previous government, or the United States, as well as for journalists and human rights activists. There are also reports that the group has covertly detained, forcibly disappeared, and even executed their perceived enemies.'

The appellation, Taliban 2.0, itself is apologetic. The Taliban is wrongly seen by its apologists more as a Pashtun tribal Islamic nationalist group rather than as a global Islamist terror outfit even after its partnership with Al Qaeda in launching terror globally. In that context, it is necessary to understand that the Taliban shares the same Salafi Islamic theology and ideology which is the driving force behind global terror outfits like Al Qaeda and the ISIS. Their source of inspiration and goals are the same and identical.

Taliban 2.0 Virtually Confirms it is Only Taliban 1.0—Only Sharia Law Will Be Supreme

The Supreme leader of Taliban 2.0, Hibatullah Akhundzada, has declared in his first statement the future policies of the new Afghan government. He said it will uphold Sharia law, protect human rights and respect international treaties, but subject only to Sharia law. The declaration is clear that Sharia law will reign supreme and everything else will only be subject to that. The distressing images of Afghan journalists being beaten by the Taliban for reporting on the womens' protest against the Taliban in Kabul, the arrest of journalists working for a Kabul daily and Akhundzada's statement being silent on the commitment to sever its ties with Al Qaeda and other foreign terrorists groups, clearly indicates that the reincarnated Taliban will be no different from its earlier avatar.

Six terrorists named by the UNSC are in the new Taliban cabinet. Apologists of the new Taliban like the US and EU have expressed concerns about their inclusion.

It is necessary now to understand the true nature and character of Islamist terror. Is it only an anti-establishment phenomenon for which the extremists seek inspiration from Islamic scriptures as most discourse tends to dismiss it, or is it more?

Islamic Terror, Theological and Ideological

While the West spent much labour and energy on the domestic, political, and geopolitical aspects of Islamic terror, research and scholarly works of strategic think tanks on the dominant theological and ideological motivation for terror are not too many. With the result, the core drive behind Islamic terror is even now not in the main discourse. In this background, a research and scholarly work titled 'Inside the Jihadi Mind: Understanding Ideology and Propaganda', sponsored by the Tony Blair Institute of Global Change, needs a mention. It is a detailed survey of the theological state of mind of Islamic people across the world and a study of the jihadi mindset. It brings out the core truth that jihadi terror is theological and ideological, and not simply political. Here is the relevant part of its executive summary to explain the theology which gave birth to the Taliban from which it cannot be separated.

> The ideology of global terrorism can only be countered if it is first understood. The combination of theology and political objectives needs to be uprooted through rigorous scrutiny and sustained intellectual confrontation. After the 9/11 attacks, Osama Bin Laden's Al Qaeda had approximately 300 militants. ISIS alone has, at a low estimate, 31000 fighters across Syria and Iraq. Understanding how ideology has driven this phenomenon is essential to containing and defeating violent extremism. Within the last decade, polls have found that:
>
> Over a half of the Muslims surveyed in nine Muslim-majority countries around the world believed that they would live to see the start of the Apocalypse. Today, ISIS exploits this and believes, and fights to hasten the apocalypse.
>
> Over two thirds of the population of three large Muslim majority countries agreed with the need for a caliphate. Today, jihadis claim to deliver on their desire.
>
> At least 40 per cent of Sunnis in five Middle Eastern and North African countries did not recognise Shias as Muslims. Today, Jihadis are killing Shias in their thousands.
>
> Three quarters of the respondents in four large Muslim majority countries agreed that there was a need to 'stand up to America and affirm the dignity of the Islamic people'. Today, Jihadis fight the West and aliens to 'deliver' the world from a 'Zionist-Shia-Crusader' conspiracy. We know that this does not make for comfortable reading. But the Muslims themselves suffer the most from jihadi violence. And unless we are honest about the nature and appeal of the jihadi ideology, we cannot uproot.

> The researchers analysed a cross-section of 114 propaganda sources ranging from April 2013 to summer 2015 from three Salafi-Jihadi groups: ISIS, Jabhat-al-Nusra and Al Qaeda in the Arabian Peninsula. The report provides an evidence base for what is already assumed by many, that the ideology of Salafi-Jihadism is a vital motivating factor for extremist violence and, therefore, must be countered in order to curb the threat.

The Centre for Strategic and International Studies (CSIS) estimates the jihadist population worldwide to be at 2,30,000. The CSIS says: 'Despite nearly two decades of US-led counterterrorism operations, there are nearly four times as many Sunni Islamic militants today as there were on 11 September, 2001. Based on a CSIS data set of groups, fighters, and violence, the regions with the largest number of fighters are Syria (between 43,650 and 70,550 fighters), Afghanistan (between 27,000 and 64,060), Pakistan (between 17,900 and 39,540), Iraq (between 10,000 and 15,000), Nigeria (between 3,450 and 6,900), and Somalia (between 3,095 and 7,240).'

The theology and ideology of all Jihadi groups inspires their cadre to die and kill adversaries who are impediments to the apocalypse common to all of them, including the Taliban. Some tend to distinguish the Taliban from Al Qaeda or the ISIS, on ideology. But Taliban ideology is derived from the same source as that of others.

But the US, which is one of the prime targets of global jihad, and no one, for that matter, seems to have a clear strategy to fight jihadism and the radicalisation of the Muslim mind effectively, and to deal with the large armies of jihadists, who are invisible and diffused. A large number of radicalised minds support them.

Common Origin of Taliban's Deobandi Islamic Theology and ISIS-Al Qaeda Wahhabi Theology

The ideology of Taliban is derived from the Deoband School of Islam of colonial India, the ISIS-Al Qaeda's, from Wahhabi theology. The difference between them is without distinction.

The Indian Deobandi and the Arabic Wahabi schools are sourced in the theology of Ibn Taimiyyah, the celebrated founder of Salafi Islam.

Taimiyyah was the only scholar in Islamic history to challenge Prophet Mohammad, advocating inner Jihad Akbar (Greater Jihad) over the outer Jihad Kabir (Lesser Jihad). Taimiyyah's adherents had continued teaching Salafi ideology in Medina. Between the 14th and 19th centuries, Salafi Islam was underground. In the 19th century, Al-Wahhab from Arabia and Shah Waliullah from India studied in the Salafi School in Medina. While Al Wahhab went to Saudi Arabia and initiated Salafi-Wahhabi Islam and partnered with the House of Saud, Shah Waliullah came to Deoband in India and established the Arabic mosque where he taught Salafi Islam. He even wrote to Shah Abdali in Afghanistan to come and conquer India, as after the death of Mughal Emperor Aurangzeb, Islam had become weak. After him, his work continued in the name of the Arabic mosque in Deoband. But during the Khilafat agitation, to escape the British government's notice, the name Arabic mosque was renamed the Dar-ul-uloom Deoband.

The common origin of Wahhabi and Deobandi Islam was brought out by Charles Allen, a renowned historian of the British Raj in India, in his book *God's Terrorists: The Wahhabi Cult and the Hidden Roots of Modern Jihad*. Allen traces the history of Wahhabism, the guiding ideology of Islamist modern terrorism. Wahhabism was founded in the 18th century, but its seeds were sown centuries before by Taymiyya, who re-invented and re-weaponised the concept of Jihad. Here is the brief account of how Allen traces the common Salafi origin of the Wahhabi and Deobandi schools.

In Prophet Mohammad's times, jihad was an obligation put on Muslims to strive for their faith until the entire world had converted or submitted to the Islamic authority. But as Islam transformed into a multi-ethnic world religion, the literalist view of jihad gave way to pragmatism. The pragmatists cited the famous declaration of the Prophet in Hadith on his return from the Battle of Badr, that it marked the end of his military campaign against the polytheists, the Lesser Jihad (Jihad Kabeer) was over; the Greater Jihad (Jihad Akbar) had started. This statement was interpreted in Islam as meaning that the outer and less important physical struggle for Islam was over and had given way to a more important inner, moral struggle.

After the Mongols devastated the Islamic heartland in the 14th century, Ibn Taymiyya found that the Greater Jihad idea had weakened Islam. He stood for a literal, and was against a liberal, idea of jihad. He defied the Prophet himself on the pragmatic Greater Jihad. Citing two verses in the Quran (Chapter 2 verse 193; Chapter 8 verse 39), Taymiyya argued that the Prophet's division of the jihad in the Hadith as lesser and greater was not authentic because it contradicted the words of God in Koran. He declared that the (indivisible) jihad against Islam's adversaries was the finest act a Muslim could perform. Taymiyya also classified infidels of Islam in four categories: the Christian; Muslims with infidel habits unless brought back to Islam; Muslims not carrying out Islam's rituals, and those who rejected Islam while still claiming to be Muslims. He declared that no peace was possible with the first two and the next two must be mercilessly killed.

Taymiyya's theology was rejected in his time. He was branded a heretic and even imprisoned. But, says Charles Allen, Taymiyya's theology continued to attract adherents. A most famous adherent of his was Muhammed Ibn Abd Al-Wahhab, who founded what is now known as the Wahhabi strand of Islam in the early part of the 18thcentury. This most virulent strand of Islam, rejected in the 14th century, was reincarnated four centuries later. Allen says that Al-Wahhab was schooled in Medina under Muhammed Hayat and his father from Sind in India, both followers of Ibn Taymiyya. They encouraged their students to 'view the militant jihad as a religious duty'. When Al-Wahhab was studying in Medina, Shah Waliullah from Delhi too was in Medina studying the Hadith under a Taymiyya disciple who was the master of

Al-Wahhab's teacher. Al-Wahhab and Shah Waliullah, both young, went back to their respective countries to implement these radical teachings. In Delhi, Waliullah called for 'a return to the first principles of Islam'. He attempted to restore 'Muslim rule in Hindustan' by even inviting Afghan ruler Ahmed Shah Abdali to invade India and destroy the Hindu Marathas in battle to bring back the golden days of Mughal Emperor Aurangzeb. But Ahmed Shah was defeated and the Maratha gained dominance in northern India.

But Waliullah's Medina-mate, Al-Wahhab, went beyond. Allen says he 'was able to construct and apply almost unchallenged, a brand of confrontational and heartless Islam, the like of which had not been seen since the days of Mahmud Ghazni, the butcher, who led twelve loot-and-destroy raids on India in the eleventh century, justifying his actions in the name of Islam.'

Al-Wahhab's book, *Call to Unity*, which later became a four-volume affair, expounded the Wahhabi theology. It declared that there should be but one interpretation of the Quran and the Hadith—Al-Wahhab's—and none else. Pointing out that Islam rose only by Jihad against the idolaters and polytheists, it concluded that loving the true Muslims and hating the infidels was the only way—the Wahhabi way.

A turn came in Islamic history in 1744 when Al-Wahhab allied with Muhammed ibn Saud, a reputed warrior and leader of a sub-branch of the powerful Aneiza tribe. They mutually recognised each other—Saud as the secular leader (Emir) and Al-Wahhab as the religious head (Imam). The rulers of Saudi Arabia are the descendants of Muhammed Ibn Saud. Thanks to Saudi Arabia owning up Al-Wahhab's theology, Ibn Taymiyya, outlawed long ago, now occupies a place of honour next only to Al-Wahhab's.

There is only as much difference between Al Qaeda and Taliban as between the disciple brothers ('Gurubhais' in Indian idiom) Al Wahhab and Shah Waliullah, schooled under Ibn Taymiyya's Salafi institution in Medina. Understanding this common umbilical Salafi theological and ideological link connecting the Taliban and Al Qaeda is necessary to judge how, in the company of Al Qaeda, the Taliban 1.0 graduated from being a barbaric force in Afghanistan in the 1990s into a global terror outfit in 2001.

Taliban 1.0 Graduated from National Terror to Global Terror

The Taliban 1.0, when it seized power and ran a barbaric government in Afghanistan, was not, and indeed was not seen as a threat to the world. It was at best seen as a national and regional terror outfit. The perception that Taliban's Islamic terror was a national and regional threat changed overnight on 9/11, which transformed Islamic terror into a global threat because it hit the US. The Taliban did not become a global threat overnight. It graduated over a period of time as it got linked to both the Islamic and non-Islamic worlds beyond Afghanistan.

The West, when it leveraged on the jihadi spirit of the Islamists and set them against the Soviets in Afghanistan in the 1980s, saw it only as a political enterprise. It probably underestimated the apocalyptic ideological potency of Islamic theology and its appeal to a vast number of Muslims. Though both Islam and Christianity are apocalyptic religions, Christianity went through a long modernisation and secularisation process to marginalise the belief in it. But Islam, which had not undergone such a historic process, has retained its apocalyptic beliefs. Unlike Christianity, which had a global outreach outside politics through the church, Islam, despite its geographic reach, did not out have a matching trans-national and trans-political outreach mechanism like the church. Also, unlike Christianity, Islam underwent a violent separation of powers between the state and the church, later firmed up by democracy. Islamic history did not undergo any modernisation, secularisation or democratisation process, except in individual cases.

It was the organised, funded, and technologically and militarily weaponised geopolitical Islam, weaponised by the US for its Afghanistan campaign against the Soviets, that organised the mind of the theological and political Islamists for global Islamic apocalypse.

It is the Taliban-Al Qaeda combine which inherited this process from the Afghan campaign. The combine saw the West, headed by the US, as the greatest threat to Islamic beliefs as Western anthropology of modernity lured the Muslims away from their core beliefs.

Apocalyptic Islam needed a global enemy to become global. Al Qaeda smashed the Twin Towers symbolically to show to the West and the world who its target was. They taught the West on that single day that the ideology of Islamic terror was global. Taliban 1.0 was snuffed out by the West precisely for the reason that it hosted Osama Bin Laden, whose brainchild was Al Qaeda.

It is from that background that the Taliban 2.0 will always be seen as a threat and will, therefore, always face threats. As the Taliban 2.0 rule starts, it faces the gravest questions about its true nature and the threats to its rule which the Taliban 1.0 never did when it seized power in the 1990s.

Here are some of the threats Taliban rule will face:

Taliban Emirate is the not the end of the Project, it is the start.

Catherine Zimmerman, writing in Hill TV web, correctly captures the implications of the Taliban rise. She says, 'But the Taliban's ideological beliefs align it closely with Salafi-jihadi groups that use violence to advance their aim of enforcing a fundamentalist understanding of Islam. These beliefs led the Taliban to protect Osama bin Laden in 2001—though the group may have officially disagreed with his actions—and to defy the United States after the 9/11 attacks. Twenty years later, the Taliban is savvier, but the core beliefs of its members remain the same. The danger of these Salafi-jihadi beliefs is that they do not stop at Afghanistan's borders. The Taliban's Islamic Emirate is not the end of the project; rather, it is the start. The vision always has been global and the Taliban has played host willingly to those seeking to replicate the Islamic Emirate's success elsewhere in the Muslim world.'

It is an extremely profound and realistic assessment of the Taliban's rise.

The Islamic Text that United the Fighter Taliban Can Divide the Ruler Taliban

By the very nature of Jihadi ideology and the organisation of the Taliban, it can oppose and attack the perceived enemy under one unified leadership, but it cannot remain united and rule under one leadership.

Even purely political parties split on ideological and personal differences. Ideological text becomes the pretext for organisational splits as Islamic texts, capable of interpretations ranging from an extreme view that motivates Muslims to kill all non-Muslims to Islamise the world, to a moderate view that persuades Muslims to live with non-Muslims, can be used by any Muslim to set Muslims on the boil. The Islamic text-based Taliban is also bound to be divided between differing views of what is true Islam and how to handle Muslims deviating from true Islam and non-Muslims. Any division within the Taliban, which is bound to arise as it turns into a political movement, is bound to be based on the divergence of views founded on the text. As the Brookings Institution says, 'the challenge of maintaining cohesiveness across its many different factions of varied ideological intensity and material interests is tougher now that the Taliban is in power.' This is entirely true. Uniting to fight an enemy is easier than ruling.

Extremist Ideological Taliban vs Political Establishment Taliban

Though there can be nothing like moderate Taliban as distinct from an extremist Talban, there will be differences between the Political Establishment Taliban whose agenda will be to rule Kabul and relate to the rest of the world, and the Extremist

Ideological Taliban whose main agenda is Islam. In case the Political Establishment Taliban adopts moderate means and focusses on governance, it will not be able to rein in the militias that have got used to drugs, human trafficking, gun culture and violence. That is how the perceived moderate Taliban establishment rule, which is seen as Taliban 2.0, will face hostility from the theological and ideological extremist Taliban which is the original Taliban 1.0.

This clash is implicit in the ruling arrangement between the Establishment Taliban and the Extremist Taliban. The reported tussle between the Taliban in Doha and Taliban in Kabul is indicative how both may come to a head soon. The ruling arrangement proposed for Afghanistan, vesting supreme authority over the nation in top religious leader Mullah Hebatullah Akhundzada and day-to-day management of government in Mullah Hasan Akhund, also has the potential for a clash.

The Akhundzada-Akhund arrangement seems perilously close to the Iranian model. This leads us to the issue of whether the Iranian model will work in Afghanistan.

Sunni Caliphate in Taliban 1.0 vs Shiite Imamate in Taliban 2.0

Reports say that the new government in Kabul will be based on the lines of the Iranian leadership, with Mullah Akhundzada as Afghanistan's supreme authority. The supreme leader is the highest political and religious authority in Iran, ranking above the president, and having the power to appoint the heads of the government, the judiciary and the military. He has the final say in all political, religious and military affairs pertaining to the country. It is here that the potential for clashes within the Taliban abounds. In Taliban 1.0, Mullah Omar was the supreme leader and the head of the state. Now, the position of supreme leader and head of state is separated. This leads to the more profound question whether the Shia Iranian model will work for Sunni Afghanistan.

The Iranian model seems to have been copied to make Taliban 2.0 different from Taliban 1.0 to make it more acceptable to other nations. Afghanistan, which is autocratic, is nowhere near Iran, which is democratic. There is a vast difference between the Shia and Sunni political cultures apart from their adversarial relations. While the Sunni faith rests on the Caliph, the one ruler over the Caliphate, the Shia faith works on the imamate or imamah. The imamate is a religious and political ideology based on guidance received from Imams. Distinguished Arabic language authorities define the word 'Shiite' as meaning a group of people developing a consensus on an issue. Therefore, there is the element of consensus in the Shia faith which the Sunni faith abhors. The Imamate is theologically consultative and consensual while the Caliphate is fundamentally authoritarian.

While Taliban rule 1.0 was a Caliphate, Taliban 2.0 is envisaged as an Imamate. Both belong to two different paradigms of the same faith. It is impossible for the Shiite Iranian Imamate to work in Sunni Afghanistan that is used to an authoritarian Sunni Caliphate model. The adoption of the Shia Iranian model for a Sunni Afghanistan will itself create conflicts and complications for Taliban 2.0. To make it all worse, the new Imamate model in Afghanistan proposes not only two centres of power, but also two capitals, that is, while the government headed by Baradar will function from Kabul, the supreme leader, Akhundzada, will function from Kandahar. This physical division of authority is bound to cause both mental and psychological tension. Having a Shiite Imamate in place of a Sunni Caliphate in Afghanistan is a dangerous experiment. The very perception of a Shiite Imamate model displacing the Sunni Caliphate model in Afghanistan where there is intense hatred for Shias can, and will, create complications.

Jihadi Terrorist Groups Operating in Afghanistan—A Clear Threat to Taliban Rule

According to the UN, twenty groups were fighting along with the Taliban to oust Afghan security forces, which was ominous news. The diverse groups which seemed to have united to defeat the Afghan government could never unite to rule the country under, or with, the Taliban.

There are six major terror groups operating in Afghanistan. Of the six, three—Al Qaeda, ISIS and Lashkar-e-Taiba (LeT)—are classified as proscribed. The other three, Taliban, Tehreek-e-Taliban Pakistan (TTP) and the Haqqani Network (HN) are classified as active insurgent groups. The terror attack on Kabul Airport in August 2021 when the US forces were present in the airport, clearly portends the kind of things to come, not only for Afghanistan, but also for the world. Reports say that this attack, which claimed the lives of 13 American soldiers and 170 Afghan civilians, was the combined work of the Haqqani group and Al Qaeda. It is clear that Taliban rule will be incapable of preventing such terror groups from operating in Afghanistan and in other nations. Afghanistan is now an open ground, like it was in the 1990s.

An article titled: 'How Will Taliban Deal with Other Terror Groups' (Carnegie Endowment for International Peace 31August 2021) says that the militant landscape in Afghanistan is complicated, to say the least. The three main groups—the Taliban, the Haqqani Network (HN) and Al-Qaeda—are closely aligned. They have multi-generational ties between them that date back to the anti-Soviet Afghan jihad, which have been reinforced over time by the experience of fighting the US and NATO troops, as also by family bonds, including intermarriages.

The Taliban and the HN are integrated at the top: Sirajuddin Haqqani, the leader of the HN, is also a deputy to the Taliban supreme leader. While the HN fights under the Taliban umbrella, it retains relative operational autonomy in its primary zone of operations in eastern Afghanistan. When asked if the HN was a group distinct from the Taliban, one of its main leaders responded: 'We are the Taliban.'

The Taliban and the HN also have the same external patron, Pakistan's Inter-Services Intelligence (ISI), which has supported these groups as a hedge against Indian influence in Afghanistan. According to the UN Sanctions Monitoring Team, the HN also acts as the primary liaison between the Afghan Taliban and Al-Qaeda.

The three groups have an adversarial relationship with the Islamic State Khorasan (ISK), in part because the ISK has exploited their internal conflicts to poach their disaffected members.

Taliban's Ties with Al Qaeda: US Defence Intelligence Agency says 'Al Qaeda Awaits Further Guidance from the Taliban!'

The US Defence Intelligence Agency (DIA), has in its report (18 May 2021), said that the Taliban has 'maintained close ties with Al Qaeda'.

The DIA's analysis is cited in a report prepared by the Department of Defense's Lead Inspector General for Operation Freedom's Sentinel in Afghanistan. Referring to the report, the Long War Journal (LWJ) brought out by the Foundation for Defense of Democracies (FDD) reported that on the same day as the report was released, Zalmay Khalilzad, the US Special Representative for Afghanistan Reconciliation, was informing the Foreign Affairs Committee of the US House of Representatives that the Taliban had made substantial progress on its countr-terrorism commitments. However, he failed to provide a single example. Khalilzad's claim is contradicted by the DIA's assessment as well as other official reporting since the US State Department entered into an agreement with the Taliban on 29 February 2020.

The LWJ reported that when Khalilzad was questioned on whether or not he was able to negotiate a commitment from the Taliban to separate from the Al Qaeda, he simply summarised his terse three-page plus agreement with the Taliban, which specified that 'the Taliban will not host, will not allow training, will not allow fundraising, will not allow recruitment of terrorists, including Al Qaeda that would threaten the security of the United States and our allies.'

Again, when questioned on what commitments the Taliban was upholding and what it was not, Khalilzad was found equivocating.

The LWJ reports further that Al Qaeda has celebrated Khalilzad's deal with the Taliban as a 'victory' for the Mujahideen. It adds that contrary to Khalilzad's assurances, the DIA assesses that the Taliban and Al Qaeda 'have reinforced ties over the past decades, likely making it difficult for an organisational split to occur'.

The DIA reported that Al Qaeda 'is likely awaiting further guidance from the Taliban'. The two continue to fight side by side against their common foes inside Afghanistan, despite some erroneous reports suggesting that the Taliban was going to disband foreign fighter units.

While the DIA's reporting is inconsistent with Khalilzad's assurances, it is in line with other official assessments. Despite the warnings that the Taliban-Al Qaeda nexus has not been broken, Khalilzad negotiated a deal with the Taliban, keeping his political masters in the dark.

In May 2020, the Lead Inspector General for Operation Freedom's Sentinel reported that the Taliban leadership was 'reluctant to publicly break with Al Qaeda'. In a 27 May 2020 analysis, a monitoring team working for the UNSC reported that the Taliban 'regularly consulted with Al Qaeda during negotiations with the US and offered guarantees that it would honor their historical ties.' That same UN report cited multiple points of contact between senior Al Qaeda and Taliban leaders, as well as other details concerning how the two organisations are intertwined.

In January 2020, the US Treasury Department reported that Al Qaeda was 'gaining strength in Afghanistan while continuing to operate with the Taliban under the Taliban's protection'. It further stated that Al Qaeda 'capitalises on its relationship with the Taliban through its network of mentors and advisers who are embedded with the Taliban, providing advice, guidance, and financial support'.

The Department of Treasury said that Al Qaeda 'maintains close contacts with the Taliban'. And this remained true as of May 2020, i.e., a few months after the 29 February agreement signed in Doha, between the US and the Taliban, as Al Qaeda and the Taliban 'maintained a strong relationship and continued to meet regularly'.

The Department of Treasury also referenced intelligence showing that senior Haqqani Network officials 'have discussed forming a new joint unit of armed fighters in cooperation with, and funded by, Al Qaeda'. The Haqqani Network, led by Sirajuddin Haqqani, is an integral part of the Taliban and also closely allied with Al Qaeda. Sirajuddin is the Taliban's deputy emir.

The Taliban, however, has refused to admit that Al Qaeda operates inside Afghanistan, let alone break with the group. The Taliban regularly lies about the presence of Al Qaeda and affiliated jihadists. On the other hand, the Thabat News Agency, which likely serves as an Al Qaeda media arm, regularly claims conducting operations inside Afghanistan in Thabat's weekly newsletter. In addition, American and Afghan forces have repeatedly targeted Al Qaeda figures and fighters in Taliban territory since 29 February 2020. There are also multiple reports indicating that Al Qaeda and its affiliated groups continue to assist the Taliban in its insurgency. Against all of this evidence, Khalilzad is yet to produce a single example of the Taliban's compliance with the counter-terrorism assurances he had negotiated.

Possible Defections to Islamic State Khorasan (ISK)

If Taliban rule appears to be moderate, it will risk desertions from within its ranks on ideological grounds. The Taliban's principal rival is the Islamic State Khorasan (ISK), whom it has battled for years. The ISK has claimed responsibility for the Kabul airport attack in which 13 US soldiers and over 180 civilians were killed, besides leaving many others injured.

According to the report, the ISK's core elements are former Taliban commanders whom the group's past leader, Mullah

Akhtar Muhammad Mansour (killed by the United States in 2016), had expelled because they were too brutal, too sectarian, and too independent.

Reports also say that possible defections of Taliban factions, or foreign fighters in Afghanistan, could boost the Taliban's principal rival. While reports say that the ISK cannot currently bring the Taliban regime down, it could become an envelope for any future defections.

An article titled: 'How Will Taliban Deal with Other Terror Groups' (Carnegie Endowment for International Peace 31 August 2021) traced the origin of ISK. It said that the ISK, a regional affiliate of the Islamic State (IS) operating mainly in Afghanistan, was formed in 2015 by disaffected commanders of the Tehrik-e-Taliban Pakistan (TTP), which seeks to overthrow the Pakistani state.

These commanders had escaped to Afghanistan following Pakistan's military offensives in districts adjacent to eastern Afghanistan in 2014. Their mission is to restore historic Khorasan, comprising Afghanistan and Central Asia, as a part of a global Islamic caliphate. The ISK, an operationally autonomous network, has attracted former members of various jihadist groups in the region, including the Taliban, Al-Qaeda and the Haqqani Network. At its peak, ISK successfully recruited thousands of fighters and captured Taliban-controlled territory in Nangarhar, Kunar and Jowzjan provinces of Afghanistan. By 2018, it had suffered significant leadership and cadre losses because of relentless US airstrikes, Afghan military operations, and to some extent, Taliban offensives. But the group is far from defeated. In fact, experts believe it has reconstituted itself as a decentralized network of sleeper cells concentrated in urban centres like Kabul and Jalalabad to avoid further attrition and detection.

According to the UNSC, in the first four months of 2021 alone, the ISK carried out seventy-seven attacks in Afghanistan, representing a significant uptick from 2020. The group's latest deadliest attack was the 26 August suicide blast at Kabul airport. The group's purest claim to the mantle of global jihad, extreme tactics (such as mass public executions) and lethal attacks have helped it lure a variety of extremist militants to its ranks.

Issue of Foreign Fighters in Taliban and in Afghanistan—Clear and Present Threat to Taliban 2.0

The Taliban still has thousands of foreign fighters, including Chinese, Chechens, Uzbeks and others, all with interests in their home countries. The Taliban denies these fighters' existence, so its promise to keep them well behaved and never to let them run off to trouble other parts of the world is roughly as credible as its promise to rule without rancour or without serving gonad sandwiches to captured enemies. Nikkei Asia writes, 'But even as the US and the allied forces have almost completely withdrawn, the Taliban have made rapid territorial gains, capturing swathes of the countryside, towns and border crossings, mainly with the support of Al Qaida and allied groups, including the East Turkestan Islamic Movement (ETIM), a Uyghur Muslim rebel group; Tehreek-e-Taliban Pakistan (TTP) and Central Asian militant outfits such as the Islamic Movement of Uzbekistan (IMU) and the Jamaat Ansarullah, a militant outfit also known as the Tajik Taliban.

The Taliban insists the reports are untrue. 'We do not have foreign fighters in our ranks,' Suhail Shaheen, a Taliban representative, told Nikkei Asia. 'Such reports or claims are aimed at misleading the people of the world about the ground realities in Afghanistan.'

But government officials, tribal elders and local journalists say foreign fighters, particularly Tajiks, Uzbeks, Pakistanis and Uyghurs linked with Al Qaeda allies, have been spotted in Taliban ranks during recent advances in Afghanistan. Afghanistan's Ambassador to the United Nations, Ghulam Isaczai, explained at a recent Friday briefing at the UN Security Council that 'the thousands of attacks by the Taliban since mid-April has the direct support of more than 10,000 foreign fighters representing 20 groups, including Al Qaeda, ETIM, TTP and IMU.'

Writing on the impact of thousands of foreign fighters being in Afghanistan and being drawn to the decades-old Salafi-jihadi sanctuary, the EU *Politico* magazine says

> A complex network of alliances, partnerships and competitors runs through the country, a network the Taliban can influence but cannot control. In the mix are transnational terror groups such as Al Qaeda and the Islamic State, but also the Pakistani Taliban and the Haqqani Network—a longtime Taliban and Al Qaeda bedfellow. Lesser-known groups include the Islamic Movement of Uzbekistan and the Turkistan Islamic Party. Each is capable of spawning radicalised recruits for terror attacks against the West, and none has pledged not to recruit and train in their Taliban-provided sanctuaries.

The presence of foreign fighters with their own ideological loyalties, particularly linked to Islamic movements in countries like China and Pakistan that the Taliban wants to maintain good relations with, will pose increasingly serious problems for the Afghan dispensation. With its difficult geography, Afghanistan is likely to become open for terror groups to have a field day and with Islamic terror landscape more populated with radical groups now than in the 1990s, more infighting among them within Afghanistan and outside from Afghanistan can be expected—even though they are linked by the same extremist ideology.

Afghanistan as Global Threat—Emerging as Safe Haven for Global Terror Groups

According to the Global Terror Index (GTI), over the last six years there has been a considerable drop in incidents of terror around the globe. and deaths from such attacks have fallen for the fifth consecutive year since peaking in 2014, by 59 per cent to 13,826 per cent in 2020. The geographic reach of terror has also been reducing and there is no new area currently involved in terror. Over 96 per cent of deaths in 2019 occurred in countries already in conflict. But the GTI notes that the Taliban remained the world's deadliest terrorist group in 2019 and Afghanistan and Nigeria are the two countries that have posted a tally of more than 1000 deaths from terror. The South Asian Terror Portal shows that even though extremists killed came down from 10,634 in 2019 to 5539 in 2020, and to 6307 in 2021 (till 31 August), civilian killings rose from 817 in 2019, 847 in 2020 to 844 in 2021 (till 31 August). The killing of security personnel rose from 728 in 2019 to 1217 in 2020, and reduced to 787 in 2021 (till 31 August).

This indicates that post-February 2020 US-Taliban peace deal, there has been fall only in extremists' death, not in the deaths of civilians or security personnel. The UN press release (6 August 2021) says that with the departure of foreign troops, the Taliban and their foreign associates are fighting to turn the country once again into a safe haven for transnational terrorism. It adds that the scale, scope, and timing of the Taliban's offensive is akin to an invasion unprecedented in the last 30 years and, since mid-April, different groups have launched more than 5500 attacks in thirty-one of thirty-four provinces. It concludes that twenty groups, including Al Qaeda and the ISIL, are fighting alongside the Taliban against the Afghan population and security forces.

The Taliban has been ominously silent about disengaging with Al Qaeda, while the Haqqani Network is represented in strength in the new government. It has made the Haqqani leader, who is a proclaimed global terrorist wanted by the US dead or alive, as interior minister. This is clearly the indication for the kind of support the new government will provide for terrorists operating from Afghanistan.

Taliban 2.0 as a Regional and Neighbourhood Threat

While Taliban 2.0 in Afghanistan will be a huge security risk for its neighbourhood and even beyond, it will not be a net and undiluted advantage for even its friends like Pakistan and China.

Apart from India, which is a special case given, besides ideological bias, Taliban's strategic relations with Pakistan.

Russia—Welcomes First, Ignores Later, Finally Falls in Line with India

Initially, Russia appeared to celebrate the defeat of the US-backed Afghan government and the departure of American troops from Afghan soil. A gleeful Taliban invited Russia to its inaugural ceremony, but with Taliban 2.0 coming out in its original colours, Moscow's stand shifted and it began seeing Afghan developments with serious concern. It began strategic discussions with India and refused the Taliban invite.

Before the shift in stance, despite Russia's official position that the Taliban was a terrorist outfit, Moscow's envoy to Kabul, Dmitry Zhirnov, had praised the Taliban's conduct and said the latter had made Kabul safer in the first twenty-four hours after the US exit. Russia's state media had portrayed the departure of US troops from Afghanistan as a significant coup.

But within days, Dmitry Peskov, President Putin's Spokesman, said: 'The situation is developing, time is running out, the situation remains extremely tense and we still follow it most closely and retain our concerns.'

The directive, which came on the orders of President Putin, marked an abrupt shift in the Kremlin's stance to the Taliban's takeover. Russia sent four military planes to evacuate 500 Russians and others.

Moscow is now keen to prevent the spillover of Afghan Islamist extremism into Tajikistan, Uzbekistan and Turkmenistan, with a potential risk for Russia itself. Russia is also worried about the flow of Afghan narcotics through Central Asia and on to markets in Russia. In the end, Russia has aligned itself with India on Afghan developments, which is a diplomatic success for New Delhi and a huge setback for Afghanistan and Pakistan.

Tajikistan wants the Collective Security Treaty Organisation (CSTO), the Russian-led military alliance which includes Central Asian nations other than Turkmenistan and Uzbekistan, but along with Armenia and Belarus, to come together and combat the security challenges, if any, arising from the situation in Afghanistan.

China's Danger—More Than 80 km Border with Taliban

China seems to be concealing and understating its risks of Taliban 2.0 threat to it by posturing and trying for strategic positioning with the new dispensation. Reports point out Beijing's unease with the potential fallout in Afghanistan was reflected in statements from its foreign ministry, which has repeatedly criticised the US for acting 'irresponsibly' in its 'hasty withdrawal'.

China's critical Xinjiang province, where it suppresses the Uyghur Muslims uprising, shares an 80-km-long border with Afghanistan ruled by the Taliban, which has in its ranks Uighur Muslim jihadists. Uyghur is China's homegrown terror. It has had no cross-border help like Kashmir terrorists in India had, and still have, from across the border. The presence of US forces in Afghanistan had ensured that China was safe from across the border. It is that security which has been shaken after 20 years by the sudden Taliban rule in Kabul. China's security risks are not limited to the terror in Xinjiang. The expanded geopolitical role of China under Xi Jinping in the South and Central Asia region—particularly the Belt and Road Initiative—has made China a sitting duck for terrorists to target Chinese interests in the region.

China's growing interests beyond its borders, which has changed the character of Beijing, makes her more vulnerable than even India to the explosion of terror that is likely to engulf the region after the Taliban establishes itself in Kabul. What risks the new Kabul regime and its cohorts pose to China in Xinjiang and elsewhere, needs to be examined.

International Centre for Counter-Terrorism says 'Uighur Foreign Fighters: An Under-examined Jihadist Challenge'

A November 2017 policy brief for the International Centre for Counter-Terrorism (ICCT) titled: 'Uighur Foreign Fighters: An Under-examined Jihadist Challenge' says: 'Uighurs, specifically individuals of Turkic descent from China's northwest province of Xinjiang, have become a noticeable part of the constellation of globally active jihadist terror groups. Uighur jihadists first came to the world's attention when the United States and its allies invaded Afghanistan in 2001. While continuing their cooperation with the Taliban under the banner of the East Turkestan Islamic Movement (ETIM), Uighur jihadists have now spread to Southeast Asia and the Middle East. ETIM members are part of the Turkestan Islamic Party fighting with the Al-Qaeda umbrella group in Syria, but other Uighurs have joined IS in Syria and Iraq, and some local terror groups in Indonesia. However, Uighurs are currently under-examined as active participants in jihadist organisations. Publications about Uighurs have been piecemeal focusing on their struggles against the Chinese government, or narrowly describing the specific groups in which Uighurs have been participants.'

China's Attempt to Underplay Uyghur Revolt

The ETIM seeks an independent Xinjiang. Perhaps therefore, for a long time, China was unwilling to admit the Uyghur terror which began in 1990 till 2002. Even in 2002, it was not willing to credit the terror attacks to the ETIM. A Brooking Institution research paper dated September 2020 said:

> A State Department official speaking on the background with one of the authors (Millward) in late 2002 confirmed that the ETIM was a small group based in Afghanistan, and was previously known as Xinjiang specialists. The PRC had included ETIM in a White Paper cataloguing a number of 'East Turkistan' terrorist forces' and alleging that these forces had committed 200 terrorist attacks, causing 162 deaths and 440 injuries, between 1990 and 2001, although the document actually described many fewer incidents and death and casualty tolls of events described did not add up to these totals. The White Paper associated a few acts with specific named groups and did not allege that the ETIM was responsible for any of the attacks. However, the US State Department statement designating the ETIM as a terror group attributed all 200 attacks and 162 deaths and 440 injuries to the ETIM, and thus, the idea of an organised international and deadly Uyghur terrorist organisation was born.

Uyghur Terror Has Intensified

Over time, Uyghur terror has only deepened and expanded and not reduced despite the rise of China. The November 2017 ICCT policy paper says: 'Indeed, over the past two decades, Uighurs (UYghurs) have launched several terror attacks in China in pursuit of this goal. Some recent attacks have included:

- October 2013: The ETIM attack at Tiananmen Square in Beijing kills five in February 2014.
- A knife attack at a train station in Kunming kills on 30 April 2014.
- A knife and bomb attack at the South Railway Station of Urumqi kills three and wounds seventy-nine in May 2014.
- Two cars crashed into a market and attackers lobbed explosives, killing thirty-one people in Urumqi in May 2014.
- Bomb blasts (including suicide bombers) and clashes left fifty people dead and fifty injured in September 2014.
- A knife attack at a coal mine kills fifty in October 2015.

The Strength and Spread of Uyghur Extremists

What is the strength of the ETIM? The ICCT policy paper says, 'On the sidelines of a May 2017 meeting between Syrian and Chinese businessmen in Beijing, Syria's Ambassador to China startled reporters with such surprising number—5000—which represented how many Uyghurs he claimed were fighting in Syria for various jihadi groups. The figure was several times higher than the Chinese government estimate of 300 Uyghurs for the Islamic State (IS) of Syria. The precise number of Uyghurs fighting in Syria is difficult to assess. The Syrian ambassador's high figure may have been an intentional over estimation in an attempt to further encourage Chinese support for the Assad regime. In turn, the Chinese government may have purposefully underestimated the number to lessen public anxieties among the ethnic Hans Chinese that Uyghur attacks have increased in recent years. Regardless of the exact numbers,

Uyghurs, specifically, predominantly Sunni Muslims of Turkic descent from China's northwest province of Xinjiang, have become a prominent cog in the constellation of globally active jihadist terror groups.'

The ICCT brief also says, 'According to Botobekov, an expert in Central Asian Jihadist groups, there are approximately 2000 members of the TIP (Turkestan Islami Party) in Syria largely grouped in Idlib province.' The ICCT brief also says, 'However, Uyghur terrorists have now spread to Middle East and South East Asia. ETIM's members are fighting along with Al Qaeda umbrella group Jabhat Fateh al Sham (JFS) in Syria. Other Uyghurs have joined IS in Syria and Iraq while still others have joined local terror groups in Indonesia.'

Is Autocratic China Transforming Low Level Conflict Separatism to a More Dangerous Islamisation and Bloody Insurgency?

The ICCT policy brief makes an interesting point that China's attempts to suppress the Uyghur separatism by suppressing Islam itself, is triggering Islamisation in Xinjiang. It says,

> China's repressive tactics in Xinjiang such as banning certain religious names for Uyghur babies, restrictions on the length of men's beards, limits on observing Ramadan and preferential treatment for Han Chinese in employment and education, have further hardened Uyghur identity and increased Islamic radicalisation. This oppression is also a factor in the increasing Islamisation of what was previously a separatist insurgency.

The ICCT paper indicates how that could prove more lethal. It says,

> One of China's primary reasons for consternation is the sense that Xinjiang's once separatist insurgency could soon be dominated by those advocating for jihad, which could transform the nature and severity of the low level conflict into bloody insurgency. The conflict in Chechnya followed a similar trajectory during the 1990s and into the early 2000s. If a more violent and lethal insurgency

> does indeed develop in Xinjiang, it could jeopardise China's prized 'Belt and Road Initiative', the centre piece of Xi Jinping's foreign and economic policy.

The ICCT paper concludes,

> The heavy-handed policies of the Chinese Communist Party have done the government a great disservice. Even a cursory glance at the history of insurgencies in the modern era, would reveal that what begins as rather banal grievances can manifest over time and develop into more deeply seated issues between the minority groups and the ruling party. Authorities maintain tight control over the restive Uyghur population in Xinjiang can continue through repressive measures, at least in the short term. However, if the conflict becomes global, as has occurred in places like Afghanistan, Chechnya, the Balkans and now Syria, Beijing could soon find itself in the crosshairs of a religiously motivated, battle-hardened crop of returning foreign terrorist fighters—an unenviable position for any nation to be in.
>
> Several experts on China's Uyghur minority, including George Washington University cultural anthropologist Sean R. Roberts, have called the situation in Xinjiang 'a self-fulfilling prophecy', as Beijing's exaggeration of the threat it faced from Uyghurs in the early 2000s resulted in increasingly repressive policies that have intensified the discontent in the region and helped to push more and more Uyghurs toward militancy.

In contrast to an autocratic China risking the transformation of separatism into terrorism, democratically-run India has ensured that the Kashmir separatist problem, promoted from across the border, which is the not the case in Xinjiang, did not graduate into a large scale terror because India did not in any way interfere with, or harm, the Islamic identity of Kashmiri Muslims. Kashmir separatism, and later, terrorism were promoted from across the border, while the Xinjiang separatism and terrorism is home grown without any external impetus.

Democratic India helped to isolate the terrorists and the mainstream Kashmiris. This shows how by allowing dissent to express itself, democracy moderates the discourse which autocracy is unable to do.

Xinjiang: China's Most Sensitive Issue

China's Uyghur problem is real. With the disengagement taking place between the West and China, the muted voice of the West about China's human rights abuses in Xinjiang has become very vocal. This has led to mutual sanctions between the US and the EU on the one hand, and, China on the other, and also has caused the collapse of the Comprehensive Agreement on Investment of January 2021 between China and the EU that was calculated to divide the Atlantic Alliance, which, Xi Jinping invested personal time and effort in to push. That Xi Jinping risked the collapse of his pet and strategic project to resist Xinjiang's Islamist separation becoming an issue, demonstrated how sensitive China is about it.

The leverage that China had over the US and the West, through its economic and political engagement had softened their voice on Xinjiang for over a decade, is virtually lost after April 2021 and has exposed China to intense scrutiny by the West and that will make China even more sensitive about Xinjiang. In 2002, the US joined China to request the UN to declare the ETIM—read Xinjiang separatists—as terrorists as, according to the Brookings Institution paper, the Bush administration felt that closer ties with China would help the US on Iraq. That kind of leverage is no more available to the Chinese.

'China more concerned about Afghanistan than ever' says the South China Morning Post

But China's issue is more than the securing of it. Chinese Foreign Minister Wang Yi boldly said after a meeting with Taliban leaders that the Taliban would 'play an important role in the process of peaceful reconciliation and reconstruction in Afghanistan'. But, for China, with its substantial investment in the region, the security challenges posed by Taliban 2.0 are far more pressing than its strategic interests. The *South China Morning Post* stated in a report titled: 'Two decades after 9/11,

China is more concerned than ever about Afghanistan", that 'the Taliban's victory could give rise to bolder attacks by other extremist groups, threatening China's economic interests; endanger counterterrorism efforts in Xinjiang by a resurgence in extremism; and embolden violent groups in South Asia'.

Situation More Uncertain for China Than Ever Before

'The victory of the Taliban is likely to boost the confidence of extremists,' said Professor Yan Wei of the Institute of Middle Eastern Studies at Northwest University in China. He added: 'The Taliban successfully coming to power more or less encourages extremist forces in South Asia and the Middle East, especially given the fact the Taliban survived and developed under pressure from the US and other Western nations, and eventually toppled the Afghan regime even before the US completed its withdrawal.'

The SCMP report has also said that academicians were also worried about the Taliban continuing their previous policy of sheltering extremist elements from neighbouring countries, especially dissidents from China's Xinjiang region—a reference to Xinjiang's Muslim Uyghur rebels.

'If the Taliban continues to shelter extremism, it will definitely stimulate the development of it. Other groups in the region may imitate the Taliban's way of development, which was to use religious beliefs to mobilise marginalised people in rural areas.'

Huang Minxing, a professor at China's Northwest University, said 'the current situation was more uncertain than before, when the US and its allies were cracking down on the Taliban and Al Qaeda.'

Li Wei, a counter-terrorism specialist with the China Institute of Contemporary International Relations in Beijing, agreed that the Taliban's victory was likely to stimulate extremist forces in the region. He was also alarmed over the fact that various extremist and terrorist outfits had congratulated the Taliban over their victory after they had seized power in Afghanistan.

China-Taliban Relations—More About Managing Theatre

Andrew Small, a Fellow at the German Marshall Fund in Washington, in an interview with the European Council on Foreign Relations, said: 'China does not tend to perceive Afghanistan through the prism of opportunities; it is almost entirely about managing threats.'

He said that though Beijing had long been wary of the American military presence in Afghanistan, in reality, China, which shares an 80-km border with Afghanistan, has also benefited from the relative stability brought by the US over the past two decades. China is particularly concerned that Afghanistan would become a base for terrorists and extremists fighting for the independence for the largely Muslim region of Xinjiang—a priority issue Wang raised with Taliban leaders during their meeting in Aug 2021. In response, the Taliban pledged that it would 'never allow any force to use the Afghan territory to engage in acts detrimental to China.'

But the security risks are not bound to China's borders. In recent years, China has invested heavily in Central Asia through its Belt and Road trade and infrastructure program. A spillover effect of the Taliban's rise to power on Islamist militants could potentially threaten Chinese economic and strategic interests in the wider region.

'Although Beijing is pragmatic about the power realities in Afghanistan, it has always been uncomfortable with the Taliban's ideological agenda,' Small said. 'The Chinese government fears the inspirational effect of their success in Afghanistan for militancy across the region, including the Pakistani Taliban.'

That security threat was underscored in August 2021 when nine Chinese workers were killed in a suicide bombing in Pakistan—one of the deadliest attacks on overseas Chinese nationals in recent years. Islamabad said the attack had been carried out by 'the Pakistani Taliban out of Afghanistan.' It is the Chinese assets, with several billions such as BRI, minefields, oilfields, universities, colleges, and so on, that are located in Pakistan and Central Asian countries that worries the Chinese. It is estimated that over 45,000 engineers and workers of China's XPCC (Xinjiang Production and Construction Corps) and other companies are operating from Pakistan. Any threat to them will lead to them moving back to China. XPCC, a quasi military organisation with fourteen divisions (sub-divided into 185 regiments) and lakhs of workers will become idle. This will have twin impacts, one on debt trap diplomacy and two, on unemployment. Chinese State Councillor and Foreign Minister Wang Yi's visit to Turkmenistan, Tajikistan and Uzbekistan, the three states that share borders with Afghanistan, and other diplomatic overtures, are related to the spillover of security threats coming from the worsening situation in Afghanistan.

Taliban at China's Mercy or China at Taliban's Mercy?

The Taliban needs dollars from China and so it is at the mercy of the Chinese. But the position of China, which has explicitly warmed up to the Taliban, seems no better. The very fact that China has started engaging with the Taliban and started extracting statements like the Taliban sees China as its 'friend' and is hoping to talk to Beijing about investing in reconstruction work 'as soon as possible', reflect the worries that China has. China will lose if the Taliban does not stand by its statements. If it does, even then China will lose as the Taliban will surely extract costs from China. Just as the Taliban is at China's mercy, China also seems to be at Taliban's mercy twice over.

But having come this far, China will never be in a position to abandon the Taliban which, having declared China as its friendliest country, will cling to it like The Old Man and the Sea, or Sinbad the Sailor.

China is trying to convert Badakhshan into a buffer zone and is seeking a military presence in Tajikistan. But all this reflects its own insecurity over Taliban rule in Afghanistan.

It needs to be seen whether China will be drawn into the Afghan conflict even though it may like to be cautious. It had supported the Taliban covertly in the 1990s. Now, its support is overt. But it may be treading into a quagmire. Only time will tell.

Pakistan Likely to Face Risk of High Terrorism

A Brookings Institution paper says that Pakistan may find its triumphalism over the Taliban's victory souring quickly. Now in power, the Taliban will be eager to loosen Pakistan's yoke from its neck and deepen the diversification of its external relations.

The Afghan Taliban's victory may give a boost to Pakistan's own Taliban militants (Tehreek-e-Taliban). The TTP, the tormentor of Pakistan, which has killed thousands of soldiers of Pakistan and maintains ties with the Afghan Taliban and Al Qaeda, is reportedly in comeback mode. According to a UN report (July 2020), there were 6,000 Pakistani fighters in Afghanistan, most affiliated with TTP. The Brookings paper also says that other countries will continue to seek to enlist Pakistan as a broker to moderate the Taliban's behaviour and be dissatisfied when Islamabad doesn't succeed.

France24, the French Government media, says that according to analysts, the Taliban in Afghanistan is what risks destabilising Pakistan—and that the exultation in Islamabad is myopic. The Taliban's win does pose a security risk for Pakistan, a member of the cabinet admitted to the *Financial Times* under condition of anonymity.

The Afghan militants' closeness to the TTP, or, simply the Pakistani Taliban, is a particular source of concern. The Taliban and the TTP are 'two faces of the same coin', Pakistani Army Chief General Qamar Javed Bajwa and ISI boss Lieutenant General Faiz Hameed acknowledged at an off-the-record briefing in July 2021. The Taliban reportedly freed a senior TTP commander earlier this month during their sweep through Afghanistan. 'Pakistan definitely worries about the galvanising effects the Taliban's victory will have on other Islamist militants, and especially the TTP, which was already resurging before the Taliban marched into Kabul,' Michael Kugelman, a South Asia expert at the Wilson Center in Washington, DC, told France 24, 'It's a fear across the establishment.'

An in-depth report in the *Financial Times* said that recently the Pakistan government had claimed that the TTP was behind a July blast at a hydroelectric plant that killed nine Chinese workers and four others, a claim the group denied. Moreover, the TTP chief, Mufti Noor Wali, has described the Afghan Taliban's victory as one shared by all Muslims. 'Taliban's recent advancements in Afghanistan, doubtlessly, have boosted the TTP's morale and increased the group's strength,' said Aftab Khan Sherpao, a former Pakistani interior minister, who has survived three TTP suicide attacks. 'It is the beginning,' he said. 'There will be a rise in terror attacks and it will be linked with Taliban advancement in Afghanistan.' But a collapse in Afghanistan would carry risks for Pakistan, too, including a possible wave of refugees, and a boost to jihadist movements.

'The Taliban's rise is not at all a simple outcome for Pakistan,' said Madiha Afzal, a Fellow at the Brookings Institution and author of a book about extremism in the country. 'Taliban rule in Afghanistan will probably have serious adverse security repercussions. Jihadi groups operating in and around Pakistan, most notably the Pakistani Taliban or TTP, 'consider the Taliban's takeover of Afghanistan as a larger ideological victory. That portends instability in the region in the longer run,' she added.

The TTP comeback may be linked with the Afghan peace process and Pakistan's fencing of the border with Afghanistan, both of which threaten the group's sanctuary in Afghanistan. Pakistan has already raised the issue of Afghanistan's sanctuary for the TTP. The Islamic State Khorasan (ISK) has been responsible for the recent attacks in Balochistan, including eleven Shia Hazara coal miners this January, complicating Pakistan's already violent sectarian landscape.

Pakistan's strategy toward militant groups has long been two-pronged, as it were: to take overt (and successful) action against groups targeting the Pakistani state and citizenry—the TTP—without taking action against the groups it has considered 'strategic assets', including the Afghan Taliban that have sought sanctuary on its soil, and anti-India militants that its intelligence agencies have covertly supported. Underlying this approach has been an effort to hedge bets.

Finally Pakistan, which has mounted the Taliban tiger, cannot get off without being devoured by it. That is why Pakistan is pleading with the international community to help the Taliban to avoid state failure and instability. TTP is reviving itself. Pakistan cannot avoid a huge revival of terror in its territories.

Iran Too in a Complex Situation

Iran which started off as a sympathiser and supporter of the Taliban rule in Kabul, turned against Pakistan's support for the Taliban thrust towards the Panjshir Valley. Iran has also declared that Kabul does not have an inclusive government. Iran's semi-U-turn is attributable to the emergent character of the new regime in Kabul and the role of Pakistan's army and ISI.

Iran will face two big issues because of the present character of Taliban rule in Kabul—one, a threat to the Shias in the region, and two, the extensive drug trade through its borders. Iran's engagement with the Taliban has been more as a counter to the US hostility to Iran. Iran is bound to fear that the Sunni extremist Taliban might support other like-minded terror outfits like the Haqqanis and TTP that could use Afghanistan as a base for terror attacks especially against the Shias.

The *New York Times* wrote 'Frequently attacking the Shia Hazara minority, the ISK has sought to instigate a Sunni–Shia war in Afghanistan. If the Taliban fails to control these attacks, its improved relations with Iran could deteriorate—something all the more likely if the attacks set off runaway sectarian fighting that sucks in Taliban factions.'

The Brookings Institution write up titled 'Pakistan's problematic victory in Afghanistan' says that the Afghan Talibans are virulently anti-Shiite.

Taliban 2.0 and India—Matter of Grave Concern, but with Upsides

Given the Taliban-Pakistan nexus, while it will have serious security implications for India, it need not be overly perturbed at Afghanistan falling to the Taliban, as it has many geopolitical upsides. These are:

- It will reduce Pakistan's leverage on the US with the latter's withdrawal from Afghanistan.
- It will fully expose the close Pakistan-Taliban nexus with the former having to carry the can for the latter's misdeeds, particularly in the realm of human rights and terrorism.
- A Taliban governed Afghanistan will be a political, military and economic resource drain on its primary supporters, such as Pakistan.
- It will expose Pakistan itself to serious risks of terror which has been subsiding.
- Any maniacal attack by the Taliban on any infrastructure so assiduously built by India will only result in discrediting the former in the eyes of the Afghan people.

India's Taliban 2.0 Afghan Policy—The Near Term

India's policy ever since the Taliban captured Afghanistan cannot be faulted and has, in fact, been adept. India has been wise in withdrawing all of its diplomats from harm's way in Afghanistan. While not criticising the Taliban directly, it has not recognised it. It has rightly and single mindedly focused on evacuating its people. India's near-term priorities in Afghanistan may be listed as:

- Ensure the safety of its nationals and all others of interest from Afghanistan.
- Ensure that Afghanistan does not export terrorism against us or allow itself to be used against us.

- Prevent the emergence of an unfriendly Afghanistan. Promote an inclusive and friendly Afghanistan which is not a puppet of Pakistan and acts independently.

Only after a Taliban government is established and is recognised by the international community, and when this exercise is completed, we should make more definitive moves.

Taliban-Pak Link up—Likely to Target Kashmir

There are reports that Kashmir is an urgent priority of the new Pakistan-Afghanistan link up. This is what they did after the 1989 defeat and withdrawal of the USSR. India must prepare for a fitting military response. The Quad will not directly help India but India needs the Quad partners, at least notionally, on its side. The US seems to be becoming aware of the risks germinating from Af-Pak Jihadis to India and also to the US and the Western world. The US declaration of review of its relations with Pakistan is a pointer in this direction.

While global relations will be of great strategic and political assistance to India, India will have to redouble its efforts to secure itself. This is the crux of the issue. India will face the blow back from Afghanistan. We must take an urgent review of our security arrangements. Diplomacy alone will not be sufficient. India needs to build up the army and the air force literally on a war footing. Reviving the full Rafale deal and ramping up our own Tejas production are two easy steps to getting started. More Sukhois-30s could also be an added option. Delaying the retirement of middle-level officers and men by at least three years will go a long way in addressing the shortage of human resources. Our defence budgets need to be raised in significant measures to three per cent of the GDP. At present, we are at levels last seen in pre-1962 and we know that did not turn out very well.

Our approach to Taliban 2.0 must, of course, be conditioned on the nature of the Taliban government as well as indicators about its policies towards India and the extent to which these are influenced by Pakistan. Some indication will no doubt be derived by our interactions with its leaders. Recognition should only be accorded if we are convinced that the Taliban government will not act against Indian interests.

Mere verbal assertions of the sort that we have received from Pakistan in the past should not and cannot be relied upon. We should look for cast iron guarantees. In case these are not forthcoming, recognition should not be accorded. The Taliban regime cannot change its character. Not only should India withhold recognition, it must also persuade others to also do so. Last time around, India did not recognise the Taliban regime at all. India should be in no hurry in the matter. A patient waiting game will benefit us as a Taliban-dominated set up in Afghanistan will be plagued with difficulties which can be used opportunistically by us. As long as we are undecided on whether or not to recognise the Taliban, we should do what we have been doing, i.e., eschewing an open and direct criticism of it while voicing concerns about the human rights situation in Afghanistan, as well as apprehensions of it becoming a hot bed of terrorism which poses a threat the world over.

India's Taliban policy is gradually becoming clearer and less ambiguous. It is now using UNSC Resolution 2593 formulations in policy statements. The Indian Prime Minister took a straight-forward position at the Shanghai Cooperation Organisation meet and also in his address at the United Nations General Assembly. The Quad and Indo-US bilateral statement also has specific references to Afghanistan. However, our media, NGOs should be encouraged to openly and vigorously raise these issues and to directly criticise the Taliban.

Our position in the UN sanction committee should be based on merits of the case even if it means riling the Taliban. As to the resistance movement, we should have no hesitation in supporting it clandestinely with plausible deniability. Economic assistance to Afghanistan should only be accorded if we recognise the Taliban and if we reopen our mission. In the absence of this, meaningful assistance would serve no purpose.

In the unlikely event that we are convinced that the Taliban will play ball with India, we can consider making it known that should it do so, we will be open to its interpretation of the Durand Line rather than that of Pakistan and much of the international community.

India's Response to the Rise of Taliban in Kabul

India's position that Taliban 2.0 is not inclusive is in line with the broad global position, including that of Russia and China. The Taliban 1.0 regime was recognised by three countries, namely UAE, Saudi Arabia and Pakistan, and it later became untouchable for all nations. Today, no one wants to be the first nation to recognise the Taliban government. Even Pakistan, the very mastermind of the Haqqani-powered government, is unable to summon the guts to recognise the Taliban government.

With Russia turning back to take India's position, India too has had a high NSA-level meeting with Russia. Russia seems to be on the same page as India on the Afghan issue. Russia, which started off as a friend of the Taliban, refused the invite for the inauguration of the Taliban government, and now has U turned and taken the same position as India, namely that the Afghan government is not inclusive and that the risks and the interests of the two countries are identical.

The Russian President's recent statement about engaging the Taliban is also qualified by the same position that the government is not inclusive. The developments in Afghanistan have pushed India closer to the US as both face the same degree of risk from Islamist terror, which is likely to get accentuated because of the Taliban-Haqqani rule, which will give a fillip to other terror outfits, including the ISI. India has had NSA-level talks with the US. The Indian Prime Minister's visit to the US and his speeches at various fora there, all bear a distinct and clear focus on Taliban rule and the emerging common position that the US and India share on Afghanistan, the exception being that on Pakistan, unlike India, the US may still be ambivalent because it may still have ambitions left to use Pakistan to deal with the Taliban and Haqqanis and also to keep Pakistan as far as possible away from China.

India has taken special efforts to interface with Kazakhstan and Tajikistan, both of which have taken the same position as India to oppose the Taliban rule unless an inclusive and representative government is formed. Uzbekistan, Turkmenistan and Kyrgyzstan have shown some willingness to engage with the Taliban, but the whole Central Asian region is wary of the situation in Afghanistan.

Taliban 2.0, Long Term Implications for India

The long-term security implications for India in the event Taliban 2.0 proves to be a continuation of Taliban 1.0 are serious, but not insurmountable. These would take the form of Pakistan's enhanced efforts at terrorism in Kashmir and also in other parts of India. These would be executed under ISI guidance and with its support. One may also expect an increase in the quantum of narcotics traffic in India, both for local use and for export. Perhaps more serious than all this is the extent that the Taliban take over in Afghanistan emboldens local fundamentalist elements to take to terrorism against India. In these circumstances, we need to urgently strengthen our anti-terrorism grid with greater use of the latest technologies. While fortress India is no doubt strong, we must never forget that we have been taken by surprise repeatedly over the decades. Thus, constant improvement in our systems and constant vigilance is the need of the hour.

4

India and the Changing World Order: An Assessment

In Random Thoughts-2020, we had tried to think aloud about how the world might move on different issues. It is appropriate to assess subsequent developments in the background of what it had said, to judge how far our assessment has matched with how the world has actually moved on. This exercise is necessary to know where we have been right and where we have not been. Here is a brief summary of a few areas in which our understanding of the world appears to have matched with global developments that have later unfolded.

On the Possible Death of the US-China Engagement—US Announces Its Demise

We have earlier assessed that though the unprecedented rise of China had set alarm bells ringing in the US since 2008, it needed the rise of Trumpism in the US to raise questions on the impact of the US-China engagement and argue how China got one-sided and unfair advantage from it. We had said that when the US mainstreamed an isolated and ideological China under the Kissinger Formula during the Cold War period and in its aftermath, that it became a positive engagement which led to China's rise, and also that it was at great risk of deterioration, if not termination. We had also pointed out the systemic mismatch and conundrum between Marxist ideological China and the ideology-free market model of the West. It is against this background that we had apprehended that the death of US-China engagement would have far reaching consequences not only to these two nations, but also for the whole world of trade, business, finance, and politics. Many had thought that if, in the fiercely fought US Presidential election—almost as if it were an ideological battle between America First and Globalism—Joe Biden and globalism would win, the anti-China heat would moderate and the China-US engagement might survive. But we thought otherwise and argued that Trumpism in the US was sure to last beyond Trump as it had transcended bipartisan divisions.

As we had thought, the change from Trump did not arrest or reverse the deterioration of the US-China engagement and it is now officially pronounced to have come to an end. The Foundation for Defense of Democracies (FDD), in its 'Biden Administration Foreign Policy Tracker' (Late May-3 June 2021), has brought out from official statements, the death of the engagement between the US and China. The FDD Tracker said:

> The contours of the Biden administration's China policy are coming into clearer focus. In a series of blunt remarks, the White House's Indo-Pacific coordinator, Kurt Campbell, stated that 'the period that was broadly described as engagement has come to an end.' Campbell further remarked that the 'dominant paradigm' between China and the United States would now be one of competition, not collaboration. Campbell blamed Chinese policies under President Xi Jinping as the catalyst for the administration's policy shift, citing the threat posed by military clashes on China's border with India, Beijing's "economic campaign" against Australia, and the rise of China's "wolf warrior" diplomacy. This unexpectedly assertive approach closely mirrors that of the previous administration. It also occurs after President Biden ordered the US intelligence community to redouble its efforts to ascertain COVID-19's origins, in part because of China's refusal to participate further in the World Health Organization's pandemic investigation. Still unclear is whether the Biden administration will proceed with a Trump-era plan to ban American investors from trading securities in subsidiaries of blacklisted Chinese companies. Such a decision, which could come in the next few weeks, carries major economic implications for the world's two largest economies. There are already indications that major Chinese companies such as Huawei are shifting their business operations to counter U.S. sanctions.

With the US virtually ending the policy of engagement of China in May 2021, the early June G-7, NATO and EU Summits fell in line and reinforced the trend toward the end of the engagement of the G-7 with China. The Trumpist policy on China is now not only the policy of the US, but also, the broad policy of the entire West, including the G-7 and EU-27.

On the Final Victory of the West over the Rest—NATO Admits It is the Opposite

Had the West stopped at seeing this as only the defeat of the Socialist bloc, that would have been practical and probably correct? But that is where it got excited by theories like the end of all conflicts and the final victory of Western values over that of the Rest. In the euphoria of the collapse of socialist economics, the West embarked on the over ambitious project of globalization, while the WTO rested on the assumption and conviction of the superiority of the West over the Rest, and this was where it erred. Western market economics certainly won against socialist economics, but it was not the victory of the West over the Rest, because the world was not, and will never be, completed only by and between the two materialist ideologies of Marx and Market.

'Thirty years ago advanced democracies were told that they'd reached the 'end of history,' and that the continued advance of freedom was inevitable,' wrote Anders Fogh Rasmussen, former NATO secretary general, in a Wall Street Journal op-ed in which he urged greater cooperation among democracies. 'The opposite has been the case: Freedom has retreated as America retreated from its place as the global leader. We may not see a better opportunity again to recover from the West's crippling disease of democratic self-doubt.'

On the Danger of the Marx-Market Conundrum—Admission and Proof

We had pointed to the irreconcilable contradiction between the established deep Marxist state and the pretended Market Economics in China and how that has helped China to vault over disciplines of the transparent market with non-transparent state. We had said that if there was any convergence between free market economist Milton Friedman in his Capitalism and Freedom (1962) and Left economist Amartya Sen in his Development as Freedom (1999), which won for him the Nobel Prize, it was on the relation between democracy and the market economy, and how one was a necessary condition for the other. The US flouted this basic rule of market economics in two stages. First, to break the Communist bloc and to gain the balance of power it was losing to the USSR-led socialist alliance, and second, by coalescing China and giving annual extensions of Normal Trade Relations since the early 1970's and Most Favoured Nation treatment to it from 2001 once it joined the WTO, thus partially recognising the Marx-Market mix; and thereafter, in its post-Cold War euphoria of the final victory of the West over the Rest, the US facilitated the integration of China into the WTO. The induction of China into the WTO eminently suited the geopolitical and strategic interests of the US/West.

The world was, and is even now, far too diverse to be packed within the campus of two materialist ideologies, one of which had succeeded against the other, and the other which had failed against the first. But on the self-generated belief that there was no competition for it from anywhere, the West went ahead to include Marxian polity in market-centric globalisation and the WTO structure. In its excitement, the West was oblivious to the fundamental fact that while both market and democracy individually and together complement, are transparent and verifiable, Marx is not, and a market aligned with Marx too is not, and cannot be.

Joseph Nye 2021: 'With China today, we have half a trillion dollars in trade and millions of social interchanges. Moreover, with its 'market-Leninist; system, China has learned to harness the creativity of markets to authoritarian Communist party control. It announced its intent to use this system to dominate ten key technologies by 2025. We and our allies are not threatened by the export of communism—few people are taking to the streets in favor of Xi Jinping thought—but by a hybrid system of interdependence.'

On WTO Becoming Even Irrelevant—Movement Away from Multilateralism to Bilateral and Regional Trade Pacts

Long before Covid-19 struck the world, the US Trade Representative stated in his 2017 report to the Congress, 'The US erred in supporting China's entry into the WTO...on terms that have proven to be ineffective in securing China's embrace of an open, market-oriented trade system. It is now clear that the WTO rules are not sufficient to constrain China's market distorting behavior.'

The EU Trade Commissioner observed, 'There needs to be a thorough and quite radical reform...if nothing happens in the coming years (the WTO) will be more and more weakened and it will become irrelevant.'

This demonstrated the underlying tensions between nations which are transparent and a non-transparent China, particularly when it rises and tends to acquire power that challenges the former. That the US, which promoted the WTO, has fatigued even before the Covid-19 onset, is evident from its refusal to participate in the appointment of judges for the Dispute Settlement Mechanism (DSM) of the WTO. The DSM, which is celebrated as the crown jewel and heart of the WTO, has been rendered dysfunctional, as it now has only one judge instead of three. That the US had also threatened to block the approval of the budget of the WTO also showed its exasperation about the multilateral organisation.

The US/EU complaint that China has not embraced an open market oriented system and its behaviour is market distorting, only stops short of pointing to the underlying, but the unstated fact is that China, with its Marxian polity, cannot operate in an open market economic system within, nor can it participate in a global market system honestly.

The implicit decision by China to bury its market status case in the WTO, which had held that China is a Non-Market Economy, will probably break the WTO as anti-dumping actions against China will multiply. It is highly unlikely that the WTO can be reinvented to become an effective mechanism for multilateralism, particularly with the participation of non-transparent single party dictatorships in it. Multilateral treaties like the WTO are likely to weaken through unilateral actions and even disappear into oblivion, though how soon, will depend how fast alternatives are put in place.

With globalisation weakening and the epitaph of WTO likely to be written over a period, multilateralism may yield space to plurilateral and bilateral trade, and economic relations. But dismantling integrated financial architectures and supply chains will be a painful and highly disruptive process unless calibrated properly.

On the China Challenge Reinforcing and Reviving the Transatlantic Alliance—That is Precisely What is Happening

The leadership of the US, with the support of the G-7 and NATO, which was the fulcrum of post-Cold War world order, had got psychologically and geopolitically undermined under the Trump regime and forced Europe to have questions about American leadership. Trump's universalism forced French President Emmanuel Macron to talk of a Euro alliance with a defence budget matching its responsibilities and strength. Our previous assessment had noted that 'the China challenge is likely to revive and restore the Transatlantic Alliance' and 'the election of the US President in 2020 will have a far reaching impact on the Alliance'.

The three summits which took place in June 2021, namely G-7 meet at Cornwall UK on 11–13 June, to which India along with South Africa and Australia were invited; the NATO meet at Brussels on14 June and the US-EU summit on 15 June, have shaped the strong response of the Transatlantic Alliance to an autocratic China. The geo-political ecosystem at the start of 2021 to the TransAtlantic was less than encouraging with the

EU virtually seeking a third way between US and China, which had greatly undermined the TransAtlantic as the efforts to revive it began with a change of regime in the US.

The background to TransAtlantic efforts in June needs to be recalled to understand how it appears to have been restored from the Third Way syndrome neutral to the US and China into what is clearly a US-EU alliance statedly to engage and also, unstatedly, to contain China. But here are some important developments that may explain how the TransAtlantic divide of the last four years was dissolved in an unprecedented show of rapport seen in the June summits.

Over-Confident China Misjudging Its Strength and Transatlantic Alliance's Weakness, 'Shoots Itself in Foot'

Everything changed dramatically in March 2021, when the US, EU, UK and Canada sanctioned several Chinese officials for human rights abuses against the Muslim Uyghur minority in China's Xinjiang province. China reacted promptly, even violently. Denouncing the sanctions 'as based on nothing but lies and disinformation', China announced its sanctions against 10 European individuals, including five members of the EU Parliament and four institutions, saying they had 'maliciously spread lies and disinformation'.

This single issue brought together all 27 European nations, besides Britain, Canada, New Zealand and Australia, to firmly stand with the US. This virtually meant the death of the CAI. Theresa Fallon, the founder and director of the Centre for Russia Europe Asia Studies (CREAS) in Brussels, and concurrently, a member of the Council for Security Cooperation in the Asia-Pacific and a Nonresident Senior Fellow of the Chicago Council on Global Affairs, wrote in an article titled: 'China shoots itself in the foot on EU-US relations' 'After March 22, Beijing did everything it could against Europeans, as official Chinese statements and state media angrily branded the Germans Nazis and Namibian genocidaires, then accused all of Europe of being racist. Years of caution have been replaced by a level of Beijing's wickedness that Europeans had not noticed before'.

While the US and EU sanctions were against the Chinese officials involved in human rights violations in Xinjiang, China's angry and disproportionate counter sanctions penalized a long list of politicians, researchers and institutions, including a key member of Germany's Green Party. German Chancellor Angela Merkel was the principal driving force behind CAI. The likely new government in Berlin, following the recent elections, will take a more China-sceptic view.

A commentary on Voice of America (VOA), prior to the elections, said 'China may have sabotaged its own prospects for securing a sought-after investment agreement with the European Union where support from Germany is seen as crucial to its approval'.

The CAI needs final ratification by the European Parliament. And that is precisely where China went ridiculously wrong. Green Party lawmaker Reinhard Buetikofer, who heads the European Parliament's Delegation for Relations with China, was put at the top of a list of EU individuals and institutions targeted for Beijing's sanctions last month.

According to Reinhard Buetikofer, that could leave the CAI deal 'as dead as a doornail'.

Subsequently on 20 May 2021, the EU Parliament voted overwhelmingly, by 599 votes for, 30 against, with 58 abstentions, to 'freeze' the massive CAI deal with China following the recent tit-for-tat sanctions over Beijing's treatment of its Uyghur population in Xinjiang province. According to the resolution, the parliament, which must ratify the deal, 'demands that China lift the sanctions before parliament can deal with the CAI'. Some EU Parliament members warned that the lifting of the sanctions would not in itself ensure the deal's ratification.

France and Italy Stun G-7 and NATO and Stump Germany

The speech which raised eyebrows from those listening in, including the assembled press, was Emmanuel Macron's. They knew that Macron had told an earlier summit in Brussels that he didn't think China was NATO's business. That same summit turned around to declare for the first time that China poses 'systemic challenges' to the international order.

But a transcript of what Macron actually said at NATO is telling. Of China, he said: 'It is much larger than just the military issue. It is economic. It is strategic. It is about values. It is technological.'

Italy stunned fellow G7 members when it signed up to Beijing's controversial Belt and Road Initiative in 2019, but its newly installed Prime Minister Draghi seemed to have caused a policy shift. He has been cool on the partnership for several weeks now, but emerged from the G7 session so alarmed that he pledged to review Italy's deal. 'It's an autocracy that does not adhere to multilateral rules and does not share the same vision of the world that the democracies have,' he said.

Dramatic Transformation from Signing CAI to Revival of Transatlantic Alliance

It is clear that the Transatlantic Alliance is getting revived, driven by developments starting with the inauguration of the Biden regime in the US. Two further and almost simultaneous developments, one explicit and the other implicit, appear to have made the turnaround from CAI to TransAtlantic—the explicit one being the sanctions and counter sanctions by EU/US and China, and the implicit one being the emerging view that the lab leak theory of the Coronavirus at Wuhan was no conspiracy after all and that it needed to be probed after the WHO commission refused to categorically endorse around the same time, in March, that the virus was natural evolution.

Again, it is implicitly clear that behind the scene developments must have worked to ensure that the US and EU acted together against China on the Xinjiang human rights issue, knowing fully well that it is a red rag to the bull for China, which was bound to react the way it did with disproportionate counter sanctions and in violent language. Even the further developments appear to have been well rehearsed. After the mutual sanctions of March 2021 played out in April, and after the EU Parliament froze the CAI deal on 20 May European External Action Service Secretary General, Stefano Sannino, and US Deputy Secretary of State, Wendy Sherman, met on May 26 in Brussels to reaffirm the strength of the EU-US partnership on key foreign policy and security issues.

Welcoming the upcoming EU-US summit on 15 June, as 'an important step in the revitalised transatlantic partnership', the 'two sides underscored the shared EU-US interest in strengthening the rules-based international order and pledged further close cooperation in support of democratic values, global and regional stability, and universal human rights'. Saying that both sides held the first high-level meeting of the EU-US dialogue on China, they reiterated that the EU and the United States' relations with China are multifaceted and comprise elements of cooperation, competition, and systemic rivalry. They highlighted issues of shared concern, including ongoing human rights violations in Xinjiang and Tibet, the erosion of autonomy and democratic processes in Hong Kong, economic coercion, disinformation campaigns, and regional security issues, in particular the situation in the South China Sea. They discussed the importance of Taiwan's meaningful participation in the work of international organisations, including the World Health Organization forums and the World Health Assembly.

Though the press release mentions three elements, cooperation, competition, and systemic rivalry, significantly most of the issues mentioned in the press release other than 'climate change and non-proliferation, and on certain regional issues', relate to only competition and systemic rivalry. It is again significant and a matter of concern for India that the India-China border issue figures not specifically but impliedly in regional security issues.'

G-7 Summit 2021 Ends with a Resurgent Transatlantic That Explicitly Takes on China—Trump's China Policies Virtually Adopted by Biden's US, G-7 and EU

The G7 and the Transatlantic Alliance very clearly indicated that they had shed their reservations and are willing to take on a belligerent China. Reuters reported that the re-emergence of China as a leading global power, considered to be one of the most significant geopolitical events of recent times, alongside the 1991 fall of the Soviet Union that ended the Cold War, has also unnerved the United States.

On the issue of a probe into the origin of the virus, Joe Biden said: 'We haven't had access to the laboratories', and added that it was not yet certain whether or not 'a bat interfacing with animals and the environment... caused this COVID-19, or whether it was an experiment gone awry in a laboratory'. 'We remain seriously concerned about the situation in the East and South China Seas and strongly oppose any unilateral attempts to change the status quo and increase tensions,' he said.

Biden said democracies were in a global contest with 'autocratic governments', and that the G7 had to deliver viable alternatives. 'We're in a contest, not with China per se, ... with autocrats, autocratic governments around the world, as to whether or not democracies can compete with them in a rapidly changing 21st century,' Biden told reporters. President Joe Biden casts China as the main strategic competitor and has vowed to confront the latter's 'economic abuses' and to push back against human rights violations.

After discussing how to come up with a unified position on China, the final communique issued by G7 leaders was highly critical of China and delved into, what is for China, some of the most sensitive issues, including Taiwan. The communique, a most significant development in contextual geopolitics, clearly targets China on issues it is highly sensitive about.

- It declared China as a security and systemic threat to the world—a massive U-turn from engaging China that began decades back.

- It declared 'We will promote our values, including by calling on China to respect human rights and fundamental freedoms, especially in relation to Xinjiang and those rights, freedoms and high degree of autonomy for Hong Kong enshrined in the Sino-British Joint Declaration.'
- It insisted on 'a transparent, expert-led Phase 2 Covid-19 Origins study, including in China, to be convened by the World Health Organisation (WHO)'.
- It underscored 'the importance of peace and stability across the Taiwan Strait and encouraged the peaceful resolution of cross-Strait issues'.
- It expressed concern about forced labour in global supply chains, including in the agricultural, solar and garment sectors.

The Center for Strategic and International Studies (8 June 2021) said that it was not until April 2019 that China appeared on NATO's agenda, mostly in response to increasing pressure from the Trump administration. At a foreign ministers meeting in Washington, then US Secretary of State Mike Pompeo notably urged NATO allies to adapt to 'Chinese strategic competition,' in particular, in the field of 'technology and 5G.'

The China Challenge and the Need for a New Technology Paradigm—West and Rest Efforts to Counter China's Tech Challenge

Alluding to China's notorious agenda of dominating the Internet and technology, and collecting and misusing consumer data for surveillance, it was noted that in the post-Covid-19 world order, democracies of the world need to create a new, transparent and accountable paradigm of oversight and control of future technology and the internet', and added, that 'New cooperative models for democracies to work on research and development and development standards and technologies is required'. In its majority report, the United States Senate Committee on Foreign Relations dated November 2020 titled: 'United States and Europe—A Concrete Agenda for TransAtlantic Cooperation on China' says under the head Technology:

> China's massive market, as well as the political focus and economic resources directed towards the development, manufacturing and regulation of emergent technologies, means that the United States and Europe are at the risk of being subjected to PRC technological infrastructure and the intrusive way the CCP uses such technologies. This threat is particularly acute in areas such as research and development, data and digitisation, and standards setting. Losing their technological advantage would present severe challenges to US and European economies, militaries, and shared values such as individual freedom and privacy. The United States and Europe should thus:
>
> - Prioritise areas where there are little to no regulatory obstacles for increased transatlantic cooperation and technology development Create a technology coalition of advanced democracies
> - Seek to harmonise regulatory practice in key areas and
> - Take other steps to regain a competitive stance in the global technology race.

The *Foreign Affairs* magazine (3 August 2020) said even more explicitly that 'The D10 (democratic 10 nations, including India proposed by Boris Johnson), should take on a narrowly defined yet highly significant endeavour: jointly developing 5G networks that don't rely on Chinese technology. This project would benefit all D10 countries, but none could accomplish it alone. It requires extensive inter-governmental cooperation, financial investment, and policy ingenuity. If the ten countries can execute this project successfully together, the institution through which they have done so could easily evolve to address a broader and more ambitious agenda.'

It further said, 'In the security realm, the D10 could coordinate the enforcement of norms, such as freedom of navigation, sovereignty and territorial integrity. It could establish collective defense frameworks against cyber attacks and other non-military threats—for instance, members could agree on joint economic and political consequences that they would impose on any country that interferes in one of their democratic elections. The D10 would also be a natural forum for coordinating multilateral sanctions and setting and policing behavioral standards in cyberspace.' This is precisely what we had in mind and stated it in RT-20.

On Possible Alliance of Democracies as Future World Order—G7 Move, and the Convergence of Views in the West

We had perceived earlier that a global alliance of democracies as the fulcrum of the future world order might emerge. The majority report, the United States Senate Committee on Foreign Relations (November 2020) quotes the High Representative of the European Union for Foreign Affairs and Security Policy as saying,

> Given everything that is happening in the world and the rise in authoritarian powers, it is important to have cooperation with like-minded democracies. The EU-US should be at the heart of this effort, but we should be working closely with Japan, India, South Korea, Australia, New Zealand, Canada and others.

In the Introduction to the report, even earlier opinion has been building up in the West about the need for a broad coalition of democracies.

The *Foreign Affairs* magazine (3 August 2020) in an article titled, 'A Council of Democracies Can Save Multilateralism', Boris Johnson's 'D-10 Is the Club the World Desperately Needs', said that as the world's economic center of gravity has shifted toward the Indo-Pacific, it has become impossible for institutions with global ambitions to credibly claim to lead without meaningful representation from that region.

It said that with the G20 being too disparate in political outlook and capability to solve international problems, and the UN Security Council being hobbled by the resurgence of aggressive authoritarianism in China and Russia, the world desperately needs a new institution that is both global in reach and unified in vision. It commended that Johnson's D10 is just the type of body the world needs, a group of capable, committed and cohesive democracies that could muster the political will and real resources. It expands G7 by bringing in the most internationally minded major democracies, South Korea, Australia, and India in Asia, saying that India is Asia's other emerging giant, and after its recent clash with China high in the Himalayas, it may elect to pursue closer ties with the United States.

As the world's largest democracy, the *Foreign Affairs* magazine sees India as a vital partner and a potentially pivotal player in counterbalancing against China in the Indo-Pacific region. It also cautions that while the United States and its democratic allies should not pressure states to make a binary choice between the United States and China, or Russia, they should incentivize nations to work closely with leading democracies.

The *Foreign Affairs* magazine also said: 'The D10 could chart a path out of this abyss by helping to address wealth and income disparities within countries while also making supply chains more resilient. Many domestic economic problems that democratic societies face actually stem from features of the global economy: D10 members could help rectify them by working together to crack down on tax havens, illicit finance, and other kleptocratic practices that fuel inequality. They could also design alternative supply chains for critical products—such as pharmaceuticals, medical equipment, computer chips, and aircraft parts—that can come online rapidly in times of crisis.'

An article titled, 'An emerging new alliance of democracies' in the Washington Post, which never considered India as worthy of mention as a democracy, mentioned Anders Fogh Rasmussen, former NATO secretary general, as approving Boris Johnson's idea of the G7 nations plus his three guests forming a new bloc of 10 major democracies.

'The idea of a 'D10' grouping ideologically committed to combating the march of authoritarian states chimes with

Joe Biden's plan to hold a summit of democracies,' wrote the Guardian's Patrick Wintour.

In a paper titled, 'Retooling America's Alliances to Manage the China Challenge', the Brookings Institution said: 'Given the allied divergences laid out above, as well as the varied nature of the challenge China presents, no single forum will bring all of the right players to the table. Although practical coordination on issues like trade and technology are more likely to emerge through smaller coalitions, Washington would be well served by bringing European and Asian allies together in a broader strategic-political forum. The D-10, for example, is likely best suited to serve as a high-level political coordination mechanism, creating closer alignment between allies in international institutions or ensuring they can respond with a unified voice to crises such as the crackdown in Hong Kong.'

5

The Indian Picture: Economic, Internal Security, Border Issues with China and the China-Pakistan Axis

Commencing from the first quarter of 2020, India has been facing multifarious and intense challenges—External Security, Internal Security, Economic Issues, Geopolitical Shifts and a Covid-19-hit Health Sector—all at the same time.

Never in its history post-independence, has India faced such comprehensive challenges simultaneously. Some of them have far reaching transnational and geopolitical ramifications. It is necessary for us to understand the depth and the impact of these challenges to evolve appropriate strategies for handling them. Any inappropriate way of handling would be a repeat of historic blunders like the idealistic, unrealistic, impractical and un-strategic handling of neighbourhood relations, external security, and internal economic challenges particularly, by the fledgling free India's government of the 1950s and 1960s—the effect and impact of which the country is enduring even now.

Here is an overview of the challenges and the probable responses, given the ecosystem in which the country is positioned. While in recent decades both India and China had comparable demographic strength, with China's lead getting narrower in recent times, the West preferred autocratic China over a democratic India purely for growth and profit. While both India and China had demographic advantages, India's democracy was considered as burdensome and difficult to handle, while China's autocracy was considered to be stable and easy to handle—after the reforms initiated by Deng Xiaoping in the late 1970's and following the death of Mao Zedong. While demography was in favour of both, the West had an undisclosed view that democracy was against India. But with the West having burnt their fingers with autocratic China, it is now turning to a democratic India.

China vs India: Why India Only Grew, When China Flew

For those who debate 'why China and why not India', here is an insight. An article in *Forbes* magazine (2019) titled: 'Politics, Productivity & Population: Why the Chinese Economy Flew and India's Just Grew', summed up how China surpassed India by a wide margin. It said:

> The GDP per capita for China and India in 1985 was approximately \$293 per person. According to 2017 data from the World Bank, China's GDP per capita has ballooned to \$8,827 and India's has climbed to \$1,942. Both countries have made tremendous progress, but the growth in China has been miraculous. Why such a significant difference? How did China outpace India? The answer lies in the differences between politics, productivity and population trends.

Saying how political factors favoured China over India, the article compared the two, and said about China, 'The Chinese Communist Party (CCP) governs the country with few barriers. When the government decides on a course of action, few obstacles stand in its way. For example, China spent more than a decade building the Three Gorges Dam, the world's largest hydropower project. The massive undertaking displaced more than 1.2 million people and flooded 13 cities, 140 towns and 1,350 villages. The dam, despite its enormous social and environmental cost, provides China with a source of clean energy and brought thousands of jobs to the Chinese interior. When it comes to rapid development on such a scale, an authoritarian political system is a definite advantage.'

On India, it said: 'India is a democracy. It has regional parliaments and a federal parliament with many assemblies. This system is all-inclusive, but a nightmare for development. It can take decades to make a decision. For example, it took

16 years for the Indian parliament to pass a tax reform bill (2016). A project like damming the Yangtze River could not happen in India. Plagued by corruption at all levels, the divided political landscape would kill the project before it began. Politics prevent spending on infrastructure.'

In comparison to the Yangtze project in China, look at the Narmada Dam chronology:

- 1961: Jawaharlal Nehru laid the foundation.
- 1979: World Bank agreed to fund it.
- 1987: Construction began.
- 1989: Narmada Bachao agitation started.
- 1995: Supreme Court (SC) stayed it.
- 1999: SC allowed construction up to a height of 88 metres.
- 2000: It allowed 90 metres.
- In 2002: It allowed 95 metres.
- In 2004: It allowed 110 metres.
- In 2006: It allowed 122 metres.
- Finally in 2019, the full height of 139 metres—after 48 years!
- The Yangtze project displaced 1.2 million, while the Narmada project displaced between 60,000 to 150,000. China completed it in a decade, but India took five decades.

This explains not only why China flew and India only grew, but also why the West preferred to ally with a China that could fly and not with an India which only could grow.

Pretending to Bet on China Becoming a Democracy in the Future, the West Preferred China over India, Always a Democracy

The reason for China's flying rise was that the West, particularly the US, found its autocratic order more suitable for the rapid growth of the market and demand which the West and, it thought, the world needed. The West found autocratic China more comfortable and welcomed it with both hands into the WTO, made huge investments in it and even glorified China as almost an equal power. The intent of the West was more profit-oriented than founded on any principle, including democracy and human rights, which China couldn't care less about. So long as the going with China was good, the West would target India on human rights and completely overlook China on Xinjiang and other human rights violations. The West found India's democracy cumbersome and preferred China in the long term, economically. Even though the West pretends now, that it gambled on the premise that autocratic Communist China would head towards democracy and market, but that failed to materialise and, (*The Economist* magazine 3 March 2018), the West had no answer as to why it preferred an autocratic China, trusting it to become a democracy, over India.

Today the West and Its Allies are Reworking Their Maths to Decouple from China

Today, the rise of an autocratic China is a nightmare for the West. The West is realising that discounting India's democracy politically and economically, and preferring China's autocracy, both ways was wrong.

Having declared China as a systemic adversary, the West and its allies are furiously reworking the math and cost-benefit to decouple themselves from the complex multilateral trade, commercial, financial and technical architecture they have built with China during the decades of bonhomie with it. The decoupling will mean an ever-increasing supply chain shift from China in the coming decade and more, as coupling has taken at least a decade, if not more, to cement.

The shift will not be limited to trade and commerce, as the collapse of mutual trust between China and the West and its allies will need comprehensive decoupling, touching all aspects of geopolitics. And that perhaps, is bound to lead to a change in the world order that is being talked about, unless China retracts from its aggressive look outside and regressive face within—which is more unlikely than likely.

The limited medium-term beneficiary of this shift will be India, which being the only comparable replacement for China, could also be a huge long-term beneficiary. But this cannot be without equally high short and medium-terms risks for both the West and India, and it will also involve bureaucratic and policy changes as well.

The West and the World Need India's Democratic Polity and Demographic Strength for Growth, Stability and World Order

The post-World War II order led by the West was founded on the Cold War between socialist and free market nations, which was not exactly the dividing line between democracies and autocracies, as many socialist nations like non-aligned India were democracies, while some Middle Eastern and Latin American nations that are aligned with the West were autocracies. In the Cold War order, the West never regarded India as part of its democratic circle, treating it more as a socialist adversary than as a democracy. In the post-Cold War order, which was regarded as the success of the free market and liberal democracy over socialism, the West virtually ceased to have any ideological position other than leading the world without opposition. It was not averse to having, and could rationalise having, autocratic China as a strategic partner in trade, economics, and geopolitics. This was because of China's huge demography and regressive autocracy, which the West felt was the right combination for faster growth, and not that of India, which though having a comparably huge demography, also had a slow democratic polity. Indian demography was branded an elephant, both for its big size and slow pace.

The West and the world needed, and will continue to need, a huge demography to drive its and the world's growth on which its stock market value rests. In the perception of the West, demography was the strength of both India and China, but it saw autocracy as China's strength and India's democracy as a sign of its weakness.

Now, however, it perceives things the other way round. It sees autocratic China as a danger and democratic India as an ally. With the world polity delicately balanced, almost

50:50 between democratic nations of all hues and autocratic countries of all kinds, the huge demographic strength of India and its vibrant democracy are being perceived by the West as necessary for growth, stability and the world order, particularly when it is decoupling from China.

The West and the world would not have cared for either China or India had their population been just a tenth of theirs. Indian democracy and demography, in the emerging perception of the West, are the right replacement for the Chinese demography and autocracy for future world order. Several reports and studies that appeared between March and May 2021, which included the UBS Evidence Lab CFO Study, the Bloomberg report, the Information Technology and Innovation Fund research and the Qina Report, all of which uniformly pointed to the US and the West, shifting from China to India, as will be explained in detail later on.

In these studies, the report of the Information Technology and Innovation Fund (ITIF) makes extremely significant geopolitical analyses of global shifts and the likely scenarios that may emerge. Describing the worst- and best-case scenarios, the IITF report says that in the former, tensions between India and China are reduced and the many business synergies between these two neighbouring nations come to the fore, in which case, the heart of the global economy would shift to the East, and there would be little the United States could do about it. In the second scenario, the interests of India and the United States become increasingly aligned, as the economic, military and international relations challenges from China grow, in which case, democratic norms could prevail across most of the developed world, as developing nations start looking to the 'Delhi model' instead of the 'Beijing model'.

It concluded that in any event, America's tech dependence on India was bound to rise, as economic and geopolitical stakes could not be higher. This leads us to the next issue, how should India handle the shifts?

India should obviously opt for the best-case scenario mentioned in the IITF report unless it is forced into a worst-case scenario by China taking aggressive military measures against it as the IITF report mentions.

India Needs to Balance between the West and China

Even as the demographically strong India is bound to be courted by the West, and India should not be averse to working with them, here is a caveat. India needs to avoid risking beyond limits in being part of such an effort. While the West would endeavour for an alliance of democracies and market economies for building the future world order, half the world will continue to be under autocracies. Market economics may overlap between democracies and autocracies. Also, the West continues to regard itself as a Class A liberal democracy and regards other democracies particularly Indian democracy as illiberal and a Class B democracy.

The West would regard India only for statistical purposes to claim as the G-7 nations meeting in June 2021 did, that 2.3 billion people are under democracy. If India is excluded, the balance of the West approved democracy is just a billion. Unless there is greater alignment between India and the West beyond accepting India for statistical purposes as a democracy, and on quality and equality, and unless the West drops its double standards of judging democracies, democracy cannot be the bond between the West and India.

This will call for change in Western perception of ultra individualism as the supreme test of the foundation of liberal democracy, because such perception excludes cultural and civilisational diversities that distinguish different nations and their democracies from the Western. Therefore, merely because the West welcomes India into the statistical club of democracies, if it agrees to join, and gets perceived as anti-China, India would be risking a great deal that would not be in its interest.

While India will be the beneficiary of the global supply chain shift because of the decoupling taking place between the

West and China, India needs to maintain a balance between both by forming strategic relations rather than joining alliances.

Alliances are remnants of the Cold War and no one wants the return of the Cold War. It will not be in India's interest to be part of an explicitly anti-China order, or to have a sworn enemy of China's size and power along its 4000-km-long treacherous and mountainous border. India would need strategic trade, economic and political relations with individual nations which would aspire to work with such a huge demographic economics and avoid any treaty with them that would make China their avowed enemy, while being prepared militarily to face any threat from Beijing.

India's delicate balancing act is particularly needed because of Pakistan's visceral hatred of it and its willingness to be China's 'Shikhandi'. India on its own, by design or omission, should not invite open enmity with China. The first principle of managing adversarial relations is 'don't declare anyone as enemy' and the next is 'never allow anyone to declare you as an enemy'. The first one is in one's hands, though the other is not. GeoPolitics opens up medium to long-term opportunities for India—to gain on India's demography and democracy.

Western nations, for their own strategic reasons, were forced to open up medium to long-term opportunities for India like they did for China decades back. India, therefore, needs to take full advantage of these favourable tail winds that will make her move forward fast. She must realise that the reason for change is that the West needs India more than the latter would need the former for balancing the world order in favour of democracies which are facing effective competition for power for the first time from autocracies.

Autocracies never had legitimacy in post-war global affairs, but thanks to the rise of China, autocracy is gaining recognition. The legitimacy that China provides for autocracy is the real geopolitical issue for the West. Minus India, democratic geography and demography will be in danger of being marginalised. This is an advantage for India. India's policy making must be fully conscious of the fact that in the fields of trade, finance, economics and technology, the West would need India's youthful demography and transparent market economy for not only its own growth, but also of the world. India needs to strongly assert, artfully and gainfully negotiate on the basis of these two civilisational assets of high value and not to fritter away the high energy flowing from them.

Concrete and core national interests must predominate Indian policies and strategies, and not abstract global interest predominating over national. India must carefully draw up a balance sheet of its strengths and weaknesses and choose its strategic partners to add to its strength and reduce its weakness.

While India's culture and tradition would not allow it to play the cloak and dagger strategic politics of China, it needs to follow 'Chanakya Neeti' in which national interest predominates. India must also align national discourse and debate in accord with its global strategies and not allow domestic political divisions to distort them. This practical and strategic approach is necessary till India can gain enough from global changes before it enables itself to give back to the world.

Economic Issues: India's Medium- and Long-Term Prospects

India's current economic issues are indeed compounded by the marginal performance of its economy, even before the Covid-19 pandemic, with the unforeseen huge socio, political and economic toll that the pandemic imposed, adding further pain. Undoubtedly, India will have extensive short-term economic issues complicated by Covid-19 induced health issues. But in the medium-term, India will gain the advantages which it lacked and which China had over it for the last two decades. In the long run, India is likely to gain advantages which China may lack. The medium and long-term advantage which India will gain has much to do with how the world, particularly the West, looks at China in comparison to India. This is the medium and long-term advantage which India has been awaiting for two decades.

Indian Economy: Short-term Issues

India's GDP growth before the pandemic had hit a low of 4.5 per cent and during the pandemic year 2020–21, it turned hugely negative to 7.3 per cent. When the economy began rising, a Tsunami-like second wave hit and damaged India several times worse than the first. That virtually wiped out the recovery India had begun making from the third quarter of 2020 and threw it back. But with the second wave abating, the GDP for the first quarter of fiscal 2021–22 was estimated by the Reserve Bank of India (RBI) to grow at 22 per cent, but that is on a low base of the pandemic hit quarter of 2020–21.

With the GDP growing at 8.7 per cent, it was estimated that India would be back to where it was at the end of 2019–20, which meant that Covid-19 made us add not a rupee to our GDP. The burden of loss of growth which hit small businesses and the poor, had to be substantially borne by the government by way of relief measures, which damaged India's fiscal position and increased the government debt from 51.6 per cent to an expected 61.7 per cent by the end of fiscal 2021–22.

Success of Indradhanush Covid-19 Vaccine Mission

If there was any hope today of overcoming the pandemic and achieving faster economic recovery, it was the extraordinary success of the Indradhanush Mission of the government to indigenously produce the anti-Covid vaccine. Anti-Covid vaccine producing nations and pharma giants are few, but almost seven-plus billion people the world over, of which one-sixth is in India, needed the vaccines. For India to get vaccines from outside in the past, it has taken not years, but decades after the pandemics broke out. Given the past experience of depending on the world to supply vaccines against pandemics, it would not have been possible for India to get anti-Covid vaccines from outside for 100 per cent of its population for decades. Our experience has been that it has taken 40 years to vaccinate 100 per cent of India with imported vaccines and we could not start vaccinating our people even after others had completed vaccinating theirs.

India daring to take on the challenge, and its success in developing the vaccine, has put her in a different club in the pharma world and in geopolitics. It also became a real and declared global test for the very idea of AtmaNirbhar Bharat, which was declared by the government when the pandemic hit the world. The government had actually taken a huge risk in saying it would produce indigenous vaccines, as had it not achieved it, within and outside India, it would have become a laughing stock. Now with the development of at least five indigenous vaccines, the world looks at India with awe, as long back she had been written off in the branded drug market after China began to dominate it, thanks again to the West.

Against this background, when the Indian government conceptualised and drove the idea of indigenous vaccine, no one within India or outside, believed India could do it.

India has now vaccinated over a billion people in the aggregate. This huge leap, which is amongst the best in the world in terms of vaccinated population, would not have been possible but for indigenous vaccine development.

Before the onset of the second wave, India had exported 66 million vaccine doses, which it had to stop due to the harsh second wave. *Nature* magazine says that the world needs around 11 billion doses to fully vaccinate 70 per cent of the world's population against Covid-19. But more than 80 per cent of the doses had gone to high-income and upper-middle-income countries, and only one per cent of people in low-income countries have been given at least one dose.

Given these hard facts about vaccine availability, distribution, and administration, had India not developed its own vaccines, the question that surfaces is what would have been India's vaccination programme on which its economic recovery depended?

The Covid-19 infection rate can be seen inversely proportional to the vaccination rates. Unless the vaccination rate was expedited, there was no way the infection could be contained and, unless the infection was contained, the economy could not recover. It means economic recovery is directly proportional to the vaccination rate. In short, had India not produced the vaccines and ramped up the rate of vaccination, there could have been no hope for short or medium-term recovery.

Two-Three-Year Medium Term Outlook

The medium-term outlook for India's economy seems strong for various reasons, domestic and global. The medium-term growth prospects are led by exports, pent up demand of the pandemic period manifesting in the current year, rise in Startups, IPOs and FDI, huge global shift, and other favourable factors.

The Indian economy has undergone several major reforms in six years, some of which certainly were shocks that affected growth in the short run—demonetisation, GST, digitisation, Jan Dhan Yojana (JDY) and Direct Benefit Transfer (DBT), and Mudra credit, to name a few.

Demonetisation, JDY and DBT were major reforms which made GST possible. But all this meant closing wrong ways for doing business and governance. That also affected growth as, informal funds generated by wrong activities were funding MSMEs which got starved of funds on the one side and on the other, the GST too suddenly attempted to formalise informal businesses and formal funding for that sector, which did not match their needs.

This certainly affected growth, but that was the cost to pay for the extensive formalisation of the huge informal economy. But, before the economy could fully benefit from the transition from informal to a formal mode of business, the pandemic struck which added to the pain of deep reforms and also threw out of gear the entire range of economic activities. There are clear and positive indications that the Indian economy is gaining momentum. Some pointers are:

- Exports Rise: The rising exports, in which the impact of the global shifts is also seen, tend to indicate its emerging role in the short to medium-term growth prospects of India. The exports in the first quarter of 2021–22 is $95 billion, and in July it was $35 billion, August $33.23 billion and September $33.44 billion. Exports for the first half of 2021–22 was $197 billion, which is 57 per cent over the first half of 2020–21 and 50 per cent over pre-pandemic levels. Overall, India's exports surpassed the target of $400 billion in 2021. The rolling average for the last ten months to July has risen by $12 billion and the year-on-year rise is $66 billion.

- Rise in GST Collections: GST collections, another important indicator, is picking up in fiscal 2021–22, with an average of Rs 1.10 lakh crore in the first quarter and Rs 1.17 lakh crore in the second quarter, which is five per cent more than in the first quarter.
- Huge Rise in Household Financial Savings: During fiscal 2020–21, bank deposits rose by Rs 20 lakh crore against the previous year's rise by Rs 14.5 lakh crore. Even the Jan Dhan bank accounts belonging to the marginalised sections showed a rise of Rs 24,000 crore, from Rs 1.2 lakh crore to Rs 1.44 lakh crore, which showed that even low-income group people could save money, which indicated that there is particularly rural or low income distress in the country as portrayed by some studies. Data shows a huge rise in household financial savings in 2020–21 as compared to the previous year.
- Pent up Past Demand: The high level of savings in 2020–21—unspent money—with the people indicates two things, namely, one, there is pent up demand because of consumer restraint during the pandemic, and two, as the people have enough to spend, the aggregate demand is likely to go up substantially as the pent up demand of the previous year will also materialise this year. This is already becoming manifest in housing as the demand for houses has risen, which has pushed up stocks of housing companies by 19 per cent to 80 per cent in the first six months of 2021. Housing data shows that as compared to the first five months of 2020–21, sales,

new launches, have all risen, while unsold stocks have come down. Even unsold stock of houses of pre-pandemic levels of 1067 million square feet has come down to 905 million square feet. This also indicates that the pent up demand is manifesting.

- Jump in Equity-Linked Investment: A huge jump of Rs 22,880 crore (by 277 per cent) in the equity-linked mutual fund investment in July 2021 indicates that the rise in stock index, which was largely credited to the flow of hot money into the Indian stock market, is substantially driven by domestic savings now.
- Manifold Rise in IPOs: Total Initial Public Offerings (IPOs) in the stock market in the first four months of fiscal 2021–22 is over Rs 27,000 crore and a further Rs 70,000 crore is stated to be in the pipeline, which would take the aggregate close to Rs 1,00,000 crore for the current year against Rs 31,000 crore for the whole of 2020–21. The three time rise in savings in equity-linked mutual funds shows there is a huge jump in domestic investment in IPOs.
- Rise in Foreign Investment: Foreign investment into India during fiscal 2020–21 was $82 billion, a rise of over $7.2 billion over the previous year. Foreign Direct Investment in the first quarter of 2021–22 is $11.36 billion as against (-) 528 million in the 1st quarter of 2020–21, when the pandemic hit the world and India. In contrast, the foreign portfolio investment (FII) into India turned negative (of $1.00 billion) in the first quarter of 2021–22. Yet, the Sensex rose by over 2000 points. This is significant as there was always a direct relation between FII and the stock market—if the former fell, the latter would too. But the first quarter Sensex rise proves otherwise. It means domestic savings is moving into the secondary stock market.
- Sensex Doubles in Two Years: An intriguing feature of the Indian economy during the pandemic year has been the relentless rise in the stock index—the Sensex—from 27k in April 2020 to 57k in August 2021. This is partly because of

the huge liquidity and partly because of the global shift from China to India.

- 18.6 Million New Employment in July 2021: A total of 18.6 million jobs have been created in the month of July 2021, mostly in small trade and construction businesses.

Rise in Rural Jobs and its Implications: A significant change that is taking place in the structure of the employment market is the rise in rural jobs. This seems to be a trend and unrelated to the pandemic. There has been a sustained rise in rural jobs from 35.3 per cent in 2017–18, 36.1 per cent in 2018–19, to 38 per cent in 2019–20, even before the pandemic. This is a new factor to be studied deeply and not tested by any pre-existing assumptions. While the traditional explanation would be that because the high wage urban jobs are reducing, there is movement back to villages for low wage rural jobs. It is not correct to compare the better urban wages and lower rural wages and conclude that people who have lost urban jobs are moving to rural areas, because the cost of living in urban areas is more than in rural areas. The normal assumption is that a rise in rural employment means the slowing of development because people opt for low rural wages. This is how most commentators dismiss the rise in rural jobs. The theory is self defeating. When urban jobs rise, they say it is because of rural distress. When rural jobs rise, they say there is urban distress and that is a reversal of development. It is on this basis that the theory that urbanisation means development is founded. This theory needs a review for three reasons – (1) Electronic highways have connected rural areas more efficiently than highway roads, (2) Agricultural reforms have promoted agri-related jobs in rural areas, and (3) The growth of agri-related company formation in fiscal 2020–21 was upwards of 20 per cent, which implies a rise in rural activity. Given the rise in the formation of agri-related companies, the rise in rural jobs does not seem to be out of urban distress, but more likely due to the growth in the agri-sector. Also, the agri share of GDP has gone up to 20 per cent in 2020–21. The rise in rural jobs, therefore, cannot be dismissed as being due to the impact of the pandemic on the urban economy, because the rise is anterior to the pandemic. That the rise in company formation relates to a later part of 2020–21 also does not contradict the fact that agri-growth was anterior, but actually supports it. This is because in most businesses, companies are not formed first, but formed after individuals, firms and families have done their business for a few years. They then opt to turn it into companies which are a larger form of organised business. Therefore, there are a number of dots to be connected to understand the rise in rural jobs.

- Number of Active Companies Rise: The Ministry of Corporate Affairs data shows that the number of active companies grew 12.1 per cent during 2020–21 over the previous to 1.34 million, the fastest in a decade. Registration of new companies grew 11.6 per cent, of which, agriculture and social service companies grew 20 per cent plus, which is significant for the rural economy.
- India No. 2 in the World in Start-ups: In terms of numbers, India stands next only to the US, with over 11,000 start-ups. The UK, Canada, Germany, Australia and others fall way behind. This is yet another indicator of the rise in economic activity.

Geopolitical and Global Supply Chain Shift

The geopolitical and supply chain shifts are likely to hugely favour India in the medium-term. Here is a brief account of how geopolitical changes are shifting supply chains.

Geopolitically, autocratic China was seen as stable and safe supply chain for 28 years (1993–2021), and democratic India was seen as unsafe and unstable (1989–2014) because of rickety coalitions.

But geopolitical changes since the advent of Covid-19 and more particularly, since the second quarter of 2021, have made China appear unsafe now and India safe. In fact, there appears to be a scramble for shift from cheap sources to safe sources.

In September 2020, the FICCI and Dhruv Advising Study showed that India would benefit to the extent of 70 per cent due to businesses shifting from China.

In January 2021, a UBS Evidence Lab CFO study reported that 70 per cent of China-based CFOs and 86 per cent of US-based CFOs said that they would be shifting part of their business from China. The study further revealed that from almost zero, India should reach 20–30 per cent of the global supply chain in two to three years, which matches with our medium-term outlook.

In March 2021, Bloomberg said that with US President Biden calling for a China-free supply chain and a Quad membership, India would be well positioned to absorb the supply chain shifts taking place due to Washington's strategic decoupling from China. It mentioned that while Amazon, Samsung and Apple are already in India, everybody spoken to seems to be keen to move out of China.

In April 2021 (13/4), the Supply Chain Management Review said that as the US seeks to counter a rising China, no nation is more important than India, with its vast size, abundance of highly skilled technical professionals and strong political and cultural ties with the United States.

But America's increasing reliance on India for information technology (IT) services is very similar to its dependency on China for manufacturing, according to a new report released recently by the Information Technology and Innovation Fund (ITIF), the leading think tank for science and technology policy.

In April 2021 (29/4), *Supply Chain Dive* magazine reported that according to a recent Q2 Barometer report by Qima, a provider of supply chain compliance solutions, the US and global buyers view Vietnam and India as alternative sourcing locations to China, Respondents listed both countries among their top three 'buying geographies'.

Roughly a third of global buyers and 38 per cent of US buyers named Vietnam as a place they intend to increase sourcing from this year. And 'an influx of US-based buyers' increased inspection and audit demand in India 72 per cent YoY, indicative of the uptick in buying interest, according to the report.

In May 2021 (19/5), the *Global Trade Review* reported that India, Japan and Australia trade ministers met digitally and formed the Supply Chain Resilience Initiative to squeeze China out of the critical technology supply chains like semi-conductors, batteries, and rare earths.

In August 2021 (10/8), the Tata Group announced that it had 'already set up a business to seize and promote hi-tech manufacturing of electronic precision manufacturing and assembly testing of semiconductors' which included manufacture of 5-G network in the medium term. This showed the action on the ground on the shift that is taking place and its likely outcome for India in the medium-term.

Driven by the explosion of domestic drives pent up during the pandemic and by geopolitical and economic shifts, (2–3 year) medium-term prospects of the Indian economy seem bright.

Long Term Outlook—the Core vs the Additive

While it is extremely hazardous to judge the long-term outlook, it can be said with reasonable confidence that the Indian economy is poised for long-term growth. India is most likely to be the first choice of the West and the world because of its civilisational assets in the shape of a vibrant democracy and a youthful demography, which will enable it to grow in a global ecosystem which is for the first time turning her favour.

India, with one-sixth of humanity inhabiting it, cannot be dependent on the world, nor can it remain isolated from the world. China's over dependence on global demand and exports, unsupported by adequate domestic private consumption and demand for driving its economy, has been its weakness.

China is trying to overcome that by focusing on domestic demand. As late as 2020, China's domestic private consumption is 39 per cent of its GDP. In contrast, India's domestic private consumption has been averaging 60 per cent of its GDP. This constitutes the inherent strength of the Indian economy. For India, the country is the core and the global is the additive, while for China, global is the core and country is the additive. The idea of Atma Nirbhar is based on only the nature of the Indian economy which has India as the core. What India needs is substantial external additives to support and supplement its core. The geopolitical changes, including the supply chain shifts which are in the offing, are bound to strengthen the external additive which India has been lacking for reasons of the geopolitical climate favouring autocratic China in the last three decades and the neglect of democratic India by a democratic West. With the geopolitical shift, the long-term outlook for India is extremely bright.

India: Internal Security Issues

In statistical terms of the number of attacks and casualties, India's internal security has improved in the last six to seven years. The incidents have come down from 523 in 2014 to 299 in 2020, to 206 in 2021 so far. The fatalities have halved from 1012 in 2014, to 591 in 2020, to 375 in 2021 so far. Civilian casualty has come down by three fourths, from 400 in 2014 to 106 in 2020, to 70 in 2021 so far. Casualty of security forces has come down from 167 in 2014 to 106 in 2020, to 75 in 2021 so far. The number of insurgents killed has also come down marginally from 441 in 2014 to 385 in 2020, to 230 in 2021 so far. Suicide attacks have become rare.

External challenge-I: Motives of China's Moves at the Border and Outside—to Make India a Political Risk and Undermine its Value as a Safe Alternative to China

Talks between India and China to unlock the Ladakh border stand-off following the unprovoked violent clashes initiated by China in June 2020. Efforts by Chinese and

Indian Army officials, aided by diplomatic initiatives, to ease border tensions, have been a painfully slow process. But despite distrust and apprehensions on the Indian side about China's intentions of engaging in the adventure, some de-escalation seems to be taking place. According to the latest reports, India and China had completed withdrawal of forces from the Gogra region of eastern Ladakh after a year-long 'sensitive' standoff. The disengagement, which included both sides removing all temporary structures and other associated infrastructure, and returning the landform to its pre-standoff state, is reported to have taken place in August 2021. With the Gogra agreement, India and China have now concluded agreements in four of the six flashpoints—Galwan, the North and South Banks of the Pangong Lake, and Gogra. Depsang and Hot Springs are still locked in a stalemate and are the most sensitive areas in Sub-Sector North from the point of view of India's security.

While China strategically keeps the talks going, its intentions seem to be deeper and complicated. The idea seems to be not to ease the tension but to keep it on, if not intensify it. China's motives at the border are not so much to assert its border rights as to keep the mind, the time, and efforts of India occupied and kept away from a full thrust on critical issues, including internal security and economic development.

The highly split Indian politics is also encouraging and helping the Chinese in their efforts, assisted by an army of wolf warriors engaged by China, in and outside India, to distort the Indian discourse on both China and on the border. To understand why China is causing tension on Indian borders, it is necessary to know what China's global game is and how a rising India is connected to that game.

China's game is global. It has issues with different nations, not just with India. Its competition is with the West, particularly the US. China feels India is a regional challenge to its supremacy and indeed it is. A rising India is more an impediment to China because of its legitimacy, which China lacks. India, democratic and non-aggressive, is in the eyes of most nations, more legitimate than China, which they see as autocratic and aggressive.

Xi Jinping's China has been trying to play a positive global role, showcasing the BRI project and offering and making investments in other countries, to overshadow and overcome the disadvantages of its autocratic and aggressive image, which Western powers were doing during the Cold War period. This has been paying off for China in the last few years, with many countries, even Italy, joining the BRI project to the chagrin of the West. China has certainly gained a lead over not only India, but also divided the West. And, taking advantage of the stress of the Western nations since the 2008 crisis, a presumptuous China has begun perceiving its own single party autocracy and the oxymoronic Marx and Market cocktail as a global alternative to the Western concoction of liberal democracy and market society, which it regards as failing and not a successful model for the world.

This is a serious and dangerous game from which China does not seem to have a retreat option. In the kind of risk China has taken to position and push itself ahead of even the West, India is not presently a challenge to China militarily or economically.

Why then is the Chinese Army at India's borders? It is certainly not to reinforce its border claims by forcibly redefining it. The border dispute, which has been hanging for decades since before the 1962 war, needs no urgent army action. The reason why China is at India's doorstep is because of the change in Western perceptions about China that it is no more safe with it and is looking at India as a safer alternative, as also a change in China's worldview that the time has come for it to shed its reservations of becoming a global power for which India may be an impediment, if not a competitor.

China does not see India as a military threat in the short or the long run, but given the changes in the West qua China, it certainly would see India as a medium to long-term economic competitor. Therefore, it has to undermine India as a safe and peaceful destination for those seeking alternatives to China. China might not mind other nations growing but not India, as given the latter's demographic size and quality, its rise might well prove prejudicial to China's interests.

Therefore, with Pakistan at its beck and call to work with it, China's moves at the border seem to be calculated to create the threat of a possible two-front war against India that will increase political risks in the minds of countries and investors seeking out India as alternative to China. In short, China would not want India to be a safe alternative to it in the calculations of other countries, particularly the West.

But China's efforts to disturb India, on the border and otherwise, may also prove to be its undoing. In its own interest, China should work for the best-case scenario described in the ITIF report cited earlier, namely that if there is reduction in the tensions between the two, 'the many business synergies between these two neighbouring nations come to the fore—in which case, the heart of the global economy would shift to the East, and there would be little the United States could do about it.'

That will be the rise of the East and the decline of the West which Xi Jinping has talked about. In case of tension between the two, the IITF said, the interests of India and the United States will become increasingly aligned as the economic, military and international relations challenges from China grow. In which case, democratic norms could prevail across most of the developed world, as developing nations start looking to the 'Delhi model' instead of the 'Beijing model'.

It may not be in its own interest for China to have tense relations with India. President Xi seems to realise this, for he advised the PLA senior echelons along similar lines after his first visit to India in 2014, during which the PLA had intruded into Chumar.

On the other hand, India has to give deep consideration to its China policy which is no more, in substance, a bilateral one. Even though India has overcome its psychological disadvantage of the 1962 war setback, China's vast military and economic growth and the emotional loyalty of Pakistan to China makes India's position unenviable in external, even internal, security in Kashmir, and elsewhere through Islamic identity.

The strategy of China seems to be simply to keep the Damocles' sword of war at, or even beyond the border—and the possibility of the two-front war—hanging over India so as to keep India's mind occupied with the threat, and thereby, bargain with India not to move too close to the West.

In the past decade and more, India has always bilaterally managed its issues with China, but of late, it has been increasingly drawn into the complicated China vs the West issues.

While China has a Pakistan to use as Shikhandi—the famous proxy warrior of Mahabharata, who sidetracked the mighty Bhishma while Arjuna targeted him as his main adversary, as a proxy warrior against India, India has no such proxy warrior to sidetrack China.

Therefore, while entering strategic relations with the West, which has declared China as a systemic competitor, India needs to be careful in not risking open enmity with China by its own commission or omissions. If China openly chooses to declare India an enemy, that is a different matter, but India should not implicitly or expressly do so. India should consciously be a part of Asia in culture and geopolitics and not a part of the West. India should be more in tune with China's neighbouring Asian nations, which face an adversarial China, and not adopt the stances and policies of nations geographically distanced, which have declared China a systemic adversary. In his famous treatise Sukraniti, Shukracharya says: 'One should not declare anybody to be one's enemy nor oneself to be anyone's enemy.'

How the two giant neighbours handle their relations in the medium-term will decide the geopolitical ecosystem of the world, and also the future of the rule-based geopolitical and economic order which has sustained the world after the Cold War.

External Challenge-II: China-Pakistan Axis—Pakistan as China's Shikhandi

On 4 July 1999, Pakistan agreed to stop the Kargil War under pressure from then US President Bill Clinton. Clinton was triggered into action when he, as claimed by the US, received intelligence that Pakistan was preparing to nuke India and yet refused to be blackmailed by Islamabad to get into mediating on Kashmir. Pakistan's then Prime Minister, Nawaz Sharif, buckled before Clinton.

But today, Pakistan no longer shares the same relationship with the US. At that time, China was no competitor to the US for a space in Pakistan's mind. Now, if it were to choose between the US and China, what Pakistan would do is a question mark. This is being widely debated in the US as to where Pakistan would stand in case of a US vs China stand-off.

Pakistan Prime Minister Imran Khan himself said a couple of months back that Pakistan is under pressure from the US and Western powers about its over-close ties with Beijing, and added that Pakistan's relation with China is time tested and nothing can change it. Therefore, Pakistan's preferences are clear. Further, the sudden development of Taliban rule in July/August in Afghanistan has put Pakistan in an advantageous position and changed its equation with the West. The West would need greater cooperation from Pakistan to handle the likely re-emergence of global terror. Pakistan's relations with China are entirely founded on China's enmity to India and the age-old principle of an enemy's enemy is my friend doctrine, which is entirely at play in the Pakistan-India-China triangle.

But Pakistan's love for China is totally conditional on continued enmity between India and China. If, theoretically, China and India settle their border disputes and enter into a no war pact, Pakistan would stand so weakened that it will cease to be a threat for India.

6

India's Strategic Engagements: Select Important Strategic Partnerships with Israel, Russia, France and Japan

Post-Cold War Geopolitics: Strategic Partnerships as Substitute for Alliances—India as a Late Entrant

India, with its semi-idealistic non-alignment which torments the Indian psyche even today, has missed the select strategic engagement and partnership bus which evolved during the Cold War era as a flexible alternative to the firm alliances of the Cold War days. A business idea borrowed into geopolitics, strategic partnerships became fashionable and practical during the post-Cold War days. Strategic partnership is an idea that emanates from players seeking power geopolitics. Power matters in global relations and it comes at a cost. Till the Pokhran atomic test, India, which had neither economic nor nuclear power, unlike China of the 1960s, was not even seen by the world as a strategic nation. With its status as a de facto nuclear power, India became an inevitable seeker, in a sense, even a sought after strategic partner. Strategic relations entered the dictionary of Indian diplomacy rather late. India entered major strategic partnerships only in the 21st century, starting with the partnership with Russia in the year 2000, which explicitly used the term strategic, entered after the Pokhran blast. A study says that China, which started its first strategic partnership with Brazil in 1993, has achieved close to seventy strategic partnerships by 2014, while during that same period, India has secured only some twenty such strategic relations.

Over the last couple of decades, India has entered valuable and reliable strategic partnerships with different nations, important among them being with Israel, France and Russia, Japan and the USA. These relations, individually and cumulatively, have strengthened and safeguarded India's vital interests. Here are a few of them illustrated, not necessarily in the order of importance.

Israel

The relationship with Israel, which was almost adversarial for four decades, dramatically turned in a short period of five to six years into a strategic relationship, and has now emerged as one of the most reliable of strategic partnerships for India. It was always said that Israel was one country the people of India viewed positively but the state of India viewed negatively for external reasons. When Israeli Prime Minister Ariel Sharon visited India in 2003, he referred to India as an important friend of Israel and said that 'Israel regards India to be one of the most important countries in the world.'

An International survey conducted in 2009 at Israel's instance, revealed that Indians admired Israel more than even Americans. While Indian public opinion was positive towards Israel, Indian foreign policy, influenced more by external factors, did not reflect it. As the external situation began changing over years, Indian state policy slowly got aligned with the general public's positive view of Israel. But the dramatic and long-awaited turn in India's relations with Israel happened only after Narendra Modi became the Prime Minister of India in 2014, and when Benjamin Netanyahu was the Prime Minister of Israel. The relationship has reached a stage which, most observers agree, is autonomous of the political changes in India or Israel, which cannot be said about other countries. How this turn occurred is an instructive essay on how the foreign policy of a nation has to align in the long run with public opinion. Israelis, like Indians, suffered from aggressive religions, races and civilisations. Both suffered loss of independence and fought to get it back in their own unique way. For two millennia, Jewish persecution was religiously, politically and socially sanctioned in Christian and Islamic religions and civilisations. No one would utter a word about it till the second half of the 20th century. It was only in India that Jews were treated with dignity, and it was an Indian monk who first talked about the persecution of Jews in the world.

Whole World Persecuted Us, India Protected Us, Says Israel

Swami Vivekananda told the World Parliament of Religions in 1893: 'I am proud to belong to a nation which has sheltered the persecuted and the refugees of all religions and all nations of the earth. I am proud to tell you that we have gathered in our bosom the purest remnant of the Israelites, who came to Southern India and took refuge with us in the very year in which their holy temple was shattered to pieces by Roman tyranny.'

When the Swami spoke of the persecution of Jews, an anti-Jewish campaign was raging in Europe. Even in the US, where he proclaimed that the persecuted Jews came to India and India protected them, by the 1890s, anti-Semitic feeling had crystallized around the suspicion that Jews were responsible for an international conspiracy to base the economy on a single gold standard.

Writing about their sojourn in India, the Israeli consulate in Mumbai brought out a booklet in 1968 titled: 'Indian Jews in Israel', in which the editor's note said how the Jews were treated in India and how they were treated elsewhere. It said: 'While most others came to Israel driven by persecution, discrimination, murder and attempts at total genocide, the Jews of India came because of their desire to participate in the Third Jewish Commonwealth, because of their unshakeable faith in the Redemption of Israel. Throughout their long sojourn in India, nowhere and at no time, were they subjected to intolerance, discrimination or persecution?'

The Israeli government itself confirmed what Swami Vivekananda said more than 75 years after he had said that in the very land in which the Jews were persecuted. This marks the millennial relation between Indians and the Jewish.

In 2013, the first-ever National Convention of Indian Jews saw the participation of about 5,000 people from all four major groups of Israel in the Ramla municipality in the Central District of Israel. Four annual conventions have been held since. The 'Know India Programme' has been effective in binding Indian origin Israeli youth to India. Prime Minister Modi addressed a gathering of around 8000 PIOs and Indian nationals working in Israel at the Tel Aviv exhibition grounds during his visit in July 2017.

Hindu-Jewish Civilisational Dialogue

India's relations with Israel were also supported by religious and civilisational dialogue between the Israeli Rabbinate and the Hindu Dharma Acharya Sabha, in 2007 held in Tel Aviv and in 2008 in Delhi respectively, which led to historic declarations through which both religions agreed that the Hindu philosophy of Advaita transcends multiple gods and Idol worship, which the monothieistic Judaic faith does not approve of.

The declaration emphasised that in philosophical terms, Hinduism, which is externally seen as idolatry, is intrinsically as monotheistic as its ultimate idea of Brahman is the single source of supreme power, and therefore, there is no theological issue between both faiths. This is an important declaration, as Israel is a declared Jewish state and Judaism is a national principle and a way of life in Israel.

Turning Points in Indo-Israel Relations—From No Relation to Close Relations

The first and most important turning point was Narendra Modi's visit to Israel in 2017, the first by an Indian Prime Minister. It led to a floodgate of openings in political, military, and economic fields. Israeli Prime Minister Benjamin Netanyahu's visit to India in 2018 was equally important. It was the second by an Israeli Prime Minister, which led to a joint statement that unequivocally stated that both countries shared a common vision for the relationship. This was the second turning point.

Both leaders said they believed that in the next 25 years, India and Israel should strive to raise bilateral cooperation in diverse sectors to a qualitative level in consonance with their strategic partnership.

In 2019, India, which had always been against Israel on Palestine, voted in support of Israel at the United Nations (UN) Economic and Social Council (ECOSOC) to deny observer status to 'Shahed', a Palestinian human rights organisation, declaring it as a terrorist organisation linked to the Hezbollah and the Palestinian Islamic Jihad. This was the third, and a historic, turn in the Indo-Israel relations.

In May 2021, yet another turning point was when India voted against the resolution moved by Pakistan and Palestine for an independent international commission of inquiry into the events which led to the current Gaza crisis. This was the fourth turning point. Welcoming the cease-fire, India reiterated that none of the parties should attempt the unilateral change of the existing status quo in East Jerusalem and its neighbourhoods. This was post Netanyahu, which showed that the New Delhi-Tel Aviv relationship had been institutionalised and would not be affected by political changes either in India or Israel.

Friendly Israel Assisted Whenever Unfriendly India Needed Its Support

Israel has always been friendly to India and extended immediate support whenever the latter faced difficulties and sought help from the former. During the 1962 Sino-Indian war, when India sought Israel's help, the latter shipped arms and ammunition to the former. In 1965 too, Israel supplied ammunition to India during its war with Pakistan. In the 13-day war against Pakistan in 1971 that created Bangladesh, India got Israeli arms and instructors secretly through the tiny principality of Liechtenstein. Israel was one of the countries which did not condemn India for the Pokhran nuclear tests in 1998. Israel Aerospace Industries (IAI) had supplied Unmanned Aerial Surveillance Vehicles to the Indian Army in 1996 and the Indian Air Force and India became the first operational user even before the Israeli military inducted it. India did not adequately respond to Israel.

Defence Supplies, Training, Joint Venture, Co-Development and Technology Transmission

Israel, with its state-of-the-art defence industry, is willing to partner India in all spheres of defence activities. Over 40 per cent of Israeli defence exports come to India. Over two decades, from 1998, Israel has emerged as the second largest arms supplier to India. The critical equipment it had supplied included UCAVs and Loitering Missiles, fabricating AWACs and different missiles, some of which were also used for India's 2019 surgical strikes. Israel also provides cyber security solutions for India's critical infrastructure. India and Israel are involved in co-development of weapons and Artificial Intelligence. Israel trains Indian Special Forces on counter-terrorism. In Kashmir, Israel trains Indian police officers and equips security forces with surveillance technology and foliage-penetrating radar. There was even talk of replicating the 'Israel model' in Kashmir.

Both countries are working together on a Five-Year Joint Work Plan for strategic cooperation on agriculture and water. Further, they agreed to deepen cooperation in innovation, business, trade, space, homeland security, cyber, higher education, research, science, technology, tourism and culture. In 2018, both Prime Ministers welcomed the completion of all formalities for the launch of the India-Israel Industrial Research and Development and Technical Innovation Fund.

Stronger defence relations have led to closer political ties and understanding over the years. India condemned the indiscriminate rocket firings from Gaza but maintained silence about Israeli airstrikes.

Indo-Abrahamic Alliance?

The emerging relations between India and Israel, India and the UAE, and Israel and the UAE have the potential to become an Indo-Abrahamic Alliance. This triangular pact could transform the region's politics and economics, as also at the global level. The Abrahamic Accord 2020, the aggressive positions taken by Turkey and the distancing taking place between Pakistan and the UAE, seem to make the Indo-Abrahamic Alliance a distinct possibility. The Greek call for establishing a trilateral dialogue with India and the UAE could over time expand to include Israel, given the Greeks role in the eastern Mediterranean.

With Riyadh nurturing good relations with Israel on the one hand and with India on the other, Saudi Arabia's moves can also make the Indo-Abrahamic bloc in West Asia a reality. The US may also like such an alliance, as given its stakes in the region, Washington may see in such an alliance the possibility of unburdening itself in the crucial region.

France

India's strategic relation with France has developed in the last few years and is another important partnership.

French President Emmanuel Macron declared in 2018, that, 'The purpose is to make India our first strategic partner in the region and I want you to make France your first strategic partner in Europe and in the Western world. We share the same vision of the world.'

The French-India strategic dialogue takes place every year, alternating in France and India. In the strategic talks for 2021, the focus areas have been Covid-19 vaccines, cooperation in the Indo-Pacific area, nuclear, space, maritime safety, environment, digital economy and the defence sector.

With India signing agreements with France to buy fighter aircrafts, helicopters and submarines, bilateral defence and strategic ties have become comprehensive and deep. Indeed, at the handing over ceremony of the first batch of Rafale fighters to India in September 2020, French Defence Minister, Florence Parly, stated that the agreement had deeper meaning than a normal military sale: 'In strategic terms, it means India will have an edge over the entire region to defend itself…'

Both countries have often demonstrated their growing closeness. India promptly condemned the Paris knife attack over the freedom of expression issue. India also extended diplomatic support to France when Macron was attacked by Turkey, Pakistan and other Muslim nations over French security policies. Bilateral trade with France tops $13 billion with the trade balance in India's favour. French companies are some of the top investors in India, particularly in renewable energy, defence, infra and smart cities, and pharmaceuticals. The French fad with human rights issues has also been changing with France coming under terror attacks.

France, which has overseas territories in Reunion and Mayotte Islands in the Indian Ocean, is a stakeholder in the region, which gives it an area of 28 lakh square kilometres as an Exclusive Economic Zone under the 1982 UNCLOS Treaty. Because of its stake-holding presence, France has emerged as a key partner of India in the Indian Ocean. India has signed a logistics-sharing agreement with France which enables both to use each other's military facilities in the region. This is important in the context of China's growing interest and capability in the Indian Ocean. With China's increased military presence in the region, including in Bangladesh, Pakistan, Sri Lanka, Maldives and Djibouti, India's agreement with France is a deterrent to Beijing's growing ambitions, as the French Navy has permanent bases in Djibouti and Abu Dhabi, besides in the territories of Reunion Island and Mayotte.

Also, the French position today is not always aligned with the Anglo-Saxon nations' position like in the case of the AUKUS deal. It is necessary to deepen the strategic partnership with France, even to handle the G-7 and the EU, like China did with Italy and Germany.

With France, India has had very little conflict. Human rights is an area where India would not share the aggressive proselytisation of France. All human rights lectures emanate from countries which have had no internal security threat from external ideologies, to countries which have threats from external ideologies. With France currently facing terror and with the proposed French global security law, the French position on human rights has changed from being an offensive campaigner for human rights to a partly defensive one, which is advantageous to India.

Russia

Russia and India have a traditionally long, durable and mutually enriching relationship. Built on rich legacy, the India-Russia strategic partnership is truly strategic, with a strong component of Make in India and several joint ventures. The Indo-Soviet and the India-Russia partnership has been the only constant factor in an otherwise volatile world—a time-tested partnership that in many ways has weathered many a geo-political storm through the decades.

The year 2020 marked the 20th anniversary of the Declaration of Strategic Partnership signed by then Prime Minister Atal Bihari Vajpayee and President Vladimir Putin. Over the subsequent years, annual summits between the leaders have strengthened this partnership, with not a single annual summit being skipped.

Through the next decade since 2000, bilateral ties were upgraded with Putin as the chief guest for the Republic Day parade in 2007. In 2010, the strategic partnership was elevated to the level of a 'Special and Privileged Strategic Partnership'.

Prime Minister Modi and President Putin share a personal friendship and have met several times, including during the first Informal Summit in Sochi in 2018 and during Modi's visit to Vladivostok for the Eastern Economic Forum. India joined the Shanghai Cooperation Organisation (SCO) in 2017, adding to a growing list of multilateral platforms where India and Russia are cooperating. An informal meeting between Modi and Putin in 2018 helped accelerate the depth and the content of the partnership between both nations. In 2019, Putin signed an Executive Order that awarded the Indian PM Russia's highest state decoration—The Order of St. Andrew the Apostle—for his distinguished contribution to developing a privileged strategic partnership between Russia and India and for friendly ties between the Russian and Indian peoples.

In the last two decades, India-Russia strategic ties have acquired a qualitatively new character with enhanced levels of cooperation in almost all bilateral areas, including political, security, defence, trade and economy, science and technology and culture. Far East Russia and associated connectivity projects, besides cooperation in the Arctic region, have emerged as the next frontier for partnership.

India has a longstanding and wide-ranging cooperation with Russia in the area of defence. The India-Russia military technical cooperation has transcended the buyer-seller framework to one involving joint R & D and production of advanced defence technologies and systems like BrahMos Missile System as well as licensed production of SU-30 aircraft and T-90 tanks in India. It has been extended to the production of AK Series Assault Rifles at India's Ordnance Factory Korwa under the 'Make-in-India' program. The two countries hold annual exchanges and training exercises between their armed forces, and in 2020, they held a naval exercise in Bay of Bengal. A logistics pact for their navies is on the table for the next annual summit.

A key involvement of Russia in India is the largest nuclear power plant at Kudankulam in Tamil Nadu, scheduled to have 6 VVER-1000 reactors to produce two gigawatts of electricity. The first two reactors were connected to the grid by 2017. The third and fourth are 50 per cent complete. All reactors are expected to be commissioned by 2027. The Rooppur Nuclear Plant is being built as a collaborative effort between India, Russia and Bangladesh.

Another key area is defence production. BrahMos Aerospace (signifying India's Brahmaputra and Russia's Moskva rivers), a joint venture between Russia's Mashinostroyenie and India's DRDO to produce the fastest cruise missile in the world, first test fired the BrahMos missile in 2001. It has been inducted into the Indian Army, Navy and Air Force. After its success, a hypersonic version—BrahMos-II (which travels at six times the speed of sound)—has been developed and tested. An aircraft carrier, which served in the Soviet and Russian navies from 1987 to 1996, was acquired by India 2004. After the successful completion of her sea and aviation trials in 2013, she was formally inducted into the Indian Navy as INS Vikramaditya.

The third key area is hydrocarbons. Today, Russia is one of India's largest investment destinations in the oil and gas sector. Gas utility GAIL has contracted 2.5 million tonnes per annum of LNG from Russia's Gazprom for 20 years. India has embarked on the path of becoming a gas-based economy and a steady partnership with Russia is an important pillar in that vision. India is working on a long term oil supply agreement with Russia. Sakhalin-ONGC Videsh Ltd acquired a 20 per cent stake in Sakhalin in 2001. It further bought Imperial Energy a few years later and has recently invested in Vankorneft and TasYuryah. In return, the Russian firm Rosneft has bought a majority stake in Essar Oil for USD 12.9 billion. India-Russia cooperation in the field of peaceful uses of outer space dates back to about four decades, and the first Indian in space flew in a Soviet spacecraft. Both sides cooperate in the peaceful uses of outer space, including satellite launches, GLONASS navigation system, remote sensing and other societal applications of outer space. ISRO and ROSCOSMOS signed a MoU on Joint Activities in the field of Human Spaceflight Programme during the 19th bilateral summit. Indian cosmonauts for the Gaganyan Mission are being trained in Russia under a programme also signed during the 19th annual summit. The program is on schedule despite the pandemic.

Russia, which recognises India as a country with advanced nuclear technology and an impeccable non-proliferation record, is an important partner in the area of peaceful use of nuclear energy. A MoU on the Action Plan for Prioritisation and Implementation of Cooperation Areas in the Nuclear Field was signed during the 19th annual summit. Russia has backed India's application for membership in the Nuclear Suppliers Group (NSG) as well as for a permanent seat in the UN Security Council. Both sides are exploring various third country projects as part of their global partnership and share strong counter-terror cooperation.

Russia becomes even more an important and balancing ally, with India, under stress from China on the border, and being perceived to be with the US. It is necessary to deepen the strategic partnership with Russia as a counter-balance to that perception and also as a friendly buffer between India and China. With no conflict direct or indirect between Russia and India, it is their and our relative positioning in regard to others that will have to be factored into the efforts to deepen the partnership.

Even as we develop close ties with the US, we need to be mindful of reassuring Russia that this is not at the expense of ties with Moscow; on the whole, Indian diplomacy has done a good job of this. Also after the Russia-Ukraine War, it would be prudent to ensure that Russia is not forced completely into China's corner. For its part, Russia has also taken care that its close partnership with China does not impinge on Indian interests.

Japan

India and Japan share long, historic, cultural and religious relations, the symbols of which are visible in the public and private life of Japan. The Japanese government site on Indo-Japanese relations says: 'Exchange between Japan and India is said to have begun in the 6th century when Buddhism was introduced to Japan. Indian culture, filtered through Buddhism, has had a great impact on Japanese culture, and this is the source of the Japanese people's sense of closeness to India.'

Indo-Japanese ties are cultural and civilisational unlike in the case of others, and provide an enduring basis for their strategic relations, comprising economic, security and defence.

The present momentum to the Indo-Japanese relations began with Japanese Prime Minister Yoshiro Mori's visit to India in the year 2000, when he and Indian Prime Minister Atal Bihari Vajpayee decided on the establishment of the 'Global Partnership between Japan and India'. Japanese Prime Minister Junichiro Koizumi's visit to India in 2005 started the annual Indo-Japan meetings. In 2006, Indo-Japan relations acquired a strategic character during Prime Minister Manmohan Singh's visit, when the Indo-Japan relationship was designated and elevated to a 'Global and Strategic Partnership'.

Relations between the two nations became intimate in every sense of the term when, in September 2014, Prime Minister Narendra Modi visited Tokyo and he and Japanese Prime Minister Shinzo Abe decided to upgrade bilateral ties to a 'Special Strategic and Global Partnership.'

The two prime ministers shared very close personal relations which added to the pace of the fast-evolving relationship between both countries. Japanese Prime Minister Abe visited India towards the end of 2015 and during the summit meeting between him and Prime Minister Modi, both resolved to transform the Japan-India Special Strategic and Global Partnership, to use the words of the Japanese government, 'into a deep, broad-based and action-oriented partnership, which reflects a broad convergence of their long-term political, economic and strategic goals.'

Together they announced the 'Japan and India Vision 2025 Special Strategic and Global Partnership Working Together for Peace and Prosperity of the Indo-Pacific Region and the World' in a joint statement which was designed to serve as a guidepost for the 'new era in Japan-India relations.'

In the 2016 summit meeting in Japan, both Modi and Abe revealed that their interaction had substantially advanced the 'new era in Japan-India relations,' and hoped these ties would lead to the prosperity and stability of the Indo-Pacific region. It would be the result of coordinating the vision of a free and open Indo-Pacific and the 'Act East' policy. Again, when Prime Minister Modi visited Japan in 2018, he and Abe reiterated their unwavering commitment towards a free and open Indo-Pacific.

Indo-Japan Relations Ideal for Strategic Partnership

The Indo-Japan strategic relationship is the most stable one for India besides the one with Russia. For stable strategic relations, three conditions are a must and the fourth condition is an add-on. One, there should be no direct or indirect conflict between the partner nations. Two, neither of them should have an intrusive ideological or civilisational approach that invades the sense of the other's political or cultural sovereignty. Three, their relationship is necessary for mutual benefit. Fourth, they have an unvarying common aim or adversary. All four conditions are present in the Indo-Japanese strategic relationship. In addition, they share a long civilisational relationship which, as the world is seeming and seeking to shift to a civilisational paradigm, will also get upgraded as a civilisational alliance. Indo-Japan relations is an ideal strategic relation. The strategic relation with Russia satisfies the three necessary conditions.

Comprehensive Indo-Japan Strategic Partnership

The Indo-Japan Strategic Partnership is one of the most comprehensive partnerships, but short of an alliance, covering a wide range of areas from geopolitical, geo-security, regional security, trade, finance development projects, technology to cultural and civilisational exchanges. The vast and expansive limbs of Indo-Japanese strategic partnership are illustrated here: Strategic and Geopolitical Dialogues: Annual Foreign

Ministers Strategic Dialogue, Annual Defence Ministers Strategic Dialogue, Dialogue between National Security Advisors and Secretariats, Annual 2 + 2 meetings of foreign and defence secretaries and vice ministers, Japan–India–U.S Trilateral Ministerial Dialogue and Japan-India-Australia Trilateral Dialogue.

Defence and Security: Security Agreement concerning Security Measures for the Protection of Classified Military Information, Agreement concerning the Transfer of Defence Equipment and Technology, Japan's participation in the India-US Malabar exercise; Indian Navy's participation in the Japan Maritime Self Defense Force exercise in Japan; Maritime Self-Defense Force (JMSDF) Fleet Review 2015; Japan's Participation of JMSDF in the India International Fleet Review 2016; proactive development of exchanges by the Indian Army and the Japan Ground-Self Defense Force and for exchanges of both leaderships and staffs; The Japan Air Self Defence Force (JASDF) and the Indian Air Force (IAF) Air Staff Talk to enhance service cooperation and functional level exchanges; bilateral dialogue and joint exercises between the Japan Coast Guard and the Indian Coast Guard; bilateral dialogue on disarmament and non-proliferation; Japan–India Maritime Affairs Dialogue; Japan-India Joint Working Group on Counter Terrorism and Japan-India Cyber Dialogue.

Investment: Indo-Japan Investment Promotion Agreement and its follow up from time to time, resulting in Japan's share of FDI in India reaching one-third of the total; Development of Joint Industrial Townships by different Indian states, including the Ghilot Industrial Park, the Supa Industrial Park, the Chennai-Bengaluru, Industrial Corridor, Japanese Official Development Assistance loans for the Chennai Metro Project-IV; the Ahmedabad Metro Project-I, road network connectivity in India's North Eastern states; for the peripheral ring road for Bengaluru, and for horticulture and micro drip irrigation in Jharkhand; Shared Indo-Japan view of clean Ganga—the rejuvenation of the Ganga River. A survey by

Japan for Ganga rejuvenation, targeting Varanasi city and neighbouring cities; Smart Community Projects such as the Logistics Data Bank project in the Delhi-Mumbai Industrial Corridor (DMIC) area; Mega solar power project in Neemrana and a grid stabilisation project in Gujarat; Canal-top grid connecting the solar photovoltaic power plant in Gujarat as a model for next generation infrastructure. Champions for Societal Manufacturing Project, including Village Buddha as a valuable Japanese contribution to Make in India; Mumbai Trans-Harbour Link and Tuticorin Outer Harbour and Japan International Cooperation Agency on modernisation of ship recycling yards in Gujarat.

Science and Technology: Japan-India Joint laboratories in the areas of 'Internet of Things', 'Artificial Intelligence' and 'Big Data Analytics' under Department of Science and Technology; IIT-Delhi as partner for Department of Biotechnology-National Institute of Advanced Industrial Science International Laboratory for Advanced Biomedicine in the area of Health Research; DST & High-Energy Accelerator Research Organisation to continue the second phase of the Indian beam-line at Photon Factory, KEK, Tsukuba; Strategic International Cooperative Program between DST and JST; Cooperative civil activities in the field of space between Japan Aerospace Exploration Agency (JAXA) and the Indian Space Research Organisation (ISRO) for enhanced cooperation in Earth Observation, Satellite Navigation, Space Science and Planetary Exploration. JAXA and ISRO to work together under the framework of the Asia-Pacific Regional Space Agency Forum and cooperation to promote transfer of leading low-carbon technologies by Japan Investments to India.

Energy and Mineral Resources: Studies on appropriate measures to deploy energy storage technologies in India; Model projects organised by New Energy and Industrial Technology Development Organisation in the field of energy efficiency and renewable energy, like smart grid in Panipat city, Haryana; Agreement between the Indian Rare Earths Limited and the

Toyotsu Rare Earths India Private Limited, a subsidiary of Toyota-Tsusho Corporation Japan for supply of Mixed Rare Earth Chloride; Promotion of cooperation in the rare earths sector and the commencement of commercial production at the earliest; Cooperation to pursue concrete cooperation in agriculture and food industry, including establishing food industrial parks and developing cold chains; Memorandum of Cooperation in the field of forests and forestry between the Ministry of Agriculture, Forestry and Fisheries of Japan and the Ministry of Environment, Forest and Climate Change.

Strategic relations also extend to other sectors such as railways, maritime, skill development, information and communication technology, healthcare, and extensive and intensive cultural and civilisational relations. The expanse of the strategic partnership between India and Japan itself brings out the fact that the partnership is one of the most positive and development oriented ties India has developed, particularly in the last six years.

7

The Emerging Strategic Relations with USA

The chequered relations between India and the US for over 50 years since World War II, have now evolved into a mutually sought after strategic partnership. For deepening and expanding the future relations between these two great democracies, it is necessary to look at issues, discuss them freely and frankly and handle them with understanding.

While many issues are contemporary, some, now appearing as abstract, may emerge as concrete in the future. For a proper understanding of current strategic relations between India and the US, it is necessary to know how difficult and rollercoastering these ties have been throughout most of the second half of the 20th century. Without a look back, at the past, it would be difficult to draw a road map of how ties should move in future.

Cold War Period

US-India relations were first constrained by Cold War politics when Pakistan was part of all Western alliances. The principal determinant of Indo-US relations was the proximity between Pakistan and the US. Except for a brief period under John F. Kennedy, who considered India as a force to counter China after the latter's aggression against the former in 1962, Indo-US relations were never friendly or normal. The relationship reached a hostile phase during the India-Pakistan War of 1971, when the Nixon Administration even moved the US Naval 7th Fleet into the Bay of Bengal. Pakistan, which was playing a secret broking role between the US and China, and having excellent relations with both, was seen as very important for the US in its efforts to escape the Vietnam War and to divide the

Socialist bloc. But India's decision to sign a defence pact with Russia ahead of the 1971 war ensured that the conflict did not escalate beyond India and Pakistan. However, the downside of it was that it virtually pushed India into an indirect Cold War position, which it had always avoided till 1971, against the US.

With Pakistan leaving the SEATO and CENTO in 1973 and 1979 respectively, even though its formal defence alliance with the West had ended, a new and powerful bilateral alliance between the US and Pakistan evolved during the war in Afghanistan, owing to Pakistan's critical role in building, supporting, training and providing sanctuary to Afghanistan's Jihadis in their fight against the Soviets through the 1980s.

Even though there were lows in the relations between the two, like the suspension of aid and delivery of F-16 fighter jets in the 1990s, the intensity of Pak-US relations continued throughout the latter half of 20th century. Almost throughout the 20th century, and even after the Cold War had ended, India was never considered a serious player by the US mind, nor did it figure in Washington's scheme of things. The main, if not the sole beneficiary of the dissolution of Cold War, and the trade, tech, and financial largesse from the US and West, was autocratic China, clearly unfriendly to India, and not democratic India, despite all the lip service the US used to promote democracy.

Two Turning Points

One of the two breakpoints in the near cold relations between India and the US was the Pokhran atomic test in 1998, which led first to hostile sanctions and later to negotiations for normalising relations. The atomic test shook the whole world and particularly the entire West and its allies. But it also made India relevant in the world of power play. It was an event that made then US President Bill Clinton visit India in the year 2000, and that arrested the negative trend in Indo-US ties after decades.

Before Bill Clinton's visit, the last US President to visit India was Jimmy Carter in 1978, who wanted India to sign the

Non-Proliferation Treaty (NPT). The second breakpoint was the terror attack on America in September 2001, which was a telling message to the US that terror was not a local or regional threat, but global, and also exposed Pakistan as a nation supporting extremists, creating a trust deficit. Added to the role of Pakistan in providing safe haven for terrorists, the closeness of Pakistan to China was also a factor that weighed with the US in becoming cautious in its dealings with Islamabad.

Sanctions Fail, Realism Prevails, Talks Begin

Indo-US relations began to improve only when Washington found that Western sanctions against India over its Pokhran explosion had proved ineffective. Despite sanctions, India's economy began rising, and stunningly posted a current account surplus of almost $25 billion in a three-year period from 2000–01 to 2003–04, despite a fall in external assistance by $6 billion—a record unrivalled till now.

In its entire trade history from 1951, India had never posted a current account surplus except very small surpluses in 1972–73 and 1976–77. And more, during the post Pokhran period of five years, i.e., 1999–2004, India added sixty million new jobs—a record neither achieved before nor bettered later. It is this performance which made US-led nations turn realistic and begin to talk of regularising India's irregular position in the nuclear world. While Indo-US relations on the nuclear issue began to thaw during the Clinton administration itself, talks began under the Bush administration on India's nuclear status.

Deepening Relations 2001–2014

The changed geopolitical conditions so fast-forwarded the process of normalisation, that in 2004, according to a biased report of the Carnegie Endowment for International Peace; titled: 'Toward Realistic US-India Relations' (2010), the Bush administration did more for India than he did for any NATO ally, including the United Kingdom. It was in 2004 that the estranged relationship between the two began to turn into a strategic partnership. The Indo-US civil nuclear cooperation accord reversed 30 years of US nuclear non-proliferation policy towards India. America began openly talking about India's obvious virtues, which it had refused to take note in the past. George Bush said: 'India is a great example of democracy. It is very devout, has diverse religious heads, but everyone is comfortable about their religion. The world needs India.'

Indo-US relations grew in economic, technical fields under the Obama regime, and America became one of the three major defence suppliers to India, yet bilateral bonhomie was still below expectations. US Chairman of Joint Chiefs of Staff, Admiral Mike Mullen, advocating strong military ties with India, did say 'India has emerged as an increasingly important strategic partner for the US.'

US officials also began saying that 'never has there been a moment when India and America mattered more to each other'. In 2010, Obama addressed the Indian parliament and supported India's case for permanent membership of the UN Security Council. In 2012, the US said that as the India-US relationship has global scope, both countries are strengthening relations between their defence and research organisations.

History Shows India's Relations as Inversely Related to US-Pak Ties

Historically, a clear link was seen in the relation between US and India on the one hand and the relationship between the US and Pakistan on the other. That the Indo-US relations was inversely related to the Pak-US relationship might be judged by the most significant fact that while in the late 1960s, the two US Presidents, Lyndon Johnson and Richard Nixon, visited Pakistan and not India, between 2010 and 2020, two US Presidents, Barack Obama and Donald Trump, visited India, but not Pakistan. While only three of nine US Presidents visited India between 1947 and 2000, every US President has visited India at least once between 2000 and 2020.

Relationship under Modi Government

Different US governments had been exceptionally hostile to Narendra Modi when he was the chief minister of Gujarat because of the communal riots that had taken place in the state in 2002. The Bush administration denied a visa to Modi in 2005 and this ban continued till he became India's Prime Minister in 2014. The US government had to reverse its decade-old ban on visas to Modi. This was how the US began U-turning and began to engage with Modi.

In June 2014, a month after Modi became Prime Minister, Robert Blackwill, former coordinator for strategic planning, Deputy NSA under George W Bush and a former Ambassador to India, said, 'Mr Modi is a determined leader. He is candid, frank. It was a mistake by the Obama administration to delay engagement with Mr Modi. I do not know why they did so, but definitely this did not help in building relationships. The old formula and stereotypes will not work if the US administration wants to engage with Mr Modi. The Indian prime minister is candid, direct and smart and he speaks his mind. The US administration also has to engage in candid conversation when Mr Modi meets President Obama later this year. They have to do something innovative to engage with him.'

Obama invited Modi to visit US in September 2014. Modi, in turn, invited him to be the chief guest for the Republic Day Parade in 2015. Between then and 2021, Modi visited the US six times. President Trump came to India in 2020. The rise of the Indian diaspora's importance in the US also contributed enormously to growing relations between the two countries.

Milestones in Strategic Engagement In Modi Era

As a first, Modi and President Obama agreed on a memorandum of understanding which provided $1 billion to help India develop low-carbon energy alternatives and aid US renewable energy exports to India.

During his second visit to India, President Obama said: 'America can be India's best partner.' Obama and Modi announced a breakthrough on nuclear-related issues to help implement the US-India civil nuclear deal. Six months later, the US and India agreed to renew the ten-year US-India Defense Framework Agreement.

In Prime Minister Modi and President Obama's final meeting in the White House, the US elevated India as a major defence partner, a status no other country holds. The designation meant that India would enjoy some of the benefits of being a US treaty ally, such as access to defence technology, though the alliance between the two was not a formal one. Two months later, the US and India agreed on deeper military cooperation after nearly a decade of negotiations. The major defence partner status was codified in US law through the NDAA (National Defence Authorisation Act) 2017 by the Trump administration.

This step contributed significantly towards the further momentum witnessed during the Trump administration on the four foundational agreements, namely—General Security of Military Information Agreement (GSOMIA); Logistics Exchange Memorandum of Agreement (LEMOA); Communications Compatibility and Security Agreement (COMCASA); Basic Exchange and Cooperation Agreement (BECA). It marked the commencement of cabinet-level two plus two dialogues and the inception of the tri-service exercise Tiger Triumph.

Though President Trump had raised sharp disagreements with India over trade, climate change, and H-1B visas, these issues were sidelined during the leaders' summit and their joint statement emphasized strengthening their defence partnership, cooperating on counter-terrorism efforts, and boosting economic ties.

During a 'two-plus-two' dialogue in New Delhi, the US and India signed the COMCASA which was under negotiation for a decade, and which gave India access to advanced communication technology used in US defence equipment, besides allowing for real-time information sharing between the two countries' militaries.

During President Trump's visit to India, when he addressed a large rally of a lakh of people in his honour, both leaders announced plans to work together on counter-narcotics and mental health. India agreed to purchase $3 billion in US military equipment and American oil company ExxonMobil announced a deal with the state-owned Indian Oil Corporation.

Top American and Indian defence and diplomats signed an intelligence-sharing agreement during the third round of their two-plus-two dialogue. The BECA, which allowed for the sharing of sensitive geospatial data to boost the accuracy of Indian drones and cruise missiles, was the final of the four foundational military agreements signed by both countries. Then US Secretary of Defense, Mark T. Esper, emphasised the commitment of the two to keeping the Indo-Pacific free and open, 'particularly in light of increasing aggression and destabilising activities by China.'

After Joe Biden's regime took over in 2021, there were questions about whether the Trump administration's policies would continue. But there was a clear reaffirmation that continuity of defence and security cooperation would transition across administrations.

Shortly after, the new US administration released, in March, an 'Interim National Security Strategic Guidance' designed 'to engage with the world once again, not to meet yesterday's challenges, but today's and tomorrow's'. The US President and leaders of Australia, India and Japan, besides other members of the Quad, met virtually and issued a joint statement, enunciating the 'Spirit of the Quad'.

That the US had included India in the maiden visit of US Secretary of Defense Lloyd Austin, reaffirmed the Biden administration's commitment to continue the US defence partnership with India. An official statement said that Austin's visit was focused on deepening the defence partnership and on enhancing the cooperation for a free, prosperous and open

Indo-Pacific and Western Indian Ocean Region—the reference to the Western Indian Ocean region was important for India. The US and India had some differences in delineating the expanse of the Indo-Pacific. In keeping with India's security concerns across the Indian Ocean, a distinct emphasis was laid by the US side on extending cooperation to the 'Western Indian Ocean region'.

The Third 2+2 Dialogue held on 26–27 October 2020, barely a week ahead of the US Presidential elections, and the Joint Statement of 27 October 2020, provided a structured platform and basic reference document for providing further continuity and predictability, which was seen as vital for forging a defence relationship.

The Austin visit in March 2021 was also reiteration of India's status as a major defence partner (MDP) of the US. Within the ambit of the India-US Comprehensive Global Strategic Partnership, India is now at par with US treaty allies, except that the US has not offered nuclear powered submarines as it did to Australia, nor F-35 aircraft to Japan and is central to maintaining a free, prosperous and open Indo-Pacific.

In the context of the bilateral and multilateral exercises, both sides agreed on cooperation not only with the US Indo-Pacific Command, but also with the Central and Africa Commands. The joint statement of the Third two plus two Dialogue, included the positioning of an Indian liaison officer at NAVCENT, Bahrain, and a US officer at the Information Fusion Centre for the Indian Ocean Region (IFC-IOR) at Gurgaon in India.

Under the four foundational agreements, India today operates some $20 billion worth of US-sourced defence equipment, including leased Sea Guardian drones, in its armed forces. Here also comes the catch. As India possesses a large inventory of Russian origin equipment, the US seems to feel that there is a mismatch in the consolidation of resources. India will have to convince the US that it would be prudent to have Indian forces get used to the US equipment as and when the same are acquired and not pressurize India which would be most counterproductive.

Technology cooperation between both countries, both bilaterally and as part of the Quad technology-alliance, to jointly develop dual-use technologies from 5G to AI, semi-conductors, and critical materials is an area of immense potential for India.

The two countries have agreed on the inaugural Industrial Security Annexe (ISA) Summit, which will give an impetus to cooperation with, and from, private industry in defence. India's revised Defence Acquisition Procedure (DAP 2020) and liberalised foreign direct investment policies in the defence sector would help in this process. There is also a suggestion from the US side for bilateral investment mechanisms like the BIRD Foundation that established non-military technology cooperation between Israeli and American firms starting in 1977. This will help technology cooperation and Indian firms and start-ups to enter global supply chains.

Pakistan: A Continuing Issue in the Indo-US relationship

Pakistan, whose sense of nationhood is defined by its hostility to India and to Hindus who are a majority in India, was always a pet project of the US during and even after the Cold War days. In the 1950s, the US made Pakistan a defence ally and in the 1970s, it engaged the latter as a secret broker to secure China's help in resolving the Vietnam imbroglio to break up the Socialist bloc.

In the 1980s, the US asked Pakistan to create a jihadi force to oust the Soviets from Afghanistan. In the 1990s, it began realising that Pakistan was a problem state, but was reluctant to give it up, or prefer India over it. After the 9/11 attack, Pakistan became suspect in the eyes of the US, but still Washington needed and began strategically using Pakistan to handle Afghanistan.

In 2009, the US gave Pakistan $7.5 billion in aid to help defeat Al-Qaida, but it soon found Pakistan sheltering Osama bin Laden. And now, after the Taliban takeover of Kabul and the role of Pakistan in helping to form an Islamist government there, the US again cannot make up its mind on what to do with Pakistan, despite Islamabad becoming closer to China.

Pakistan thus continues to be a vexing issue in Indo-US relations. At the heart of American strategic thinking is to use Pakistan as a kind of 'Mahabharat Shikhandi' against India, should Delhi adopt postures the US perceives to be inimical to its interests at some future date.

S-400: A Concern Area in the Indo-US Defence Partnership

A major issue that India has with the US, particularly in the area of defence cooperation, is over her planned acquisition of the S-400 Air Defence Missile System from Russia, which may risk it attracting sanctions under the Countering America's Adversaries through Sanctions Act (CAATSA) 2017. India's agreement to buy Russian equipment precedes India-US defence relations, which came later. The S-400 acquisition is critical for enhancing India's air defence capabilities and US sanctions will hamper and torpedo Delhi's plans to export the Brahmos missiles to Vietnam and The Philippines and deprive their capability development against threats from China. During her visit to India in October 2021, US Deputy Secretary of State Wendy Sherman had flagged the S-400 issue as dangerous and not in anybody's interest, but added that 'we have a strong partnership with India and we want to be thoughtful about the ways ahead', indicating that there might be some way forward to get over the sanctions. India cannot afford to and should not give in to any threat of sanctions on acquisition of the S-400. The US has no moral grounds to pressurise India, as when the deal with Russia was made, Washington was nowhere around. It is not in Washington's interest also to talk of sanctions, which is bound to provide an opportunity to both China and Russia to brand the former as an overbearing partner. Sanctions, if any, would be seen as intended more to promote US arms at the expense of Russian ones.

Future Indo-US Relations: Abstract Civilisational to Concrete Political Issues

The post-Cold War world order, which is now poised to change forever, is an ideal context for both the US and India to think deeply and fashion their future relations to be comfortable to both. Besides a mix of historical errors and current complexities in the Indo-US strategic partnership, the US, with its individualist liberal democratic DNA, which has less than a couple of centuries of history to grapple with, will have to rethink on how to relate to democracies like India, which have 5000 years, why even, a timeless, recall of the past. A country with a shorter memory of its past and another country with a longer memory of its remote past, have a marked thought and behavioural differences in their respective people.

A society with brief recall like the US tends to be highly individualistic with no social collective for an individual to share space, while a society with longer recall like India tends to be collectivist where an individual shares space. Here comes the distinction between high individualism which makes one independent as opposed to high collectivism which makes one interdependent.

An American thinks he is independent and an Indian thinks he is interdependent. This leads to two different paradigms.

The contractual individual's independent paradigm and the interdependent individual's relational paradigm.

A profound, thought-provoking article which appeared in the BBC in its series the Human Planet titled: 'How East and West think in profoundly different ways' is relevant for the individualist US/West to understand better the behavioural differences between societies in which individualism does not play the most constitutive role like in the US/West. The BBC article says that until recently, scientists had largely ignored the global diversity of thinking and added that in 2010, according to an influential article in the journal *Behavioral and Brain Sciences* in the Cambridge University Press Online, a vast majority of psychological subjects had been Western,

Educated, Industrialised, Rich and Democratic or 'WEIRD' for short.

The Cambridge University article titled: 'The Weirdest People in the World?' said that a review of research samples on the basis of universal conclusions had led to a finding that 'WEIRD' societies are the least representative species one could find generalising about humans. Overall, the review suggested the need to be less cavalier in addressing questions of human nature on the basis of data drawn from this particularly thin and rather unusual slice of humanity.

The Cambridge review closed by proposing ways to structurally re-organise behavioral sciences to best tackle these challenges. Some of the most notable differences that the review brought out 'revolved around the concepts of 'individualism' and 'collectivism'; whether you consider yourself to be independent and self-contained, or entwined and interconnected with the other people around you, valuing the group over the individual. Generally speaking, there are many exceptions: People in the West tend to be more individualist and people from Asian countries like India, Japan or China tend to be more collectivist'. This is the critical differential between the individualist US and collectivist India. This is extremely relevant in the context of how the relations generally between the West and Asia, particularly between the US and India, should be approached.

The interdependence of individuals, families, castes and communities in Indian society rests on relations, which transcend geographic limits, because urbanisation did not disturb relations or uproot individuals from their environment. In contrast, in the West, urbanisation disturbed neighbourhood communities and turned them into industrial societies, and alienated people from their roots. In India, powerful communal relations transcended geographic limits and continued to bind individuals and families with the community through the institution of marriage, as also through traditions linked to local deities and temples. For example, the tradition of Indian families worshipping their family deities, or offering a child's hair to the family deity; these are powerful relational links that continue even now, even with those who have gone and settled abroad, but still come to India to perform these rituals and observe these traditions.

The continuance of trans-geographic traditional relations, undisturbed by urbanisation and even globalisation, is a unique feature of Indian society, reflecting a continuing sociological model. In contrast are the urbanised and atomised societies and individuals of the West, where relationships are governed by contracts.

English scholars like Sir Henry James Sumner Maine, who was in the British government service in India, premised his theory of modernity on atomised Western industrial society functioning on contracts as modern, and dismissed Indian society which functioned on relations based on status, and therefore, not modern. If that rationale is applied to all Asian societies, even the still powerfully relation-based Japan—that the West could not deny it as a modern industrial society—will not qualify as a modern society, as it is not contract based like the West.

In simple terms, the difference between contract based and relation based society is this: In a contract based society, individuals are independent; in a relation based society, they are interdependent. The paradigm of the US is contractual, while the paradigm of India is relational. An American naturally thinks he is independent and an Indian naturally thinks he is interdependent. This leads to two different paradigms—the contractual individual's independent paradigm and the interdependent individual's relational paradigm. The US private and public discourse based on contractual individual's independent paradigm—actually unbridled liberal individualism—is incapable of comprehending the Indian private and public based on the relations and interdependence.

This difference in the two paradigms mirrors into huge private behaviour and public policy differences between India and the US. As an example, just one telling socio-economic differential caused by the two vastly different paradigms.

While it is largely the family which takes care of social security obligations of the young, elder and the infirm in India, it is the contractual state in the US that takes care of social security through public funding.

Understood in simple language, while social security is privatised in India by relationships, it is nationalised in the US by social and personal contracts. The difference between independent individualism of the US and interdependent collectivism of India is not a philosophical one but ground reality. Just as the soul of the US liberal democracy is the contractual individual's independence, the foundation of the Indian society, democracy, and state, is the interdependent individuals' relational paradigm which WEIRD study of Cambridge calls as collectivism.

Indo-US relations must be based on the understanding that rules of public and private discourse in the US founded on the contractual individual's independent paradigm cannot apply in India.

The independent individual's contractual paradigm is the basis of the liberal democracy in the US. The interdependent individual's relational paradigm is the basis of the civilisational democracy in India.

US and Indian democracies are both electoral. But two different paradigms operate in the two democracies. The independent individual's contractual paradigm is the soul of liberal democracy in the US, while the interdependent individual's relational paradigm is the foundation of Indian democracy, which is rooted in Indian civilization. It links the individual through families and caste and ever expanding circles of religions, language, culture and ethnicity, which ultimately has something in common other than merely the constitutional social contract. This commonality makes India, as Mahatma Gandhi said in his treatise Hind Swaraj, one nation.

India is so unbelievably diverse that if she is kept on one side and the rest of the world on the other, there would be more diversity in her than in the rest put together. India whose constitutional federalism is organised on the basis of fourteen officially recognised languages, accommodates over 900 living and spoken languages and dialects; over 3000 castes with some 90,000 endogamous sub-groups within; Hindus, Buddhists, Jains and Sikhs, who demographically constitute over 84 per cent of Indians, have varying religious practices ranging from idolaters worshipping millions of idols to those who reject it. This diversity constitutes the essence of Indian civilisation. These unbelievably diverse collectives of people participate in India's democratic process. These millennial old civilisational entities vote not as individuals, but as collectives. The numerical participation of hierarchically lower segments is much higher than the hierarchically higher ones. India's civilisational democracy, which comprises interdependent related individuals, cannot be judged by norms of independent individualist liberal democracies.

Examples of Inadequate Civilisational Understanding Impeding Good Relations Between US and India

An important area where more study and understanding about India is needed in the US for better relations with the former is the paradigm difference between Hinduism, of which the majority of Indians are adherents. According to the Indian Supreme Court, Hinduism is the culture and national ethos, a way of life. The religious content of India's national ethos, the Hindu religion, is non-proselytising and, therefore, non-conflicting, as it accepts all faiths as valid for their followers, which no other religion does. It is necessary because it is also intimately linked to the non-conflicting collectivism of India, as all Indian collectivism, whether it is Indic religions like Hinduism, Sikhism, Buddhism or Jainism, or social, like different communities do not convert others and, therefore, does not interfere with others.

This faith-cum-sociology, unique to India, has not been known or studied much in depth outside. This is the foundation of India's interdependent collectivism, which is the basis of her social capital. This lack of knowledge and understanding of India's uniqueness, makes American institutions like the

USCIRF and human rights bodies misunderstanding India and clouding relations between the two nations. This needs to be explained in some detail.

The interdependent relational collectivism of India and its unbelievable diversity makes her difficult to understand from the American perspective of independent contractual individualism. In India, for instance, the family is more important than the individual. This is consistent with the Cambridge review referred to above, that in Asia, the interconnectedness makes the group more valuable to the individual, where individual interest and rights yield the group. This makes, for instance, secularism in India entirely different in practice from secularism in America even though both the US and Indian governments are separated from religion. In India, as there is no church in Hinduism, even the so-called religion cannot interfere with the family, and actually, each family has a deity to worship, the Kuldevta. Each village has a deity, the Gramdevta. And each individual too, has a deity, the Ishta devta. This is unknown to the West and the US. US/Western secularism is a product of an Abrahamic religious perspective and an outcome of a long intra-Christian conflict between the Christian State and the Christian Church. Secularism in the sense of equal treatment by a religion and culture itself to other religions as in India is unknown to Christendom. There are three important and irrefutable authorities which distinguish Abrahamic religions from the Hindu pantheon of religions.

The Encyclopaedia Britannica (16th Ed) which is a product of international scholars says:

> In principle, Hinduism incorporates all forms of belief and worship without necessitating the selection or elimination of any. The Hindu is inclined to revere the divine in every manifestation, whatever it may be and is doctrinally tolerant, leaving others, including both Hindus and non-Hindus, to whatever creed and worship practices suit them the best. A Hindu may embrace a non-Hindu religion without ceasing to be a Hindu, and since the Hindu is disposed to think synthetically and to regard other forms of worship, strange Gods, and divergent doctrines as inadequate rather than wrong or objectionable, he tends to believe that the highest divine powers complement each other for

> the well being of the world and the mankind. Few religious ideas are considered to be finally irreconcilable. The core of the religion does not even depend on the existence or non-existence of the God or whether there is one God or many. Since religious truth is said to transcend all verbal definitions, it is not conceived in dogmatic terms. Hinduism is then both a civilisation and a conglomerate of religions with neither a beginning nor a founder, nor a central authority, hierarchy, or organisation.

This clearly brings out the two different ideas of religion—the Abrahamic religions and the Hindu commonwealth of religions. The first ones are doctrinally intolerant and the second ones are doctrinally tolerant.

The Fundamentalism Project of the Chicago University Press funded by the American Academy of Arts and Science, which involved numerous scholars and was edited by Martin E. Marty, an Ordained Lutheran Pastor and well-known Christian theologian, and R. Scott Appleby, an acknowledged Christian scholar, said in the first of the five volumes titled, the 'Fundamentalism Observed':

'Some traits of fundamentalism examined here are more accurately attributable to the 'People of the Book', Jews, Christians and Muslims than to their first or distant cousins in the fundamentalist family: Hindus, Sikhs, Buddhists and Confucians.'

Why are such fundamentalist traits seen in the Abrahamic traits absent in Eastern faiths? The Fundamentalism Project itself answers the query.

'Sacred texts do not play the same constitutive role in South Asian and Far Eastern traditions as they do in Abrahamic faiths, both to intensify missionary efforts and to justify extremism.'

Therefore, the doctrine of religious fundamentalism founded on the concept of inerrant texts which decides the whole range of a religions approach within and outside itself, is inapplicable to Hinduism as there is no single inerrant or invariable text.

The Indian Supreme Court has ruled that after analysing large volumes of literature, including the Encyclopaedia Britannica that Hinduism cannot be limited only to religion and it is a way of life, culture and ethos of the people of India. The Supreme Court says:

'It cannot be doubted, particularly in view of the Constitution Bench decisions of this Court, that the words 'Hinduism' or 'Hindutva' are not necessarily to be understood and construed narrowly, confined only to the strict Hindu religious practices unrelated to the culture and ethos of the people of India, depicting the way of life of the Indian people. Unless the context of a speech indicates a contrary meaning or use, in the abstract, these terms are indicative more of a way of life of the Indian people and are not confined merely to describe persons practicing the Hindu religion as a faith.'

The Indian Supreme Court rendered a judgement as far back as 1976, quoting the Encyclopaedia Britannica, that a Hindu may become a non-Hindu without ceasing to be a Hindu and there can be a Hindu who doesn't believe in God at all.

The three authorities make it clear that:

- Hinduism is doctrinally tolerant, while Abrahamic religions founded on strict dogma, cannot be.
- The core of Hindu religion does not believe in the existence or non-existence of God, or whether there is one God or many.
- Hinduism accepts all forms of worship, including that of other religions without necessitating the selection or elimination of any.
- A Hindu may become a non-Hindu by faith and yet remain a Hindu in culture.
- A Hindu can be a Hindu without believing in God at all.
- Hinduism is a conglomerate of many religions, idolatry to monism and, not a single religion.
- It has no founder, central authority or organisation like in the case of Abrahamic faiths.
- The concept of religious fundamentalism is more a feature of Abrahamic faiths and not the Hindu and other Eastern faiths.
- As there is no single text in Hinduism, sacred text does not play the constitutive role in Hinduism.

- Hinduism is not just a religion; it is also the way of life, culture and ethos of India.

None of these are the features of the three Abrahamic faiths. Since these features which make Hinduism not a religion at all in the sense of Abrahamic faiths are not understood, it results in a gap in the understanding of Hinduism based on the Abrahamic perspectives of Christendom. And that is clearly the gap in the approach of the US and US government-funded institutions like the United States Commission on International Religious Freedom (USCIRF), which causes huge misunderstanding about India and Hinduism in the US and in the rest of the world.

For instance, in Hinduism, one's parents are equal to God and even more important than God. Any elder is to be respected. And, even a stranger who comes home unannounced is equal to God. There are sacred duties attached to an individual towards his or her parents, grandparents, elders and even strangers. This makes the larger and extended families, and the community itself, into sacred institutions.

This has huge socio-economic consequences as even now most of what is known as social security in the US and West are informally undertaken by larger families—whether it is educating children, or caring for the old, or tending to the infirm. This does mean a trade-off between individual liberties and freedom as is known in the West for the larger collectives.

Again, a large number of Indians worship plants and animals—in fact, the five elements of what is today known as the composite environment, namely earth, water, fire, air and space. Even now cutting trees, polluting water or killing certain animals is considered a great sin in India and is unacceptable to Indians. That is why almost two-fifths of Indians are vegetarians. And, that is why India's share of the world's biodiversity is three to four times the share of the world's land area. Indians were once dismissed as animists, but today, nature worship is seen by many great scholars on the environment as environment-compatible and environment-promotive.

This trades off human rights even with animals and plants. The Cambridge University (WEIRD) study demonstrates precisely this as the difference between the West and Asia, which applies particularly to India. This makes an individual's life integral to the family, community and society. But that integrality is positive and not aggressive as it does not mandate conversion from other religions and actually respects other religions—unlike in the Abrahamic religions, which tend to convert, which Mahatma Gandhi said is a serious problem for Hinduism.

The gap in the understanding of Hinduism in the US causes such institutions to apply the foundations and perspectives based on the Abrahamic faiths to judge the concept of religious freedom to Hinduism, which is like applying hockey rules for cricket.

The USCIRF perspectives are a product of an Abrahamic civilisational US. It judges religious freedom in other countries from the Christian perspective of a single God, State and Church separation. With its limited perspective acquired from the experience and worldview of Christendom, the USCIRF keeps issuing judgements about India's religious freedom. If anything has irritated the Indians, particularly the Hindus the most in recent times, it is the USCIRF, whose reports, without understanding the ground rules of Indian civilisation, keep pronouncing about the religious rights violations in India, mostly condemning the Hindus based on wrong perspectives.

The USCIRF, which has no familiarity with the Hindu commonwealth of millions of religions ranging from idol worship to those who reject and even oppose it, has no business to pronounce judgements about it. The USCIRF ought to be, and is obviously not aware, that Hinduism is the only religion not organised under a church or theological school, which not only protects even the Abrahamic faiths which have the mandate to convert the others, including Hindus.

Judging India from the American sense of human rights, which is founded on the independent individualist contractual paradigm, is disturbing, for there is no voluntary trade-off between an individual and the collective—be it a family, community or society.

Because of this trade-off of rights and duties among the individual, family and community, Indian society is less rights conscious and more duty conscious. The sacred duties of an individual to his or her family and the community are the very foundation of Hinduism. These duties do mean limitations on the rights of individuals—whether it is parents, elders, youngsters or others—and even their human rights. That is why Mahatma Gandhi advised H.G. Wells to redesign his Human Rights Declaration as Human Duties Declaration if the latter wanted him to endorse it.

What Mahatma Gandhi spoke about was not his fad for duties or against rights. He argued that in one's duties, another's rights are ensured. That is the essence of the Indian civilisational position. This was completely ignored in the conception and formulation of human rights, which was entirely based on the WEIRD norms of the US and West, and which will not fit with Indian diversity. This is also an area of irritation because of inadequate understanding of the Indian civilisational ethos.

The US and India should set up joint study projects to help the former understand Indian civilisational democracy to ensure better relations.

The US, which will continue to be the most powerful country and a leader of democracies in the emerging world order, has a special responsibility to understand the differentials of India. But it should be from an inclusive and comprehensive approach. It should not be from the perspective of Western anthropology of modernity, but from the perspective of multiple modernities.

The West as the single source of modernity, which has been the basis of the US/West approach to the rest of the world and particularly India, is no longer valid. An inclusive approach is needed to accommodate the unalterable civilisational diversity of India and civilisational aspirations of the Indian people for better relations with India. And India too, on its part, must help the US understand Indian civilisation better. For this purpose, some past notions which have no contemporary validity should be discarded. It is necessary that the Indian and the US governments set up joint study projects to help the US to understand the Indian civilisational democracy, for better relations.

Post-Cold War Period: Preference for Stable Autocracy over Unstable Democracy

Indo-US bilateral relations have, in recent times, acquired geopolitical ramifications and are at a crucial and important juncture for both countries. The US has always been important to India like it has been with most other countries, including China.

In the past why India needed the US was precisely the reason why China needed the US, namely for its own development. There was less politics and more economics in both seeking a relationship with the US.

But the US then chose autocratic China over a democratic India which showed that the US, despite its avowed commitment to democracy, was more keen to do business with a stable, yet autocratic Chinese system, as opposed to an unstable and democratic Indian democracy with rickety to difficult coalition governments. The 25 years from 1989 when Indian democracy was burdened with unstable coalition governments which made decision-making difficult, China offered the most stable decision making platform for the US to ally with.

China was seen and branded by the US as the flying, aggressive dragon, while India was described as the slow and passive elephant.

The foundation of that choice was that final victory of the West over the Rest, including China which was considered as incapable of becoming a challenge to the West. Now the result of that choice and how it shaped up the world, which is explained in chronological detail in earlier chapter, is out there for all to see. One clear result of that choice was India was less important than China in the US scheme of things then and till very recently. In the post-Covid world scenario, with a rising China challenging the West, there has been a shift, with India becoming increasingly important to the US.

The need for decoupling with China is also forcing those who are entangled with China to couple with India. India, which missed the deep techno-economic coupling with the US and the attendant geopolitical advantage because of its unviable democracy, is now becoming important also because of that very democracy.

Incidentally, Indian democracy has shown that it can be stable by electing a single party majority government for two successive terms, in 2014 and again in 2019.

High Growth under Autocracy vs Moderate Growth under Democracy—Implications

The post-Cold War and free of the West ideology, preferred Marxist ideological China over democratic India because of the higher rate of growth that China had begun posting which attracted the US and West more than the moderate growth under democracy. There is a qualitative difference between democracy and autocracy—both domestically and globally. An autocracy is oppressive and regressive inside and aggressive outside. An autocracy is a greater risk to the world than a democracy, which is answerable to its people for its external faults.

For example, if an Indian government mishandles its relations with China, it will have to pay the cost immediately in the next elections, a risk which China mishandling its relations with India, will not face, at any rate, immediately. Democracy is a restraint on external aggression. That is, besides internally, externally also autocracy is a risk which a democracy is not. In a survey in August 2005, the Lowy Institute advised:

'A democratic India that grows at 6 per cent a year should be congratulated for having succeeded better than a brutal anti-democratic China which grows at 10 per cent a year.'

But such sagely advice hardly weighed with the US and the West whose euphoria of final victory of the West had blinded them to obvious truths. Even in the recent past, the US had preferred a Communist and autocratic China, and an Islamic autocratic Pakistan over a democratic India.

India definitely has the right to expect the US to introspect on how it has treated Delhi on the one hand and China and Pakistan on the other. China is a Marxist autocracy which the US tapped to bring the Cold War to an end. As the Cold War was ending, the US was working to democratise Communist countries, but the Chinese themselves revolted to shake off the communist dictatorship. Contrary to its own policies towards other communist countries, it silently supported the continuation of dictatorship while following a different policy with other countries it was in engagement with.

The Chinese army openly massacred thousands of youths seeking democracy. Yet within three years of the Tiananmen Square massacre, the US shockingly announced positive engagement with it. When the WTO was formed, the US pushed a Marxist totalitarian China into the global market economy. Later, it went as far as to equate China and itself as global powers. China milched the US and global patronage and is now challenging it. Now look at Pakistan. On its own admission, Pakistan is an Islamic Republic in which minorities are being marginalised, if not eliminated. Even when Pakistan has had elected governments, they have always been at the mercy of the military. Its army commenced the Kargil War against India without the knowledge of the elected government. Its army executed its prime minister following a kangaroo court judgement in 1979. In contrast, India has been a highly transparent democracy. The people have seen how the US had positioned and treated India in the past relative to both China and Pakistan. C. Rajamohan wrote (*The Centre for New American Security* in 2010):

'Since the inauguration of Barack Obama (sic) in 2009, supporters of strategic cooperation between India and the United States have expressed frustration at the absence of 'a big idea' that could impart momentum to the positive relationship developed between the countries during the presidency of George W. Bush. Critics of the Obama administration, in both Delhi and Washington, have pointed out repeatedly to Bush's strategic warmth toward India and its apparent absence under his successor. In addition, they argue that Obama has tended to privilege China over India while dealing with global issues, and Islamabad over Delhi on regional issues involving the subcontinent.'

$6 Trillion Relation with China vs $350 Billion Relation with India

A most telling picture emerges when trade relations between the US and China are compared with trade relations between the US and India.

From 1979 till August 2021, the US has incurred a trade deficit of $6 trillion with China, which transformed into wealth for the latter to facilitate its investments in the US treasury and investments elsewhere, including the BRI project, through which China is cornering most countries in Asia, Middle East and Europe.

Of this, $4.56 trillion was incurred till 2016. When the so-called trade war started, China did not fall but rose and added a further deficit of $1.5 trillion in the four years of the Trump regime. Now under the Biden administration, till August 2021, there has been a further $219 billion addition to the deficit. In the last nine years to 2020, deficits totalled over $3 trillion—an average of over $330 billion a year. Even in 2021, it is likely to top $330 billion despite all the uproar over China being a threat to the US and the West.

In contrast, from 1985 to August 2021, the US trade deficit with India has aggregated to $350 billion, or less than six per cent of the US trade deficit with China. The cumulative trade deficit with India in the last four years to 2020 under the Trump regime was $92 billion—an average of $23.0 billion a year—as against China's $1.5 trillion—an average of $375 billion a year. Still, even the so-called friendly Trump regime did not differentiate between China and India, and similar punitive tariff measures were taken against India.

Indians View US More Unfavourably Than They Would Otherwise Do

In 2002, the PEW survey showed 54 per cent of a polled Indian population expressing a favourable opinion of the US. In the 2005 survey, it had shot up to 71 per cent, the highest of any country polled. In the 2017 survey, however, only 49 per cent Indians viewed the US favourably, while, significantly, 47 per cent viewed Russia favourably. The March 2014 survey said that while 36 per cent Indians saw the US as a partner of India, 16 per cent saw the US as an enemy and 21 per cent saw it as neither, which meant that more Indians saw the US not as a partner.

Undeniably, therefore, there is a certain popular trust deficit in India—a democracy—which the government of the day cannot ignore. And this has to do with the inexplicable preference of the US for China and Pakistan. Even though, at least since the dawn of the 21st century, there has been no hostility between the US and India like during the Cold War period, the norms on which the US makes its preferences between India and China and between India and Pakistan is not clear. This obviously has had a bearing on Indo-US relations in the mind of Indians.

What the US Needs to Introspect for 21st Century Relations

Bilateral relations with the US, or multilateral relations inclusive of it, have never been easy to maintain or manage for even its friendly nations. Henry Kissinger's oft quoted quip 'it may be dangerous to be America's enemy, but to be America's friend is fatal' might be extreme as a view, but certainly not outlandish.

The US needs to become more reliable as a friend. The way the US has worked to befriend China through Pakistan and totally disregarded and even turned hostile to India, has exposed its profession about democracy as being just lip service.

20th Century Rules Will Not Suit 21st Century

It is not because America has had bad intentions or goals. It is because of two reasons. One, America did not and even now does not have a comprehensive philosophy which is inclusive of people whose way of life is not consistent with its own or its world view. It may tolerate and engage with the other view like it did in the case of Middle East Islamist nations or with autocratic Communist China when it sees a benefit for itself.

Liberal America is ideological, which is exclusive like autocratic Chinese communism. Liberalism, which should have been an inclusive philosophy, has itself become an unbridled one and thus, an exclusive ideology to be exported. The US idea of exporting ideological liberalism is now being copied by China which is trying to package for export its autocratic model. The US tried to export its social, political liberal ideology based on the one-size-fits-all (OSFA) anthropology of modernity through the UN and other global institutions in the post-World War II period.

As the new millennium dawned, the US began moderating and retracting from that view, when in 2005, the G-20 nations moved away from the OSFA model, followed by the World Bank in 2008 and finally in 2010–13, by the very UN which propounded and mandated it for all underdeveloped of the world.

The experience of the 20th century world has shown that no ideology is universal. No single political or economic model will suit the entire world. The rules of the 20th century, bilateral or multilateral, will not apply to the 21st century.

US Needs Inclusive, 360 Degree Understanding of the World

It is necessary for the US, which has the responsibility to soft land the world in transition from the post-Cold War order to a changed world order, to introspect on its own past and of the world led by it.

Candidly speaking, with its unique protected geography and history unburdened by the ancient past, and a difficult recall of how it came into being, America is not a country which has had the traditional cultural, social, religious and political experience and learning of other countries with a different history and difficult past.

America began on a clean slate, a luxury which no other nation has had. It is, therefore, not a country possessed of traditional diversity and peoples and the resultant experience to have a 360 degree understanding of the diverse world.

The diversity of the US is modern diversity created by it under its state-made laws. The US experience or understanding of diversity is not natural diversity. The US diversity began as a conforming diversity regulated by rules. But the diversity of other nations, particularly India's, is not an unregulated, natural diversity. The difference between the two, to use a biological example, is the difference between a biological park in which diverse plants are arranged in an order and a forest, or to use a zoological example, between a zoo in which diverse animals live in an orderly manner and diverse animals in a forest.

Traditional diversity, which is natural, is different from modern diversity which is regulated and orderly. The universalist ideology of liberalism of the US tends to apply modern rules of regulated diversity like ultra-individualism, unbridled individualism as universal political and social ideology to societies with traditional diversity which is unregulated, in fact, in some cases, even unregulatable.

This compels the US to view the world, wrongly, through its own glasses. It makes the liberal ideological US intrusive in diverse areas like human rights (that is sans human duties), individualism (sans individual's duties to families, extended families and even communities) as the establishment rule which contradicts the way of life in a traditional society. This comprehensive understanding should be the beginning of the US approach to the world.

US Needs to Study Indian Philosophy of Inclusiveness

The 21st century world is becoming multi-polar-based on not just political or economic power, but also because of civilisational, cultural and social diversity. It needs a philosophy to understand and work in a world of natural diversity. The rules of contrived and regulated diversity, which is the formula of the US, are not only inadequate to deal with the changing world, but they may prove to be the cause of conflicts and even wars. The only workable rule is to allow each nation and society to live the way it is used to without intrusive alien force as ideas or institutions.

'Influence Yes, Intrusiveness No' should be the new approach. Here, the ancient Indian model of recognising as legitimate multiple diversities that is endogamous and natural to each community and society is the only way.

India's philosophy of not just tolerating the 'other view' but accepting it as legitimate for the other, as Swami Vivekananda proclaimed on American soil in 1893, is the way forward for the world.

Over three decades of research to compile the data on mass murders in the world from the 5th century BCE to the 20th century CE, Prof. R. J. Rummel of Hawaii University found that India was free of mass killing till the 13th century, whereafter, killing began in India with external invasions. It is evident that India, which was always the most populous in the world with diversities unknown to the rest of the world, had been peaceful and harmonious for 1800 years, according to Prof. Rummel.

It is evident from Rummel's data that ancient Indian philosophy of harmony in diversity has worked in a naturally and massively diversified society. India is in that sense a mini world and even a universe. The Indian philosophy of coexistence with nature extended the idea of living with diversity to animal-dom and plant-dom also. That is why India, with a land area of just 2.4 per cent of the world, and, with a population close to 18 per cent of the world, has a biodiversity which is seven to eight per cent of the globe.

The US and India need to partner each other to formulate a futuristic philosophy for a global order. The US per capita annual consumption of meat is over 100 kilograms and India's is less than four kilograms. If liberalism is extended to promote

US food habits, as is happening because of intrusive liberalism, which is being advocated from the US and entering India, the animal biodiversity of India will be destroyed soonest.

The best way to strengthen the strategic partnership between the US, the most powerful democracy, and India, the most populous democracy, is to work on a philosophical, rather than an ideological model. This endeavour will make India and the US partners in a philosophy for global governance which will truly be non-intrusive philosophical liberalism as distinct from intrusive ideological liberalism, an approach which no nation can object or reject. This approach can make India and US allies in both thought and action.

Key to Deepening Indo-US Relations is US Understanding of Indian Civilisation

Without civilisational understanding, US institutions will tend to be intrusive of Indian society and that will undermine the deepening of strategic relations between the two. The US ought to come to terms with the fact that the rest of the world cannot be shaped in the mirror image of the US. In a world that is rising in civilisational consciousness, India too will be increasingly civilisationally conscious. India cannot, as it has been doing in the past, for too long suppress its civilisational impulses in future. The Indian civilisation and the US prescription of norms for the world and India are bound to be a divide between the two largest and greatest democracies. This will impede the perfection of their political and strategic relations. It is also important for the US to think of how to respond to the emerging civilisational paradigm in the world. There is a clear mismatch between the contemporary individualist paradigm and the emerging civilisational paradigm.

The US has to act fast on this issue, otherwise, unlike the US, which tends to be intrusive of others' civilizational disposition, China, which is now ceaselessly expounding its civilisational identity, will recognise and accept the civilisational autonomy and aspirations of different nations and exploit to its favour the emerging civilisational paradigmatic world.

The US has to increase its understanding of the world and the best civilisation to begin with is India, which is accommodative, inclusive, non-conflicting and environmentally compatible. That will also deepen strategic relations and might even turn India and US into allies. This, however, cannot happen unless the US begins to fill in the gaps between its individualism and liberalism driven world view and the Indian civilisational perspective that is a trade-off between individualism and collectivism.

As things stand, India and the US can work for deep relations, but not deeper than strategic relations. According to a spot survey conducted during a Centre for New American Security (CNAS) webinar on 18 March 2021 on the 'Future of India-US relations,' the overwhelming opinion was that while in the next ten years, India-US relations would become much stronger, there is negligible prospect of the two forging an alliance. Unless India and the US forge an inclusive philosophic alliance, an inclusive philosophic India and an exclusive ideological US can remain strategic partners, but not philosophic allies.

Any attempt to fast forward the Indo-US relations without bridging the gap between civilisational India and liberal America will not find full resonance with the people of India, as they have managed to align their traditional life with the demands of the contemporary world and gained their own modernity. They will not be able to accept or digest the current American worldview as theirs or the world's.

8

Explosive Revelations of Fraud in Ease of Doing Business Ranking by World Bank

Need for Global Audit of Diverse Global Ranking Business Affecting the Brand and Character of Nations

The Western world had developed over a century and particularly since World War II, and more particularly since the Post-Cold War, institutions and methods to rank nations and peoples on abstract subjects like cultures, values, economies, education, politics and environment on norms which were mostly West-centric and not universal. Many institutions, which are in the business of ranking, brand themselves as non-profit institutions or exclusive clubs, even though some of the rankings are by institutions like the World Bank. These rankings, most of them not supervised or monitored or audited, have had and continue to have a huge impact on the community of nations and global discourse as they grade nations, discount some, and promote some. These rankings have tended to promote largely the Western way of life as superior and the rest should follow the West, as indeed even the United Nations told the Underdeveloped Nations in the year 1951. This ranking game which has been going on uncontested and unprobed, has been, by accident, explosively exposed in the case of one of the most trusted rankings, the Ease of Doing Business by the World Bank, as a fraud manipulated by China. This fraud has forced the World Bank to give up ranking of Ease of Doing Business of nations. This is a rude awakening which calls for a probe into, and audit of, ranking businesses and actors who do this lucrative business, as to who funds them, what are their motives and what are the norms they employ to rank nations on such abstract and semi-abstract subjects as good country, soft power, transparency, freedom, fragile states, human development, human happiness, social progress and so on.

While most ranking is based on West-centric homogeneity and disregards the diversity of the world and also are intellectually inadequate, socially unrepresentative and culturally biased, there have always been apprehensions of political and corrupt influence in ranking. But what has till now been only a strong apprehension, has now been proved by evidence—namely that even at the level of the World Bank ranking, there is bribery and influence peddling to get the improved rank. This sordid and shocking story, of China and Saudi Arabia bribing their way to better ranking, coming out, may be due to the disengagement taking place between the West and China.

Explosive Revelations of Fraud and Manipulation by China in the World Bank's Ease of Doing Business Ranking Index

In a shocking development which struck at the root of the credibility of the global financial institutions, the World Bank scrapped the Doing Business rankings due to data irregularities. Reports said an audit by the law firm, WilmerHale, mandated by the World Bank, released last week, revealed the role of the World Bank's senior management in manipulating data in order to please China and Saudi Arabia. Not many statistical indicators have been as influential in the world of investment as the World Bank's Doing Business index. The bank has even made loans conditional on improvements in a country's Doing Business ranking. Against this high background of the index, the independent investigation into the Ease of Doing Business 2018 and 2020 ranking by the bank, found that Kristalina Georgieva, who served as the bank's chief executive officer from 2017 to 2019 and is now the managing director of the International Monetary Fund, applied 'pressure' to have China ranked more favourably. The WilmerHale review was written by a group assembled by the World Bank in December 2020, after a series of internal audits revealed data irregularities in reports on China, Saudi Arabia, the United Arab Emirates and Azerbaijan. It is significant that neither did the World Bank's internal audit raise any question, nor did the WilmerHale review say anything about India's rise of 67 in the index between 2016 and 2020—the very period when it found that China and Saudi Arabia were favoured. The bank had paused the annual rankings last year as the issues emerged.

The 84-page WilmerHale review, written by senior academics and economists, was published on the bank's website three weeks after it was submitted to World Bank Chief Economist Carmen Reinhart. The investigation noted that a senior staff member had changed Saudi Arabia's data to 'reward' the country. It also said that Georgieva 'became directly involved in efforts to improve China's ranking.' This included her encouraging changes to the methodology used for the ranking. The investigation indicated that Georgieva saw this as a key to remaining in Beijing's good graces, thanking one official involved in the process for doing his 'bit for multilateralism.' The investigation noted specific 'pressure' applied by the then-CEO and her adviser to make 'specific changes to China's data points in an effort to increase its ranking at precisely the same time the country was expected to play a key role in the bank's capital increase campaign.' The damning review has shaken the financial world and has exposed the extent to which China has been able to penetrate into the high reaches of the global financial system.

World Bank Admission: The WilmerHale 'Report Speaks for Itself'

World Bank President David Malpass told CNBC that the WilmerHale Report 'speaks for itself'; it is worth noting, in passing, that Malpass is a Trump appointee. Media reports said the WilmerHale review calls for a series of reforms to address the 'methodological integrity' of the Doing Business report, citing what it called 'a pattern of government efforts to interfere' with scoring for reports in past years. 'The World Bank needs introspection. It has been advocating country reforms for better governance, transparency and practices. Now, it has to use the prescription for its own reform,' said Mauricio Cardenas, the Columbia University professor and former Colombian finance minister, who chaired the WilmerHale expert panel. The report made a damning indictment that, 'We have been informed of multiple cases where national governments have attempted to manipulate the DB scores by exerting pressure on individual contributors.' Pointing to lawyers, accountants and other professionals, it said, 'World Bank staff mentioned several countries where they believe government officials have instructed contributors how to respond. And even in the absence of explicit government pressure, of course, the perceived threat of retaliation may influence the scores contributors report.'

China Bribed and Manipulated the Ranking in Its Favour

The Investment Monitor, in its report titled: 'Weekly Data: The Doing Business Scandal Shows the Perils of Mixing Politics and Data', reported how China manipulated the ranking in its favour by donating—which means, in ordinary language, 'by bribing'. It said that the WilmerHale report 'sheds light on a third constituency for whom the Doing Business ranking was produced: donors'. It says that 'in the run up to the release of the 2018 ranking, the WilmerHale report states, the World Bank was attempting to secure a new tranche of funding from donor countries. China was signalling its apprehension. Its diplomats had expressed displeasure at the country's ranking in the 2017 index. Senior World Bank officials, allegedly under the direction of President Jim Yong Kim, ordered the Doing Business team to try various tweaks to the data to bump China up the rankings, such as including data from Hong Kong and Macau, or basing the scores on China's best-performing city. When these didn't work, the index's founder, Simeon Djankov, is alleged to have been drafted in to tweak the underlying numbers.'

The Bank's Ranking Served Those Who Paid Donations and Consultancy Fee to It

Asking 'Who did Doing Business really serve?', the Investment Monitor wrote: 'Scathingly exposed how the numbers were sold. The World Bank is a subscription-based organisation, largely reliant on funds contributed by a handful of large or wealthy countries. Unlike the UN, voting power is allocated based on these 'subscriptions'. Six countries currently hold 42 per cent of the World Bank's subscriptions and 40 per cent of the organisation's voting power—the US, Japan, China, Germany, France and the UK. In contrast, 150 of the world's poorest countries collectively hold just 15 per cent of shares and 18 per cent of the voting power. China is likely to remain a significant source of future funding increases for the World Bank. Despite accounting for 18.8 per cent of global GDP, China currently holds just 5.3 per cent of World Bank subscriptions—suggesting sizeable growth potential. Not all of the World Bank's income comes from subscriptions. By the time of the 2020 report, it was Saudi Arabia threatening to tighten the purse strings. Although the Gulf kingdom is responsible for just 2.7 per cent of World Bank member contributions, it offers the bank lucrative advisory contracts. After concerns that Jordan had beaten Saudi Arabia to the top spot in the 2020 Doing Business index, the WilmerHale report states that the team was instructed to boost the latter's score, which they did by altering the underlying data. It is significant that both supposedly charitable donations and private sector-style consultancy fees led senior World Bank figures to alter the numbers. The conflicts of interest, lack of accountability and centralisation of decision-making that characterised the world's most influential and respected international index are unlikely to be entirely absent in other, less scrutinised, publications. The appeal of such indices is their simplicity, but that simplicity always masks the messiness of data collection and the arbitrariness of combining data into a single metric—inconvenient truths that make methodological opacity all the more appealing. The Doing Business scandal shows the dangers of such an approach.

Soft Power 30 and Consultancy to Governments

The Concept of Soft Power which became part of international relations discourse from about the 1980s, was expounded by Harvard Scholar Joseph Nye in his book 'Bound to Lead: The Changing Nature of American Power.' In the book, Nye said: 'A country's ability to influence the preferences and behaviours of various actors in the international arena (states, corporations, communities, publics, etc.) through attraction or persuasion rather than coercion.' He identified three dimensions of power; coercion by military force, influence by offering economic incentives and, finally, the ability to co-opt other states by the nation's appeal based on its culture and values. But the entire concept has been perverted by commercial interests which have turned juries to decide what is Soft Power and which country is higher or lower in the Soft Power Index. Just look at the character of the actors who have occupied the jury's position.

The first to list and fix the norms for the index in the year 2010, to measure Soft Power, was the media company Monocle. *Monocle* is a global affairs and lifestyle magazine, 24-hour radio station, website, retailer and media brand. The *Monocle* magazine is for young, stylish, and business-oriented jet setters, who receive free subscriptions. It was previously described as a travel-culture magazine, and a 'repository of lifestyle sensuality and gaywad uptightness'. Gaywad is slang for gay. It is this leisure, sensual and casual magazine which is the jury fixing the norms of soft power and, in whose name, the serious subject of the global soft power index runs. On the basis of that index, the global discourse of which is soft and which is not is taking place. Obviously, the concept and determinants of soft power have been commercialised.

The other index is devised by the global cement brand, Portland Communications, which is a consultancy company that is clearly a lobbying outfit. It describes its work thus: 'We help clients make an impact on the debate, on the decision and on the bottom line. Our work spans strategy, content and delivery, supported by in-house insights, digital and design teams. We work with a range of clients from large corporates in a range of sectors through to start-ups, NGOs and governments.' It goes on to say,

> We help governments and leaders shape the future, reaching and engaging the audiences that matter.
>
> Portland's Government Advisory practice helps governments and leaders to build, profile and protect reputations. We use insights, data and creative thinking to power smart communications that reach the right audience with the right message in the right place to achieve maximum impact.
>
> We are passionate about helping deliver real change, and our team brings experience at the highest levels of government. Through our offices in London, Brussels, Berlin, Paris, Doha, Washington DC, Singapore and Nairobi we have supported governments across five continents.
>
> As publishers of Soft Power 30, the world's first and only soft power index, Portland understands the value of attraction and persuasion. From measuring soft power, to developing and delivering international positioning and branding campaigns, we help nations, states and cities improve and manage their reputation.

Clearly Portland, which helps leaders and governments to profile, build and protect their reputations, also claims that it publishes the only soft power index—Soft Power 30—and, 'from measuring soft power to developing international positioning and branding campaigns, we help nations to improve the manage their reputations', which is a clear admission of conflict of interest.

Selling Ranks for Fee—Common for Both Ease of Doing Business and Soft Power Ranking

What Portland does, namely take advisory fees and give soft power ranks, is precisely what the World Bank did—namely take consultancy fees and give ease of doing business rank. The WilmerHale report condemned the World Bank for selling advice and giving rank. It called for the bank to stop selling consulting services to governments aimed at improving a country's score, noting that they constituted an apparent conflict of interest. 'The World Bank should not simultaneously engage in scoring countries' business environment while accepting payment to coach countries on how to improve their scores,' the authors wrote. The World Bank offered these 'Reimbursible Advisory Services,' or RAS, in a number of countries, including some of those implicated in the data manipulation investigation, such as China and Saudi Arabia, the review said. In December 2020, the review said, one internal audit reported that bank management had pressured nine of 15 staff to manipulate data in the 2018 and 2020 issues of the Doing Business index, boosting Saudi Arabia to the 'most reformed' spot globally and buoying the rankings of the United Arab Emirates and China, while dropping Azerbaijan from the top 10 rankings, the external advisers reported. The separate WilmerHale report said that changes to Saudi Arabia's data were 'likely the result of efforts by a senior bank staff member to achieve a desired outcome and reward Saudi Arabia for the important role it played in the Bank community, including its significant and ongoing RAS projects.' Justin Sandefur, Senior Fellow at the Center for Global Development, in Washington, and another member of the expert panel that produced audit report, said that it showed 'a governance problem' at the World Bank and that he had not seen any assurances that similar problems would not continue with other data sets.

Patently Fraudulent World-Wide Press Freedom Index

- A Paris-based NGO, Reporters Without Borders (RSF), comes out with the Press Freedom Index to judge the degree of freedom available to journalists in different countries of the world. This index places India, the world's largest, the most vibrant and liberal democracy and arguably the most plural society, down below at number 142 among 180 countries assessed for this evaluation. This is two notches below 140, the position occupied by India a year ago. The world and Indian media cry hoarse 'Indian media downgraded'. A Suryaprakash, a valued colleague at the VIF, has analysed the shoddy, even fraudulent work, done by the RSF.

- The criteria evaluated in the RSF questionnaire, which has eighty-seven questions, are pluralism, media independence, media environment and self-censorship, legislative framework, transparency and the quality of the infrastructure that supports the production of news and information. This online questionnaire is sent by the RSF to eighteen NGOs across the world and a network of 150 correspondents, and to researchers, jurists, human rights activists chosen by these correspondents. About 10 per cent of the respondents are foreign correspondents working in the country being evaluated. See how Suryaprakash has actually made the RSF ranking a laughing stock.
- Suryapraksh says that while the RSF places India at 142, it places Burkina Faso at 108, ahead of India by a number of 36. Has anyone heard of this great nation? This is the country that was identified by the US State Department some time ago in its Trafficking in Persons Report, saying that slavery continued to exist in Burkina Faso and that Burkinabè children were often the victims. It said slavery is an entrenched institution with a long history that dates back to the Arab slave trade. In 2018, an estimated 82,000 people in the country were living under 'modern slavery' according to the Global Slavery Index.
- He says that RSF places the Republic of Maldives at 79—63 places above India—in the index. See what the Maldives Constitution says. It says that Islam is the religion of the State of Maldives and 'no law contrary to the tenets of Islam shall be enacted in the Maldives'. Article 9 (d) of the Constitution declares that 'a non-Muslim may not become a citizen of the Maldives'.
- He finds the Sultanate of Oman at 135—seven places above India—in the RSF Index. Oman is an Arab, Islamic nation. Article 2 of the Constitution of Oman says the religion of the state is Islam and Islamic Sharia is the basis for legislation. The system of governance is Sultani, hereditary

in the male descendants of Sayyid Turki bin Said bin Sultan, provided that whomever is to be chosen from amongst them as successor 'shall be a Muslim, mature, rational and the legitimate son of Omani Muslim parents'. It is neither a secular state, nor a republic, and there is no gender equality because the constitution ordains that the head of state shall be a Muslim male.

- He finds the Comoros placed at number 75—67 places above India—in the RSF Index. The Comoros Constitution says that the Comorian people solemnly affirm their will 'to draw from Islam, the religion of the state, the permanent inspiration of the principles and rules that govern the union…'.
- He sees Argentina, a declared Christian state, is at number 64—78 places above India—in the index. Argentina's Constitution declares that the federal government supports the Roman Catholic Apostolic religion.
- He points to Malta, which is at number 81—61 points above India—in the RSF Index. The Constitution of Malta declares that 'the religion of Malta is the Roman Catholic Apostolic Religion'. It says the authorities of the Roman Catholic Apostolic Church 'have the duty and the right to teach which principles are right and which are wrong' and that religious teaching of the Roman Catholic Apostolic Faith shall be provided in all State schools as part of compulsory education.
- Suryaprakash points out that the pride of the first place in the RSF Index goes to the Kingdom of Norway. It is 142 places above India as the nation with the maximum press freedom. Norway's Constitution, which describes its form of government as a limited and hereditary monarchy, says 'Our values will remain our Christian and humanistic heritage'. Laying down the eligibility criteria to be head of State in Norway, it says 'The King shall at all times profess the Evangelical-Lutheran religion'. It also grants immunity to the head of state—'the King's person is sacred; he cannot be censured or accused'. In other words, it is not a secular state; it is not Republican; and one of the basic fundamentals of democracy—equality before

the law and the equal application of the laws (Art 14 in the Indian Constitution)—has no place in Norway.

- He says that Denmark, which is number three in the RSF list, declares that the Evangelical Lutheran Church shall be the established Church of Denmark, 'and as such will be supported by the State'. This means that 'it is based on the Holy Bible, various ecclesiastical symbolic books, and the teachings of the German theologian Martin Luther…'. Today, the State has a 'duty to support the Church of Denmark financially and in other ways'.
- He points to Greece at number 65 in this Index. Article 3 of its constitution declares that 'the prevailing religion in Greece is that of the Eastern Orthodox Church of Christ. The orthodox Church of Greece, acknowledging our Lord Jesus Christ as its head, is inseparably united in doctrine with the Great Church of Christ in Constantinople and with every other Church of Christ of the same doctrine'.

Taking the very criteria adopted by the RSF for the evaluation of nations, that is 'pluralism, media independence, media environment and self-censorship, legislative framework, transparency and the quality of the infrastructure that supports the production of news and information', Suryaprakash says that many nations which have been placed above India, are actually religious and would not even qualify as democracies—leave aside ensuring freedom for journalists. Saying that a democratic environment is the sine qua non for a free press, Suryaprakash points out, that strangely, there is little or no weightage in the RSF Index for promoting the fundamentals of democracy like separation of religion and State, a republican government, a constitution guaranteeing equality, inviolable commitment to freedom of speech and expression; an unambiguous commitment to pursuit of secular values, the fundamental right to equality before law and the equal protection of the laws, gender equality and the fundamental right to life and personal liberty. There is no scope for any of these constitutional values in most of the countries, particularly, in the Islamic nations mentioned above. The RSF website says the degree of freedom available to journalists is determined by the pooling responses of experts to an elaborate questionnaire devised by it. The RSF website claims that press freedom in countries is judged on six values, namely, the touchstone of pluralism, media independence, media environment and self-censorship, legislative framework that governs the media, transparency, and the quality of infrastructure that supports the production of news and information. On every test, Suryaprakash establishes that India is qualitatively and quantitatively ahead of most nations which are listed above India. Pointing out that the RSF also measures the degree to which opinions are represented in the media, it believes that there is greater pluralism in media in theocracies and Islamic states and states where even citizenship is denied to non-Muslims than in India, the most pluralistic society in the world!

Finally, Suryaprakash says that the work of RSF is subjective, biased and non-transparent and that the biggest flaw is the complete disrespect, by the RSF, for the foundational principles of democracy. He rightly says 'It seems to delude itself into believing that press freedom can exist in wholly non-democratic environments. For this reason alone, its conclusions must be rejected lock, stock and barrel. RSF must read the Constitution of India and compare it with other constitutions. It must look at the robust institutions that propel democratic traditions in India and first define democracy itself, before venturing into the preparation of a global index. In other words, it must go back to the drawing board.'

The RSF index, which places India at 142 and below theocracies, is laughable at best and fraudulent at worst.

Need for Global Audit of the Ranking Businesses under the Aegis of the UN

Unjust, unfair, biased, fraudulent and purchased global ranking can do great damage to different nations. Countries like India, which are not into the game of lobbying or buying rankings, are greatly prejudiced by unregulated rankings which are given huge publicity in the media for diverse reasons, including political and financial. There are diverse and abstract ranking businesses some of which are listed here.

General and political rankings like

1. Good Country Index
2. Soft Power 30
3. Country Brand Index
4. Transparency International: Global Corruption Barometer and Corruption Perceptions Index
5. Economist Intelligence Unit: Democracy Index
6. Freedom House: Freedom in the World
7. Reporters Without Borders: Worldwide Press Freedom Index
8. List of Countries by Consultation on Rule-making
9. Worldwide Governance Indicators
10. Fragile States Index
11. World Justice Project Rule of Law Index
12. V-Dem Institute: Democracy Indicies
13. Economist Intelligence Unit: Where-to-be-born Index 2013
14. Globalisation Index
15. Global Gender Gap Report
16. Global Retirement Index
17. Legatum Prosperity Index
18. Save the Children: State of the World's Mothers Report
19. Social Progress Index
20. Walk Free Foundation: Global Slavery Index
21. World Giving Index
22. World Happiness Report
23. The Economic Freedom of the World Index
24. The Human Freedom Index
25. The Index of Freedom in the World
26. Worldwide Press Freedom Index
27. World Index of Moral Freedom time
28. Max Range Monthly Index of Democracy

29. Varieties of Democracy (V-Dem) Institute
30. The Democracy Index
31. The CIRI Human Rights Data Project
32. Freedom in the World
33. Freedom of the Press
34. The Index of Economic Freedom
35. Polity Data Series
36. Social Mobility Index

Economic rankings like

1. World Economic Forum: Global Competitiveness Report
2. World Economic Forum: Financial Development Index
3. International Institute for Management Development: World Competitiveness Yearbook
4. Gini index: List of countries by income equality
5. Bloomberg Innovation Index
6. Global Innovation Index
7. International Innovation Index
8. Index of Economic Freedom
9. Ease of Doing Business Index
10. Indigo Index

Environment rankings like

1. Climate Change Performance Index (CCPI)
2. Environmental Performance Index (EPI)
3. Environmental Sustainability Index (ESI)
4. Environmental Vulnerability Index (EVI)
5. Happy Planet Index (HPI)
6. List of Countries by Ecological Footprint
7. Sustainable Society Index (SSI)
8. The Global 100 (G100)

Educational rankings like

1. Education Index
2. Trends in International Mathematics and Science Study

3. Programme for International Student Assessment
4. Progress in International Reading Literacy Study
5. World Intellectual Property Indicators
6. EF English Proficiency Index
7. Programming Ability Index
8. International Association for the Evaluation of Educational Achievement: Trends in International Mathematics and Science Study Educational Testing Service: 2003–2004 TOEFL Test Year Data Summary
9. Webometrics Ranking of World Universities

These rankings, most of which are abstract and not quantitative, can make or mar and even wreck a nation's brand, respect and acceptability, given the way the rankings are publicised and even made use of in global discourse and also for deciding on policies towards nations, including investment, travel and business. There is absolutely no say for the affected nations in the way they are placed in the index like in the RSF Media Freedom Index, which is laughable and yet, very much relevant in the global discourse. When aggressive nations can manipulate even World Bank-like bodies, no one knows who cannot manipulate these ranking bodies, most of which are NGOs and rely on donations and consultancy work, like Portland, which does consultancy for countries for the Soft Power 30 Index and also ranks them!

India, which is among the nations which cannot employ unethical and corrupt tactics like others, will have to take the lead to get the global powers and the United Nations to get these different bodies, and the rankings that they give, audited and a special fund must be constituted for this purpose. Otherwise, not only ranks which are bought and sold can damage nations, also the ranks which are biased and prejudiced can harm nations, particularly India.

9

A 50-Year Chronology: How the US Raised Its Own Frankenstein Monster, Bhasmasur China, a Lesson for Itself and for All Free Nations

Recalling and reliving what the post-Cold War unprincipled balance of power theory did do to the US and to other countries in the democratic world, and what it did to create China, a Frankenstein monster for itself

To understand where the world is in the context of China's challenge to the West, it is necessary to trace the 50-year history of engagement of China by the US on assumptions which were founded more on only pursuit of power and money, without ideological and philosophical considerations.

This short-sighted strategy, sans the lessons on which human history of thousands of years, rested on the foundation of the modern Western worldview that the rest of the world could be evangelised into the Western way of life through the economic and trade advantages offered by the West. The West had clearly ignored the historic fact that each nation and people has its own soul or DNA which cannot be fundamentally altered. That each nation and people, and their culture and way of life, are different and all are not the same, is self-evident in the very idea of a diverse world. But the West thought wrongly that by breaking down and atomising societies and nations into individuals through its institutions of liberal market and liberal democracy, it could alter their DNA. The West could achieve a certain degree of success with smaller societies and nations, but its bold and ambitious experiment with a huge and autocratic China, to moderate and melt its autocracy into a democracy through the institution of liberal market, resulted in a game in which China has emerged as its Frankenstein monster.

How the West went wrong is a lesson for the West definitely, but it is equally a lesson for all, so that no successful nation—be it the US or China—would attempt something similar, namely to evangelise other nations and people to turn its mirror image. Here is where the five decades of engagement between China and the US serves as an extremely critical lesson for us all.

A recall of five decades of US-China relations—two decades of successful US attempts to lure China out of the Soviet orbit, two decades of active engagement, particularly economic engagement with it, and almost a decade of unmentioned equal and strategic partnership between the two, has finally ended now where it should, in a clearly stated policy of containment of China by the US without, of course, using the 'C' word as yet. A China nurtured and built by the US at the cost of its own principles of freedom and democracy, is now seen by the US as its own Frankenstein monster—or Bhasmasur to the Indian idiom—that is now challenging its own creator. At every stage and turn in the timeline of events, the US had engaged China in its own self-interest to remain as the superpower, not in the interest of the democratic world order of which the US had always laid claim as the leader.

US Relations with China—A Timeline That Tells Everything: Reliving the Five Decades

To understand from where 50 years before, to where now the US has turned, and how the US had either assumed that China would reform and fall in line with its world view or believed that if it did not, it could control and discipline it, and how contrary to all its intelligent assessment and judgement, China has emerged as the Bhasmasur for the US, here is a glimpse of the five decade history as culled out from the Council for Foreign Relations (CFR) timeline of US relations with China—which is telling. Unless the five decades are re-lived again, it is not possible to fully realise how the US created its Bhasmasur.

1971: Ping Pong Diplomacy, Henry Kissinger Secret Visit, China on UNSC

The first sign of thaw between the two was the famous period of ping pong diplomacy, with China inviting the US team and first American journalists to enter China after 1949 in April 1971. This was followed by the secret visit of Henry Kissinger, the then US Secretary of State, in July 1971.

Shortly thereafter, the United Nations recognised the People's Republic of China, which unseated Taiwan from the UN Security Council for China to become its member. These far-reaching moves were initiated by the US not so much for the good of the democratic world, but in its own self-interest, guided entirely by the unprincipled balance of power sans the ideology of democracy. This was the starting point of building China, which the US now sees as a Frankenstein monster, that targets the US itself. *The Kissinger Transcripts: Top Secret Talks with Beijing and Moscow* clearly brings out why the US chose to have dialogue with China. The sole idea was to contain Russia and sustain American power. The Kissinger Transcript says 'it was suspicion of Moscow that had drawn Nixon and Kissinger closer to Beijing. The goal was a détente that would contain the Soviets and sustain American power', despite the fact that Kissinger himself perceived the Chinese leadership as 'tough ideologues who totally disagree with us where the world is going'.

Kissinger knew that there was an irreconcilable contradiction between the world view of the US and that of China, which is now explicit to the US. Kissinger also rationalised the US-China dialogue, for that would force the Soviets to improve relations with the US to prevent China from getting closer to the US.

During the 1971 India-Pakistan War, Kissinger viewed India as a Soviet proxy to be countered by leaning toward Beijing's ally, Pakistan, and, if necessary, by providing military support for China, notwithstanding that China and Pakistan were autocracies, even though Kissinger regarded India as 'the pillar of democracy'.

Kissinger admits to this contradiction himself. His transcript on his dialogue with the then Soviet Ambassador to US, Anatoly Dorbrynin, says, 'We then turned the conversation to India. Dobrynin said he wanted us to be sure to understand that the Soviets were doing their best to restrain India. They wanted peace in the subcontinent. It was an ironic development where they were lined up with what looked we had always thought was the pillar of democracy while we were lined up with the Chinese'—a clever admission of unprincipled association with autocrats to oppose the pillar of democracy.

See: Chapter I titled See How Those Pieces Could Be Moved to Our Advantage': Washington-Moscow-Beijing, 1971–72.
https://archive.nytimes.com/www.nytimes.com/books/first/b/burr-kissinger.html

1972: Nixon Visit to China improved US-China Relations

US President Richard Nixon's eight-day-long trip to China (in February 1972), when he met Chairman Mao and signed the Shanghai Communiqué, which set the stage for improved US-China relations by allowing China and America to discuss difficult issues, particularly Taiwan.

This was the starting point of the US betrayal of Taiwan, which became an illustration in geopolitics of how, for maintaining its own supremacy, Washington would, and could, give up a loyal friend.

1978–79: Full Diplomatic Status, Accepting One China Policy, Severing Ties with Taiwan

The most crucial development of the first decade of thawing relations between the two was the grant of full diplomatic recognition to China, acknowledging mainland China's One China principle and severing diplomatic ties with Taiwan. This led to another significant development of Chinese Vice Premier Deng Xiaoping's visit to the US. But in April, Congress adopted the Taiwan Relations Act, which preserved continued commercial and cultural relations between the US and Taiwan and also required Washington to provide Taipei with defensive arms, without officially violating the US's One China policy.

Firstly, China got UNSC membership almost for free, and now, the One China Policy again free, paying no price for either. This was in return for just an assurance not to be with the Soviets and to be a check on India, whom Kissinger regarded as a Soviet proxy.

1982: In July, the Reagan regime pledged to honour the Taiwan Relations Act, not mediate between Taiwan and China and set no date to terminate arms sales to Taiwan. In August, it signed a third communiqué with the PRC to normalise relations and reaffirm its commitment to the One China policy. Reagan's presidential campaign supported stronger ties with Taiwan, but his administration worked to improve relations with China at the height of US concerns over Soviet expansionism. In June 1984, Reagan visited China and in that same month, permitted Beijing to purchase American military equipment.

The Kissinger model continued. Richard Nixon went to China and Pakistan, but never came to India. After Jimmy Carter's visit to India in 1978, the first US President to visit India after him was Bill Clinton, after 22 years, in the year 2000. That was after India had become a nuclear power. Had India not become a nuclear power, the US President might not have cared to visit India, as the latter would never have figured in the balance of power theory at all.

1989: In June, the Chinese military crushed a Tiananmen Square student uprising for democracy with tanks. At its peak, the uprising saw a million students assembling to ask for democracy, leaving hundreds, even thousands of protesters, dead and thousands of others injured. In the mildest response to this modern day genocide, the US just suspended military sales to Beijing and froze relations.

Just compare how the US reacted to democratic protests against autocracy at Tiananmen Square with how it acted when democratic India went nuclear in 1998. The US just froze ties with China but imposed sanctions on India.

1993: President Bill Clinton launched a policy of 'constructive engagement' with China. And four years later, Clinton secured the release of Chinese dissident Wei and Tiananmen Square protester Wang Dan, both of whom were deported by Beijing to the US.

Within four years of the Tiananmen Square genocide and after the collapse of the Soviet Union, and in return for China deporting two dissidents to the US, Washington began constructive engagement with China. This was the biggest blunder of the US. One doesn't have to be a seer to understand how hardened the converged ideological criminal minds constituting the Chinese Communist Party, government and military triumvirate must have been to consciously order the massacre of unarmed and peacefully protesting youth in hundreds and thousands. And yet, the US chose the path of constructive engagement with such deep establishment that it seems to have shown no sign of remorse over what had happened, that too after the fall of the Soviet Union, when the alibi of having to divide the enemy, didn't exist. Even 30 years later, the Chinese didn't express regret over the massacre. On the contrary, 'How can you say that China handled it improperly?' asked Chinese Defence Minister General Wei Fenghe, and added, that the massacre 'was the correct policy' before an international audience in Singapore on June 2, 2019. (*Sydney Morning Herald* 2.6.2019)

2000: In October, President Clinton signed the US-China Trade Relations Act, granting Beijing permanent normal trade relations with the United States and paved the way for China's entry into the World Trade Organisation in 2001.

Admitting Marxist China into the free global market principle-based WTO was the greatest error of both principles and judgement by the US. Just about that time (2001) the World Bank came out with a collection of works of highly eminent economists, including Amartya Sen, (who got the Nobel Prize for his work on Development as Freedom) titled *Democracy, Market, Economics and Development: An Asian Perspective*, in which the editors said five principles emerged of which the first was 'Democracy and Markets are two wheels of a cart'.

So when the US admitted China into the WTO, it was aware that autocratic and non-transparent China was disqualified to join the market-based global trade institution. After admitting Beijing, the US began pleading with the former for greater transparency. It wasn't too long before the West realised that Marxist China was exploiting the market and the rules-based WTO. Finally in 2015, the US and the EU Trade Representatives approached the WTO to declare China as a non-market economy, whereas Beijing said its admission into the WTO amounted to admitting that it was a market economy. Ultimately, the WTO ruled that China was not a market economy. But a huge and irreversible damage had been done by then.

2004: US-China Trade Rose from $5 Billion to $231 Billion

The inclusion of the opaque Marxist state in the global market had led to the runaway success of China as MNCs found autocratic China attractive for investment.

We said in RT 2020:

> The stark contrast was between China and India and how they respectively were treated by the US and West. In China, it was Marx in Politics and Democracy in Economics. It was the other way round in India, Marx in Economics and Democracy in Politics—till the early 1990s, when China was almost 15 years into development mode. The increasing strategic involvement of the West with China since the 1980s when India was hooked to the USSR, the main adversary of the US, gave China a head

> start over India. The undisclosed factor that attracted the West—which actually meant the MNC lobbies—to China was, as an authoritative study put it, 'the image of political stability (single party dictatorship in China)', 'as foreign capital is a shy deer which needs trust and stability to be tamed'. This is where—apart from the geopolitical strategic alliance of China with the later winner West, and India with the later loser USSR—even as its autocracy worked in China's favour, its democracy and freedom worked against India.

US and European businesses were comfortable operating under the umbrella of a stable autocratic China to expand their commerce.

2005: In September, recognising China as an emerging power and initiating a strategic dialogue with it, US Deputy Secretary of State Robert B. Zoellick called on Beijing to serve as a 'responsible stakeholder' and use its influence to draw such nations as Sudan, North Korea, and Iran into the international system. But that same year, North Korea walked away from the Six-Party Talks aimed at curbing Pyongyang's nuclear programme and ambitions and conducted its first nuclear test in October 2006. China served as a mediator to bring Pyongyang back to the negotiating table.

After helping build China's economic might, the US began strategically partnering China for its geopolitical goals. This opened up unprecedented possibilities for China to develop its own connections and influence in geopolitical and economic think tanks in the US and elsewhere. China began investing hugely to develop and market its own worldview through hundreds of Confucian Institutes it had set up in all academic institutions in the US and elsewhere. The lift given by the US initiating strategic dialogue with it and designating China as a 'responsible stakeholder' was an invitation to the US, global think tanks and educational institutions to associate and even crave to associate with the Chinese institutions.

2008: In September 2008, China surpassed Japan to become the largest holder of US debt—or treasuries—at around $600 billion. The growing interdependence between the US and Chinese economies becomes evident as a financial crisis threatens the global economy, fueling concerns over US-China economic imbalances.

2010: China Surpasses Japan to Become World's Second Largest Economy after US

In the second quarter of 2010, China ($5.88 trillion) surpassed Japan ($5.48 trillion) as the world's second largest economy after clocking a growth of $1.33 trillion, slightly above Japan's $1.28 trillion for that year. Goldman Sachs projects China to overtake the US in 2027.

2012: US Trade Deficit with China Soars

US trade deficit with China rose from $273.1 billion in 2010 to an all-time high of $295.5 billion in 2011. With China's ban on export of rare earth metals forcing MNCs to use metals to shift to China, the United States, the EU and Japan filed a 'request for consultations' with China at the WTO, contending that it was violating international trade norms. China slammed the move as 'rash and unfair,' and vowed to defend its rights in trade disputes.

2012: China's New Leadership

The 18th National Party Congress replaced 70 per cent members of the country's major leadership bodies—the Politburo Standing Committee, the Central Military Commission and the State Council. Li Keqiang becomes Prime Minister; Xi Jinping replaces Hu Jintao as Communist Party general secretary and chairman of the Central Military Commission, and as President in March 2013, Xi delivers a series of speeches on the 'rejuvenation' of China.

What did Xi's shift to the idea of 'rejuvenation of China' mean to the world? The Hoover Institution Study explains this shift:

> For three-and-a half decades following the end of the Maoist era, China adhered to Deng Xiaoping's policies of 'reform and opening to the outside world' and 'peaceful development.' After Deng retired as paramount leader, these principles continued to guide China's international behavior in the leadership eras of Jiang Zemin and Hu Jintao. Admonishing Chinese to 'keep your heads down and bide your time,' these party leaders sought to emphasise that China's rapid economic development and its accession to 'great power' status need not be threatening to either the existing global order or the interests of its Asian neighbours. However, since Party General Secretary Xi Jinping came to power in 2012, the situation has changed. Under his leadership, China has significantly expanded the more assertive set of policies initiated by his predecessor Hu Jintao. These policies not only seek to redefine China's place in the world as a global player, but they also have put forward the notion of a 'China option' that is claimed to be a more efficient developmental model than liberal democracy.

But studies like the Hoover Institution came late because Trumpism came too late to the US. The rise of Trumpism in the US was no accident of an election, but the compulsive impact of blind admiration of China by the US, particularlarly under the Obama administration.

2013: Obama Nearly Nods to Xi Jinping Proposal for a 'New Type of Great Power Relations'

In June, President Obama hosted President Xi for a 'shirt-sleeves summit' at the Sunnylands Estate in California in a bid to build a personal rapport with Xi and ease tense US-China relations. The leaders pledged to cooperate more effectively on pressing bilateral, regional, and global issues, including climate change and North Korea. Obama and Xi also vowed to establish a 'new model' of relations, a nod to Xi's concept of establishing a 'new type of great power relations' for the United States and China.

What POTUS Obama gave on a platter was precisely what Xi Jinping was seeking, namely a 'new type of great power relations' that would make it on par with the US in global affairs. That only rationalised and encouraged global think tanks and universities to join and work with China and drove different countries to seek China's friendship, to seek favour from, or to counter the US—the most telling examples being Pakistan and North Korea.

2015: As the Only Exception, Obama-led US Warned China over South China Sea

As the only instance of the US admonishing China in almost a quarter century, it criticised latter over the South China Sea. At the 14th annual Shangri-La Dialogue on Asian Security, finding that China was creating artificial islands on the South China Sea and placing military equipment on them (despite Beijing's claims that construction is mainly for civilian purposes), the then US Secretary of Defense asked China to halt its controversial land reclamation, saying that the US opposes 'any further militarisation' of the disputed territory.

From 1971 to 2016—At Every Stage, China was Seen as the Winner and the US as the Loser

At every stage in the Timeline of events, China had been declared the winner and the US as the loser not only by Chinese, but even other geopolitical players and observers. It was almost a one-sided love for China by the US.

In 1971, it was the US National Security Adviser who went on a secret visit to China. It was the US which made China a UNSC member and discarded loyal Taiwan without any open quid pro quo.

In 1972, Nixon's visit was again without any reciprocal visit by any top Chinese leader. Nixon opened all contentious issues, including Taiwan, for dialogue, without any corresponding move from China.

In 1978–79, Jimmy Carter established full scale diplomatic relations with mainland China; accepted the 'Government of the PRC as the sole legal government of China', severing normal ties with Taiwan, reducing it to a cultural associate. Chinese Vice Premier Deng Xiaoping visited the US—the first Chinese leader to visit the US six years after the US President's visit.

In 1982, President Reagan reaffirmed the One China Policy and visited China in 1984 without any reciprocal visit by any Chinese leader and also allowed military purchases by Beijing.

In 1993, within four years of the Tiananmen Square massacre and without China expressing any remorse for the slaughter, and also without any substantial quid pro quo, President Bill Clinton launched a policy of constructive engagement with China. During the campaign in 1992, candidate Clinton criticised President Bush for 'coddling dictators' in China.

In 2000, Bill Clinton paved the way for Marxist China's entry into the market-based WTO, which proved to be disastrous for the rules-based global trading system. The US and EU had to move the WTO to get China declared a non-market economy almost two decades later.

In 2005, US raised the geopolitical stature of China as a responsible stakeholder and entrusted the high responsibility of drawing recalcitrant nations such as Iran, North Korea and Sudan into the international system.

Between 2005 and 2012, US trade deficit with China grew to $315 billion and China became the second largest economy, overtaking Japan.

In the year 2013, President Obama gave his Chinese counterpart Xi Jinping what he had wanted—a new model of great power relations between US and China which further enhanced China's geopolitical stature.

In each one of these stages, the US has been only conceding and grating without getting anything in return—leading to the unavoidable perception that China has always been the winner, while the US has always been the loser.

The advent of Trumpism, regardless of Trump's excesses, unpredictability and lack of strategy, is a historic turning point for the US.

It is Donald Trump who awakened the US out of its slumber and to the reality of an aggressive China that is seeking to change the global order. The advent of Trump changed the way of the US. Regardless of the extreme hate and criticism of Trump, there is a near consensus among many commentators that Trump is not an accident in US history. Trump was unpredictable, excessive in words and action, and lacking in strategy, particularly, concerning foreign policy and China. But the Timeline in his period was the most eventful and productive of unprecedented changes within and outside of the US.

2017: Trump Affirms One China Policy After Raising Doubts

After winning the presidential election in December 2016, Donald Trump broke with established practice by first speaking on the telephone with Taiwanese President Tsai Ing-wen and questioning the four-decade US commitment to its One China policy. But in a call with President Xi, Trump said he would honour the One China policy. The then US Secretary of State, visiting Beijing in March, described Sino-US relations as 'built on non-confrontation, no conflict, mutual respect, and always searching for win-win solutions.' Trump had high-profile summits with President Xi in April and November 2017.

2018: Trump Tariffs Target China

The Trump administration announced sweeping tariffs on Chinese imports worth at least $50 billion, in response to what the White House alleged was Chinese theft of US technology and intellectual property. Coming on the heels of tariffs on steel and aluminium imports; the measures targetted goods, including clothing, shoes and electronics, and restricted some Chinese investments in the United States. China imposed retaliatory measures in early April on a range of American products, stoking concerns of a trade war between the world's two largest economies.

2017: Trump-Xi Summit in the US

In April, a two-day summit with Xi Jinping in Florida was held, where bilateral trade and North Korea topped the agenda. President Trump touted 'tremendous progress' in the relationship and Xi cited deepened understanding and greater trust building. In mid-May, the then US Commerce Secretary unveiled a ten-part agreement between Beijing and Washington to expand trade of products and services and described the bilateral relationship as 'hitting a new high' but failed to address the more contentious trade issues, including tariffs on aluminium, car parts and steel.

2018: US-China Trade War Escalates

The Trump administration imposed fresh tariffs totalling $34 billion worth on Chinese goods. More than eight hundred Chinese products in the industrial and transport sectors, as well as goods such as televisions and medical devices, faced a 25 per cent import tax. China retaliated with its own tariffs on more than 500 American products. The reprisal, also valued around $34 billion, targetted commodities such as beef, dairy, seafood, and soybeans. President Trump and his administration believed that China was 'ripping off' the United States, taking advantage of free trade rules to the detriment of American firms operating in China. Beijing criticised the Trump administration's moves as 'trade bullying' and cautioned that tariffs could trigger global market unrest.

2018: Mike Pence Speech Signals Hard-Line Approach

In October 2018, US Vice President Mike Pence delivered a speech marking the clearest articulation yet of the Trump administration's policy toward China and a significant hardening of America's position. Saying that the US would prioritise competition over cooperation by using tariffs to combat 'economic aggression', Pence condemned what he called growing Chinese military aggression, especially in the South China Sea, criticised increased censorship and religious persecution by the Chinese government and accused China of stealing American intellectual property and interfering in the US elections.

China's Ministry of Foreign Affairs denounced Pence's speech as 'groundless accusations' and warned that such actions could harm US-China ties.

The Hoover Institution on How China's Informational Influence Undermined the US Democratic Process—a Belated Study

An educative Hoover Institution study titled: 'China's Influence & American Interests: Promoting Constructive Vigilance' (29 Nov, 2018), while brilliantly capturing the Chinese strategy from its downtrodden psyche three decades ago to a dominating mindset, has meticulously mapped the ever-expanding stealthy footprints of Chinese influence in diverse areas, geopolitics and even national politics in the US and elsewhere. The Hoover Institution Study says:

> While Americans are well acquainted with China's quest for influence through the projection of diplomatic, economic, and military power, we are less aware of the myriad ways Beijing has more recently been seeking cultural and informational influence, some of which could undermine our democratic processes. These include efforts to penetrate and sway—through various methods that former Australian Prime Minister Malcolm Turnbull summarized as 'covert, coercive or corrupting'—a range of groups and institutions, including the Chinese American community, Chinese students in the United States, and American civil society organizations, academic institutions, think tanks, and media.
>
> Some of these efforts fall into the category of normal public diplomacy as pursued by many other countries. But others involve the use of coercive or corrupting methods to pressure individuals and groups and thereby interfere in the functioning of American civil and political life.

It is important not to exaggerate the threat of these new Chinese initiatives. China has not sought to interfere in a national election in the United States or to sow confusion or inflame polarization in our democratic discourse the way Russia has done. For all the tensions in the relationship, there are deep historical bonds of friendship, cultural exchange, and mutual inspiration between the two societies, which we celebrate and wish to nurture. And it is imperative that Chinese Americans—who feel the same pride in American citizenship as do other American ethnic communities—not be subjected to the kind of generalized suspicion or stigmatization that could lead to racial profiling or a new era of McCarthyism. However, with increased challenges in the diplomatic, economic, and security domains, China's influence activities have collectively helped throw the crucial relationship between the People's Republic of China and the United States into a worrisome state of imbalance and antagonism. (Throughout the report, 'China' refers to the Chinese Communist Party and the government apparatus of the People's Republic of China, and not to Chinese society at large or the Chinese people as a whole.) Not only are the values of China's authoritarian system anathema to those held by most Americans, but there is also a growing body of evidence that the Chinese Communist Party views the American ideals of freedom of speech, press, assembly, religion, and association as direct challenges to its defense of its own form of one-party rule.

Both the US and China have derived substantial benefit as the two nations have become more economically and socially intertwined. The value of combined US-China trade ($635.4 billion, with a $335.4 US deficit) far surpasses that between any other pair of countries.3 More than 350,000 Chinese students currently study in US universities (plus 80,000 more in secondary schools). Moreover, millions of Chinese have immigrated to the United States seeking to build their lives with more economic, religious, and political freedom, and their presence has been an enormous asset to American life.

However, these virtues cannot eclipse the reality that in certain key ways China is exploiting America's openness in order to advance its aims on a competitive playing field that is hardly level. For at the same time that China's authoritarian system takes advantage of the openness of American society to seek influence, it impedes legitimate efforts by American counterpart institutions to engage Chinese society on a reciprocal basis. This disparity lies at the heart of this project's concerns. China's influence activities have moved beyond their traditional United Front focus on diaspora communities to target a far broader range of sectors in Western societies, ranging from think tanks, universities, and media to state, local, and national government institutions. China seeks to promote views sympathetic to the Chinese Government, policies, society, and culture; suppress alternative views; and co-opt key American players to support China's foreign policy goals and economic interests.

Normal public diplomacy, such as visitor programs, cultural and educational exchanges, paid media inserts, and government lobbying are accepted methods used by many governments to project soft power. They are legitimate in large measure because they are transparent. But this report details a range of more assertive and opaque 'sharp power' activities that China has stepped up within the United States in an increasingly active manner. These exploit the openness of our democratic society to challenge, and sometimes even undermine, core American freedoms, norms, and laws.

Except for Russia, no other country's efforts to influence American politics and society is as extensive and well-funded as China's. The ambition of Chinese activity in terms of the breadth, depth of investment of financial resources, and intensity requires far greater scrutiny than it has been getting, because China is intervening more resourcefully and forcefully across a wider range of sectors than Russia. By undertaking activities that have become more organically embedded in the pluralistic fabric of American life, it has gained a far wider and potentially longer-term impact.

2019: Huawei Sues the US

In March, amid legal proceedings against Meng Wanzhou, Huawei sued the United States for banning US federal agencies from using the telecom giant's equipment. In a battle with Beijing for technological supremacy, the Trump administration launched an aggressive campaign warning other countries not to use Huawei equipment to build 5G networks, claiming that the Chinese government could use the company to spy.

2019: Trade War Intensifies

In May, after trade talks broke down, the Trump administration raised tariffs from 10 to 25 per cent on $200 billion worth of Chinese goods, saying he believed China would come for a deal favourable to the US. China, however, retaliated by announcing plans to increase tariffs on $60 billion worth of American goods, saying that the US had 'extravagant expectations'.

Days later, Trump banned US companies from using foreign-made telecommunications equipment that could threaten national security, to target Huawei. The US Commerce Department also added Huawei to its foreign entity blacklist.

2019: US Labels China a Currency Manipulator

In August, after China's Central Bank let the yuan weaken significantly, and a little after Trump announced higher tariffs on $300 billion worth Chinese goods, the Trump administration designated China a currency manipulator. It meant that everything the United States imported from China would now face taxes. Beijing warned that the designation would 'trigger financial market turmoil'.

2019: Trump Signs Bill Supporting Hong Kong Protesters

In November, President Trump signed the Hong Kong Human Rights and Democracy Act after the US Congress passed it with an overwhelming majority, authorising the United States to sanction individuals responsible for human rights abuses in Hong Kong and requiring US officials to evaluate every year whether Hong Kong enjoyed a 'high degree of autonomy' from Beijing. Many pro-democracy protesters in Hong Kong celebrated the US law. China condemned the move, imposed sanctions on several US-based organisations and suspended American warship visits to Hong Kong.

2020: 'Phase One' Trade Deal Signed

The US and China signed a breakthrough deal after two-year trade war between the two, which relaxed some US tariffs on Chinese imports and committed China to buying an additional $200 billion worth of American goods, including agricultural products and cars, over a period of two years. China also pledged to enforce intellectual property protections. Days before the signing, the United States dropped its designation of China as a currency manipulator.

2020: Tensions Soar amid Coronavirus Pandemic

In January, the Trump administration barred all non-US citizens who had recently visited mainland China from entering the United States amid an outbreak of a new Coronavirus that was first reported in the Chinese city of Wuhan. Leading officials in both China and the United States blamed the other side for the pandemic. A Chinese Foreign Ministry spokesperson claimed, without evidence, that the US military brought the virus to China, while President Trump made repeated references to the 'Chinese virus', which he said had spread because of failures of the Chinese government. In April, both countries changed their tones by highlighting areas for cooperation amid the crisis. Still, Trump faulted the WHO for being biased towards China and halted US funding to that organisation.

2020: Trump Ends Hong Kong's Special Status

In July, two weeks after Beijing passed a new national security law for Hong Kong, President Trump signed an executive order ending the city's preferential trade status with the US. He also signed legislation to sanction officials and businesses that undermined Hong Kong's freedoms and autonomy. Chinese officials threatened to impose retaliatory sanctions on US individuals and entities. They denounced what they called US interference in China's internal affairs, including Washington's announcement a day earlier declaring most of Beijing's claims in the South China Sea as illegal.

2020: US-China Close Consulates in Diplomatic Escalation

In July, the US ordered China to close its consulate in Houston, Texas, alleging that it was a hub of espionage and intellectual property theft. Condemning it, China retaliated by closing the US consulate in Chengdu. Washington indicted two Chinese hackers for allegedly stealing Coronavirus vaccine research and sanctioned eleven Chinese companies for their reported role in human rights abuses in Xinjiang. Chinese Foreign Minister Wang Yi blamed the United States for tensions.

2020: Pompeo Says 'Engagement with China Has Failed'

In July, US Secretary of State Mike Pompeo delivered a speech, titled 'Communist China and the Free World's Future,' saying that the era of engagement with the CPP is over, signaling a profound shift in US policy. He also condemned its unfair trade practices, intellectual property theft, human rights abuses in Xinjiang and Hong Kong, and aggressive moves in the East and South China Seas. He called on Chinese citizens and democracies worldwide to press Beijing to change its behavior and respect the rules-based international order.

2020: December Trump Ramps Up Pressure as Transition Looms

In November-December, President Trump attempted to cement his legacy of being tough on China during his final weeks in office. Director of National Intelligence, John Ratcliffe, called China 'the greatest threat to America today,' while the Commerce Department added dozens of Chinese companies, including the country's biggest chipmaker, Semiconductor Manufacturing International Corporation (SMIC), to its trade blacklist. The State Department tightened visa rules for the around ninety million members of the Chinese Communist Party. It also sanctioned more Chinese officials, including fourteen members of China's legislative body, over abuses in Hong Kong, Xinjiang and elsewhere. The White House also banned US investments in Chinese companies that it claimed had ties to the People's Liberation Army. Chinese officials vowed retaliation against these and other actions of the Trump administration.

2021: Trump Administration Designated China's Abuses of Uyghurs as 'Genocide', Biden Administration Affirmed It

On January 19, Trump's penultimate day in office, US Secretary of State Mike Pompeo declared that China was committing 'crimes against humanity' and 'genocide' against Uyghurs, a Muslim ethnic group primarily from China's Xinjiang region. The US was the first country to apply those terms to abuses the Chinese government had committed over the past few years, which include the arbitrary detention of more than one million people in Xinjiang, forced sterilisations, and a crackdown on religious freedom. This description was subsequently affirmed by the incoming Biden team.

Trump 'No Accident in History'—He is Its Outcome

The Trump Timeline from 2015 shows the phenomenal change in US policy and psyche, which is outlasting Trump because Trumpism was no accident in US history. When Trump was in the office, writing for Deutsche Welle (DW), the German International Broadcaster site, Alexander Görlach, a senior fellow with the Carnegie Council for Ethics in International Affairs, and a senior research associate at the Cambridge Institute on Religion and International Studies, said in his article titled 'Donald Trump is no accident', 'Donald Trump is not the populist many consider him to be. On the contrary, Barack Obama was the populist who did not deliver—and Donald Trump is the reaction to him.'

Gorlach concluded, 'It is important for the future of democracy in the US to correctly classify the recent past: Donald

Trump is not an operational accident, but rather someone whom his voters consider to be precisely the kind of person who can bring back fairness to the country. For the moment, the figures prove Trump right: Employment is rising, the economy is booming, and in international relations, too, especially with China, his supporters see that he is bringing back fairness. The cosmopolitan liberals, among them the author of these lines, are going to have to digest it.'

As most pundits had predicted when Trump was in office, after he was defeated and after Biden had assumed office, Trumpism is lasting beyond Trump. It appears to be deep in American consciousness and is manifesting in US policies, both within and outside.

Trumpism in Biden's time: Biden administration affirms Trump administration view of abuses of Uyghur as 'Genocide'

The Trump administration's final day pronouncement that China's abuses of Uyghurs are a genocide, was confirmed by President Joe Biden, who used the same term genocide while campaigning. Biden also raised concerns about the abuses during his first call as president with Xi. Later, Biden's Secretary of State, Antony Blinken, also affirmed the Trump administration's declaration. Such an aggressive response to an aggressive China was unthinkable during Obama's time. The Chinese government, on the defence, denied genocide was taking place. Much after Trump's term ended, Beijing imposed sanctions on twenty-eight of his administration's former officials, including Pompeo, for what the foreign ministry called 'crazy actions' that 'seriously disrupted US-China relations.'

China Seems to View Biden as Continuity, Rather Than a Change from Trump

China too seems to perceive the Biden administration as being in alignment with Trump's policies. In an article titled 'Joe Biden's China Trade Policy: Make America Great Again, not Wall Street', the *South China Morning Post* (6.2.2021) says, 'There are signs banks will be pushed down the pecking order in Washington's new mission to bring jobs and industries home' and 'Observers say financiers have dominated US trade policy since the 1980s but their influence appears to be on the wane'. It adds, 'Call it US President Joe Biden's version of 'Make America Great Again'—a strategy to bring jobs and industries back home and one that may weaken Wall Street's long-standing influence over Washington's trade policy, especially towards China.'

Jake Sullivan, Biden's National Security Adviser, is one of several White House officials promoting the jobs-at-home theme, while the new administration touts the slogan 'The Future Will Be Made in America'. In an interview on National Public Radio in the US on 30 December, Sullivan criticised the administration of Donald Trump for what he called favouring US financial conglomerates in trade talks with Beijing. Jake Sullivan has, like Trump did, equated jobs to national security—a clear endorsement of Trumpism in US trade policies by the Biden regime.

Trump was right in seeing China as a challenge and threat, but faulted for trying to counter China without allies, actually alienating them

Till Trump took on China, China was the cynosure of the US administration, its policy makers, Wall Street, bankers and the US liberal media, all of whom admired China as a performer as all that mattered to them was numbers which showed rising stocks.

This continued even after the 2008 financial crisis in a different form. It was Trump who began to see China as a challenge and threat to the US.

Trump faulted—by making it a solo US fight against China without aligning with and bringing in the traditional allies of the US—Transatlantic powers and the European Union. In fact, he began fighting traditional allies of the US like he was fighting China. This proved to be his undoing.

Public opinion had turned against China in most democracies.

The ecosystem in the US and EU had already begun turning against China in the US and Europe. A Pew research in the last quarter of 2020 has already shown that:

> A majority in each of the surveyed countries has an unfavorable opinion of China. And in Australia, the United Kingdom, Germany, The Netherlands, Sweden, the United States, South Korea, Spain and Canada, negative views have reached their highest points since the Center began polling on this topic more than a decade ago. Negative views of China increased most in Australia, where 81% now say they see the country unfavorably, up 24 percentage points since last year. In the UK, around three-quarters now see the country in a negative light, up 19 points. And, in the US, negative views of China have increased nearly 20 percentage points since President Donald Trump took office, rising 13 points since just last year.

As compared to 2002, in 2020, the negative view about China rose from 40 to 81 in Australia, 16 to 74 in the UK, 37 to 71 in Germany, 34 to 73 in the Netherlands, 45 to 85 in Sweden, 35 to 73 in the US, 31 to 75 in South Korea, 21 to 63 in Spain, 42 to 70 in France, 27 to 73 in Canada, 61 to 63 in Italy and 42 to 86 in Japan. And, 7 in 10 felt no confidence in Chinese Chief Xi Jinping to do the right thing regarding world affairs. Being democracies, they could not afford to keep the state policy on China out of sync with the people's opinion.

This is notwithstanding that the liberal media in the US and EU had a favourable view of China, thanks to their unfavourable view of Trump. The *Cato Institute Journal* (Fall 2020) on US media's perspectives on China, said; 'throughout President Barack Obama's administration, although a majority of news stories and opinion pieces still presented the US-China relationship as positive and mutually beneficial', but 'The Trump administration's hardline trade policies led primarily to a sharp (sometimes partisan) debate, with journalistic advocates of the status quo condemning the president's apparent willingness to wage a trade war...a sizable portion of the corporate media community has still held back, according good relations—especially profitable economic relations—between the United States and China a higher priority'.

Liberal journalists rejected such labels as Wuhan virus and China virus for corona virus 'not only inaccurate, but xenophobic and implicitly racist, and they blasted both President Trump and his right-wing media allies for using them' and they also dismissed the lab-leak theory of the virus as 'as crude right-wing conspiracy theories'.

Biden's attempts to organise the Western world and other Democracies to tackle the China challenge—with elements of Trumpism and avoiding Trump's faults.

But Biden has, so far, proceeded in a more systematic and organised way to counter China, although his policies are not settled yet. He never made it a US-centric initiative. He did not commit his regime to an anti-China position till he had brought the Transatlantic allies onto the same page. He expounded his public position on China first at the G7, NATO and US-EU summits on 11–15 June. With the EU having signed the Comprehensive Investment Agreement with China after Biden got elected, it was a complicated and difficult situation for both the US and EU to come on the same page against China. But obviously a lot of behind the scenes homework appears to have been done by the US and Transatlantic allies, which seem to have enabled both to take simultaneous and strong positions on the uniting issue of human rights.

Both announced sanctions in February on Chinese officials guilty of the genocide in Uyghur. An overconfident China, obviously underestimating the growing distrust against it in both the US and the EU, responded with unprecedented verbal violence and disproportionate counter sanctions, and shot itself in the foot. With the corona virus origin issue coming back into focus at about the same time, this made it worse for China.

The verbal description of China by the Biden regime at the three June summits and the language of their communiqués and press releases unmistakably showed the elements of Trumpism. The Biden administration has made the G7, NATO and EU accept the elements of Trumpism on the China challenge and the need to contain China.

Now the agenda to counter the China challenge is the shared agenda of the US and Europe. The G7 has also initiated efforts to make a D10 (Democratic 10) as a counter to China outside the Atlantic extending it to the Indo-Pacific region.

June 2021 Hoover Institution Paper Confirms US Raised its Own Frankenstein Monster—China

A Hoover Institution paper dated June 2021 titled: 'China-US Relations in the Eyes of The Chinese Communist Party: An Insider's Perspective' written by Cai Xia, a former CCP insider and Professor at the Central Party School for many years, brings out how the US had always been unrealistic in its assessment of the CCP, which always had a hidden agenda against the US behind the veneer of engagement with the latter.

What Cai Xia writes perfectly fits in with the chronology which shows how the US was taken for a ride by China. What he says confirms the view that the US raised its own Frankenstein monster—China. Cai Xia says:

> How does the Chinese Communist Party (CCP) view the China-US relationship and what factors have shaped China's approach to the United States? As a former insider in the CCP and professor at the Central Party School for many years, I would like to offer some personal reflections on these questions (even though I am not an expert on Sino-American relations)
>
> Looking back on China-US relations over the past half a century, we Chinese should first affirm and thank the US government for its 'engagement policy' with China, which helped China end thirty years of isolation and poverty. China's rapid economic and social development and tremendous changes are inseparable from the sincere exchanges and help of the US government as well as people in American scientific, technological, educational, cultural and economic circles. This assistance provided an extremely precious historical opportunity and development space for China to integrate into international society, get in touch with and understand modern civilisation, and restore economic and social vitality. As a result, many Chinese have had the opportunity to get

out of the country and thus change their destiny and that of their families. Currently, there are more than five million Chinese who have migrated to the US. The vast majority of them came after the 1980s through study, work or immigration, becoming permanent residents, with green cards or naturalised American citizens. In turn, their close interaction with their relatives, friends and colleagues back in China have helped to broaden Chinese people's views and opened their minds.

As a result, the effects of the engagement policy over the past half century have been multifaceted. On the one hand, engagement has helped the Chinese people to get rid of poverty and isolation and enter the international community, and, it has also allowed civil society to emerge and gradually develop in China. On the other hand, the engagement policy also hastened the rapid rise of China under the neo-totalitarian rule. The CCP is determined to reframe the existing international order and norms and lead the world in the opposite direction of liberal democracy.

Since Xi Jinping came to power in 2012, he has continued the diplomatic strategy toward the US established by Mao Zedong and Deng Xiaoping—namely to take advantage of the engagement policy to gain time to achieve the CCP's goals. But with China's enhanced strength now, Xi Jinping has wrongly judged that the international configuration is 'East rising and the West is declining' and has become more aggressive and outspoken about his intention to displace the United States. As a result, in recent years, troubles and conflicts in China-US relations have continually increased and the CCP has become the greatest challenge and the greatest threat to the post-war international relations, to the liberal system of free democracy and to the security of the United States. The March 22, 2021 clash between the diplomatic officials of the two countries in Anchorage, Alaska, showed that the relations between US and China may return to the rivalrous state of 50 years ago. How the US understands and handles US-China relations affects not only the wellbeing of the Chinese and American people, but also the peace and stability of the world. As a former member of the CCP system looking back at the changes in the US-China relations over the past 50 years, I have three basic perspectives which I would like to share with Americans so that they can see more clearly the CCP and its strategies for what they are.

First, in more than 70 years since it came to power, the CCP has treated domestic and foreign affairs as "one integrated game", with the priority of strengthening the CCP's control and

> preventing the collapse of the regime. In this regard, diplomacy is an extension of domestic affairs and is seen as a device to keep the party in power.
>
> Second, as far as the CCP's global objectives are concerned, the CCP's attitude toward China-US relations and the engagement policy is determined by how well they serve the CCP's political needs.
>
> Third, international engagement and economic development have failed to soften the political character of the CCP regime. Its combination of ideology and extreme repression make it a totalitarian regime and the sophisticated digital nature of its surveillance and repression has given totalitarian control a new dimension. All this makes China a more dangerous adversary.

The US-China interface chronology is a highly instructive lesson on how relations should be mutually beneficial and not burdensome or one sided.

US Breached Bhishma's Rule for Friendship with the Adversary

It started with the fundamental rule of politics from ancient times to contemporary times that an 'enemy's enemy is a friend'. In the Mahabharata, when Yudhishtir asks Bhishma, who was advising him on statecraft, under what circumstances could there be friendship with one's adversary, Bhishma gives the example of a cat and mouse game. A mouse living in the hole in a tree led a terrified existence with a cat living in that area targeting it. The cat was caught in the net laid by a hunter. The cat offered a peace treaty to the mouse to treat it as a friend forever if the mouse could cut the net and enable the cat to escape. The mouse refused saying that the desire to eat the mouse was in the DNA of the cat and it could not change. At that time, came a snake which would chase and kill the mouse even if it entered its home in the tree hole. The mouse then offered a deal to the cat. 'If I am with you inside the net I will be safe from the snake which will be afraid of you and will not touch you'. The cat agreed and there was the strange spectacle of the cat and mouse being together. The snake hissed and hissed and moved away. The mouse came out and the cat asked the mouse to fulfill its promise. The mouse asked the cat to wait for its release. As the sun was setting, the hunter was seen returning. The cat was restless, but the mouse waited. It was measuring the distance between the hunter and the cat. It cut the net when the cat would have sufficient time to escape from the hunter, without harming the mouse. Bhishma told Yudhishtir that that was the discipline for friendship with the enemy. It had to be only need based. It could not be turned into a positive engagement.

Placing Bhishma's advice in modern-day context, US relations with Russia's enemy, China, should have ended with the Cold War; US enmity with Russia was over. But the one-sided positive engagement by the US, which began in 1993 without even an iota of remorse expressed by China on the Tiananmen Square massacre that took place four years before, was in breach of Bhishma's counsel and proved to be an unmitigated disaster.

Index

About the Author

S. Gurumurthy wears many hats. Besides being a popular writer and journalist, he is a teacher of diverse subjects. He is most celebrated for his investigative journalism and has ceaselessly campaigned against corruption at high places, exposing the bribery in Bofors arms deal and the nexus between corporates and government.

Hamish McDonald, the well-known Australian journalist, writes in his book *Polyester Prince* that Gurumurthy's investigative work must rank among the most powerful examples of investigative journalism anywhere in the world. Gurumurthy, he says, had a strong sense of probity. The *Business Barons of India* rated Gurumurthy's knowledge of economics, finance and accounts as outstanding. In his biography on the media baron Ramnath Goenka, B.G. Verghese, a highly respected editor and writer, describes Gurumurthy as a brilliant chartered accountant and an exceedingly astute amateur lawyer.

Gurumurthy is a visiting faculty member at IIT Bombay, where he teaches economics, finance and management. He is also a distinguished professor of legal anthropology at SASTRA, Tamil Nadu. A chartered accountant by profession, Gurumurthy is also a corporate adviser of high standing. He is one of the founders of the Vivekananda International Foundation and the chairman of its board of trustees.